DATE DUE

KALAMAZOO VALLEY

COMMUNITY COLLEGE

A Gift to the KVCC Libraries from

Barbara J. Roberts

EUBIE BLAKE

by Al Rose

SCHIRMER BOOKS
A Division of Macmillan Publishing Co., Inc.
NEW YORK

SCHIRMER BOOKS
A Division of Macmillan Publishing Co., Inc.
866 Third Avenue, New York, N.Y.   10022

Collier Macmillan Canada, Ltd.

Library of Congress Catalog Card Number: 79-7369

Printed in the United States of America

printing number

1   2   3   4   5   6   7   8   9   10

Library of Congress Cataloging in Publication Data

Rose, Al.
    Eubie Blake.

    Discography: p.
    Includes index.
    1. Blake, Eubie   2.   Jazz musicians--
United States--Biography.
M.410.B6247R68   785.4'2'0924   [B]   79-7369
ISBN 0-02-872170-5

*Dedicated with admiration and affection
to one of the most beautiful ladies
I've ever had the good fortune
to encounter,*

Marion Tyler Blake

Contents

Eubie's Foreword

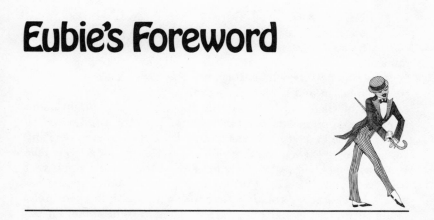

People always ask me—the first thing—how a man of my age can go on traveling and performing at this pace. They say it's unusual for a ninety-six-year-old man to keep on going this way. All I can say is that I don't know any other way to do. I'm not just going to look at those numbers, "9" and "6," and tell myself I can't play any more.

I like to travel and make audiences happy. I always did. Maybe I'm too old to change. Anyway, I've now been a professional in show business for eighty years and I've seen and known a lot of great people. I always wished I could write so I could put it all down on paper just so people could read about it—and so I could see what it looked like myself.

When Al Rose decided to write my biography, I had no idea how he intended to do it. What I expected was that he'd get me on tape telling all my stories I remembered about my life. Then I thought he'd put it together some way, and that would be my life. Well, he did get me on tape—but that was only the beginning.

When I first read the manuscript, I learned a lot about Eubie Blake I never really thought about before. Al Rose knows more about American popular music than anybody I ever met—and about old-time show business. What he wrote really shows how I fit into history. I always knew I did some things that were important not only in music but for my people. I see that there was really no way to tell my story "in 1." (That's a show business term, "in 1." It means an act where all the action is in front of the first curtain. Big acts are set deeper into the stage, with more of the curtains up.)

This book tells the whole story, not only about me but about the times I lived in and am still living in.

I have hit plenty of keys between Aggie Shelton's upright piano in her hookshop in Baltimore in 1898 and the concert grand in the White House in 1978. It seems like Al Rose was looking over my shoulder all the way, making notes about everything from Julie Witmark's wooden leg to the addresses of the grade schools that tried to educate me. I can't believe how he wrote about my mother and father! I know *I* couldn't have told him that, but when I read about them, it's just like they were standing in front of me. I never thought anyone could write my life this way. When I read it, I was proud of myself a whole new way.

Only thing is, I don't think he wrote enough about my wife, Marion. But there's no way to write enough about *her*. Maybe when people ask how I keep going I ought to point to her. I want to thank her for this.

My thanks to the publisher and Al Rose. I hope they have lots of opportunities to update this book. I thank the many, many people who have had faith in me and my talent. I'm especially grateful to everyone connected with the production "Eubie!"

Preface

On February 7, 1883, the day when Eubie Blake screamed out his first solo in a black working-class section of Baltimore, Maryland, Thomas Alva Edison was still six years away from marketing his first phonograph. The melodies this generation thinks of as standard—those tunes we associate with our holidays, social activities, public events—had yet to be written. Irving Berlin, who has provided us with "Easter Parade," "White Christmas," "God Bless America," and "There's No Business like Show Business," was to be born five years later in an obscure Russian village. Baseball was being played without the inspiration of "Take Me Out to the Ball Game." No one would be asking the pretty maidens of the Florodora Sextette "Are there any more at home like you?" for another fifteen years. The harvest moon hadn't yet been exhorted to "shine on." Franz Lehar, still a boy, had not thought of "The Merry Widow," and yet to come were Rudolf Friml's "Firefly" and the works of Victor Herbert.

People who played or sang popular music contented themselves with imitation Negro songs such as "Swanee River," "Camptown Races," and "Old Black Joe" or the scarcely more convincing "black" compositions "In the Evening by the Moonlight," "Carry Me Back to Old Virginny," and "Oh, Dem Golden Slippers," all three by an authentic colored man, James A. Bland. Down in New Orleans, ragtime was flowering, obscurely. Across the country a few leftover Civil War songs were still being sung—"Dixie," "The Girl I Left behind Me," and "The Battle Hymn of the Republic." Popular in America were the Strauss waltzes, especially "The

Beautiful Blue Danube" and "The Emperor's Waltz," and one
might easily hear the overture to "William Tell" or the strains of
"The Tales of Hoffmann." Not for another fifteen years would
American election days resound to "There'll Be a Hot Time in the
Old Town Tonight."

Imagine American society with such a dearth of popular song!
Not even "Ta Ra Ra Boomderay"!

But that was the nation as Eubie Blake found it in 1883.

He's done a lot to bring it along since then, and in the process
Eubie Blake and America have established a beautiful relationship.
I've seen it demonstrated time and again.

One evening in New York not long ago, Eubie and I were
standing in the lobby of Alice Tully Hall. He's not on the bill.
We're there to attend a concert given by pianist Bill Bolcom and
singer Joan Morris, and—

"Please, Mr. Blake, would you sign my program?"

Eubie takes the pen, writes in his crude but distinctive scrawl,
stops, and asks, "What's your name, young lady?"

She tells him and he writes it. He has a twinkle in his eye.

"How do you spell 'from'?" he inquires mischievously.

She starts to tell him: "*f—r—*"

But of course he's through writing his name and misses her look
of gratitude as he directs his attention to the next autograph seeker.

"How do you spell 'from'?" I hear him ask.

Eubie proceeds with unflagging energy and good humor, honoring each request for his signature. Standing by him as he's encircled
by admirers, you can feel him being overwhelmed with waves of
love. You feel it in the gentleness of people's voices, in the kindly
expressions on their faces, in occasional solicitous questions about
his health, and in the sound of the recurring phrase "Bless you!"

I have had occasion to see the scene repeated in St. Louis, New
Orleans, and Sedalia, Missouri, in recent years. The universal attitude doesn't vary.

Rudy Vallee scored with the middle-aged matrons of the Gatsby
era. Sinatra's crowd was mainly composed of teenage girls,
Presley's of the causeless rebels of the fifties. Now here comes
Eubie, a frail little man of ninety-six who has a little difficulty in
negotiating the stairs and who hasn't exhibited his buck-dancing

skills in public in seventy years. His profile doesn't rival Bar-
rymore's; he lacks the muscle of an Errol Flynn; and his singing
voice is a cut or two below Pavarotti's. Yet people crowd around
for a glimpse, a touch of this man. It is no particular age group
that succumbs to his magic. He draws little children, gauche teen-
agers, sober adults in their prime, and senior citizens.

They huddle around Eubie as though he were a pot-bellied stove
on a freezing night. They don't tear at his clothes. (I lost all my
coat buttons once trying to get through a mob with Vaughn
Monroe.) They don't jostle him. (I remember being flat on my
back with Sammy Kaye when an instant before we'd been
upright.) They don't scream in his ear. (My head still rings from
ten minutes with Sinatra.) They just stand respectfully and show
him as best they can that they love him. They respond to his
trademark greeting—hands clasped above his head in the manner
of the winner and still champion that he is. They all love him
because he loves them and they can see it and hear it and feel it.

The generation of the seventies knows his every move from his
countless appearances on the TV talk shows with Johnny Carson,
Merv Giffin, Bill Cosby, Mike Douglas, Dean Martin, and Tom
Snyder. He is what he always has been and always will be—a
superstar since before the word was invented.

But Eubie Blake is something more than merely a "personality."
He is, in fact, a man who has redirected the course of American
culture. He hasn't done this just through his music—his hundreds
of great popular songs like "You're Lucky to Me," "I'm Just Wild
about Harry," and "Memories of You," or his spectacular reprises
of James P. Johnson and George Gershwin, or his landmark instrumental rags such as "Chevy Chase" and "Fizz Water" or "The
Charleston Rag" (composed in 1899, the same year as Scott Joplin's
"Maple Leaf Rag"). He's had another kind of impact too. By artistic effort, determination, and awesome talent, Eubie Blake
became one of the small group of black performing artists who
paved the way for blacks to demand and win acceptance and
equality in the American entertainment industry, not only in billing and the right to perform in other than racially stereotyped roles
but also in payment according to the standards of white artists.

This book sets these accomplishments and the rest of Eubie's life in the perspective of the times he has lived through, and that means it spans almost the entire latter half of the life of this nation.

I myself have known Eubie, had his records, and admired his compositional and theatrical achievements for about forty years, and we have shared many old friends and associations—for instance, I knew Noble Sissle, Eubie's partner of many years. During the last ten years or so, I have gotten to know Eubie better and better, to the point that now we are close friends. I think I understand him as only a close friend can. And I know intimately many of the scenes in which he's made his life, made his music, and made history.

All this has been helpful in telling Eubie's story, but I've also had a lot of excellent outside help, for which acknowledgments are in order, as well as the support and encouragement of some delightful people, to whom thanks are due.

Chief among the published sources is the beautiful and sparkling book entitled *Reminiscing with Sissle and Blake* (Viking Press, 1973), by Bob Kimball and Bill Bolcom. It is loaded with fabulous pictures of performers, reproductions of theater bills and programs, and other visual treasures, and it includes a creditable but necessarily limited exploration of the highlights of the lives of the principals. I have freely used it as a checkpoint of comparison with Eubie's freshly restated testimony.

Album notes by John Hammond, Carl Seltzer, and David Jasen on various LPs have contributed to the details of Eubie's musical history. Tom Fletcher's *One Hundred Years of the Negro in Show Business* (Burdge, 1954) was a source for much early material. And I must mention, too, three other books that are gold mines of information on ragtime: *They All Played Ragtime* (Knopf, 1950), by Rudi Blesh and Harriet Janis; *This Is Ragtime* (Hawthorne, 1976), by Terry Waldo; and *Rags and Ragtime* (Seabury, 1978), by Trebor Jay Tichenor and David Jasen.

At my disposal has also been a transcript of interviews taped at the Yale University School of Music Oral History Collection. These were conducted by its director, Vivian Perlis, in January 1972. I did not use this transcript as source material—because Eubie had already told all his stories to me on tape and to others on radio and television, sometimes repeating them verbatim—but it proved to be a valuable and well-organized checkpoint.

Chief among those I must thank personally is the incredible Marion Tyler Blake, Eubie's wife of thirty-two years, who serves as his housekeeper, hostess, business manager, valet, treasurer, booking agent, secretary, traveling companion, and public relations director—all without ever losing her charm, graciousness, or efficiency. Of course, she sometimes collapses from exhaustion and needs a visit to the nearest spa to recuperate. She's of an age when ladies usually find themselves the beneficiaries rather than the suppliers of supportive services. Eubie, like a true gentlemen, doesn't tell her age, but he concedes that she's "old enough to vote in *any* election." She put a lifetime of priceless documents at my disposal and housed and fed me (a notoriously troublesome houseguest) as I accumulated some thirty precious hours of taped interviews with Eubie. I am more grateful to her than words can say.

My wife, Diana Beals Rose, is a classically trained, formerly professional musician whose technical knowledge of musical form and structure balances my own infinite ignorance. I have drawn not only on her mastery of music but on her patience in studying my manuscript for continuity. In satisfying her interest and curiosity, I have elucidated matters I had taken for granted regarding an average reader's knowledge of music.

Terry Waldo, transcriber of the rags collected in "Sincerely, Eubie Blake" (music folio, Eubie Blake Music, 1975), has made useful observations both in person and in print. In conversations with him and other great ragtime artists of our time, I have accumulated views on Eubie's music to supplement my own. It's a great pleasure to have such friends as Bob Greene, a Jelly Roll Morton reincarnation; Dr. John W. (Knocky) Parker; the incomparable showman Max Morath; John Arpin, Eubie's "Chopin of ragtime"; Mike Montgomery of Detroit, the super-archivist of ragtime music; Trebor Jay Tichenor of St. Louis; David Jasen of New York; and Rudi Blesh, the patriarch of jazz and ragtime authors. All have been pleased to act as consultants.

The manuscript for this book also benefited from the nitpicking of Vaughn Glasgow of New Orleans, who effectively attacked inconsistencies in the text and a certain habitual slovenliness in its author.

Data on Eubie's early Baltimore days, the addresses of the schools he attended, the addresses at which his family resided, and other important facts were obtained through the personal interest and aid of the Honorable William Donald Schaefer, mayor of Baltimore. Eubie and I are grateful for his substantial assistance.

Many thanks to all these people.

And in thanking them, I need also to thank Eubie himself, for the warmth and generosity with which so many people have volunteered their assistance in this project could have been engendered only by their profound affection for him and their enjoyment of and admiration for his music.

Eubie Blake's nearly a century of progress is of course atypical. Few nonagenarians maintain scheduled professional lives in full public view. But one thing we all can get from his story is an awareness of and excitement about the potential we all have for living our lives to the full. If you think about Eubie for a while, you begin to feel younger and stronger.

A Note on Eubie Speaking

When Eubie Blake speaks, one soon observes, he prefers the vernacular to the formal. "Prefers" is the proper word, too, for he is able, when called upon, to deliver himself of the most impeccable grammar and an extensive and concisely employed vocabulary of near-scholarly exactness. When he says "My wife don't like me to say 'ain't,'" the twinkle in his eye tells you he knows his "don't" is where his "doesn't" should be. During his long lifetime he has learned to communicate verbally on every level of society, with the result that there is no consistency in his use of language. My transcriptions from the tapes we made are, therefore, filled with inconsistencies. In transferring them to print in this book, I have made no effort to force an artificial consistency on his speech.

Mainly, Eubie is comfortable in the vernacular, in the jargon of an earlier time and place, the backstage argot of the twenties and thirties, but when he gets down to making serious points, especially in discussion of matters of musical theory, he suddenly becomes grammarian and pedagogue. "Ain't" is suspended in these talks. One learns that he really knows about syntax, that he doesn't confuse perfect with pluperfect or comparative with superlative.

When his recall of a circumstance is absolutely firm, he speaks in well-organized and complete sentences. When it's vague, he seeks help from his audience if others can supply a helpful date or name.

1

From the last century particularly there are bits and pieces of miscellaneous information that Eubie remembers—and that could well have been lost forever if I had not jogged his memory. It was part of my interviewing technique to name a variety of people and places that might evoke a response. In many cases Eubie did not relate at all, but in some his contributions turned out to be not only amusing but of substantial historical importance.

Once, for example, when I mentioned the name of Billy Kersands, Eubie answered by whistling a six-note melody."I never saw Billy Kersands," he told me, "but see that little tune I just whistled? Well, that's a tune that all colored show people knew, because they used to use it to identify themselves in crowds. So if you heard that tune"—he whistled it again—"you knew whoever was whistlin' it was in show business, see. Now, there's words to it too, but I never knew any more of it. The words are 'Here comes Billy Kersands.'" I had Eubie write down the words and the melody on music paper and later realized that the strain was the central theme of William Grant Still's "Afro-American Symphony," now a standard work.

Eubie's responses to questions are instantaneous. He starts with "Yes, let me tell you about that!" or "Sure, I remember him. From nineteen and eight. Big fella." Many times he anticipates questions and begins his answer before his interrogator has finished.

Eubie also has a varied assortment of facial expressions that are effective but almost indescribable, along with characteristic hand movements that are part of his communicating techniques. He stabs the air with a forefinger when he says, for emphasis, "see?" or, merely for rhetorical affirmation, "see," with no question mark implied. When he talks about playing certain pieces on the piano he places his hands in performing position and demonstrates as he discusses. If he watches you with raised eyebrows and a baby stare, that means you're making a damn fool of yourself and he's being too polite to interrupt you. A hand lifted to shield his mouth means he's saying something that's not for the ears of ladies (probably "damn"). A lengthening of his upper lip signals mock contention or mimicry of someone putting on airs. His high level of animation makes it easy for him to hold his listeners even when what he has to say is less than momentous.

He repeats things frequently, because the flood of his thought is so rapid that he will forget he has just made a point and make it an unnecessary second time. I have not transcribed his repetitions.

Eubie speaking has the same mastery as Eubie performing; for to him, in fact, it's all part of the same thing.

Getting Started

Survivor Son of Former Slaves
The Traditions of Home
The Organ in the Store

All Baltimoreans know that the name of their proud city is pronounced "*Ball*-mer," as Eubie Blake frequently explains. It is a city of distinguished cultural achievement, which is carefully documented and displayed in its Rembrandt Peale Museum. Through the efforts of the museum it has only lately begun to recognize its own stature. It has contributed leaders in all walks of life. Henry L. Mencken edited its newspaper. Another native became the duchess of Windsor. Joe Gans became eminent in the prize ring, and the city's Orioles, the baseball kind, are hallowed in its history, not to mention native son Babe Ruth.

Within this great city is a section centered around the old Belair Market. Its character and population were well established long before the Civil War. Today it would be called a black ghetto, but by the standards of the nineteenth century its residents were not so oppressed and not so aware of the absence of job opportunities as today's ghetto dwellers are. The unzoned neighborhood was filled with small shops, private residences, taverns, and houses of ill fame. The latter two kinds of establishment tended to generate a smell of bad whiskey, but this was overcome by the acrid aroma of carbolic acid, used as a disinfectant at nearby Johns Hopkins Medical Center. Still, the people who lived in the neighborhood found it a comfortable place to make their homes.

At 200 East Street, near Lexington, was Primary School No. 2, an all-Negro school. Throughout his early life, Eubie never lived more than four or five blocks from this school. He was born at 319 Forrest Street. In 1894 his family moved to 414 North Eden Street. Through the early 1900s they were residing at 1510 Jefferson Street. All of this will one day be important to the societies that distribute plaques and historical markers to show where cultural history was made. For now, we are interested in just the first of these street addresses and what happened there one February day ninety-six years ago.

The Patapsco River was frozen solid that day, because it does get cold around Baltimore, especially in February. A dozen or so middle-aged Negro women huddled in the front room of the tilted little four-room house at 319 Forrest. There was one man in the crowded parlor, trying to stand apart from the women. He stood nervously by the stairs trying to imagine what was going on on the floor above. The women were swaying back and forth and setting up a doleful murmur. The man wasn't paying any more attention to them than he had to. He was overfamiliar with their litany. Identifiable phrases surfaced with some regularity. "the Good Lord!" "Emily is such a good woman." "We *all* sinners, Lord." "Have mercy, Lord!" It went on without a break.

The man was John Sumner Blake. Blake was the name of the man he and Emily had belonged to when they were younger. The "John"—well, that was just his *name*. The "Sumner" was an afterthought of his own. Why *not* a grand-sounding name like Sumner?

He and Em had been through this no fewer than ten times before. Maybe *this* one would live. The midwife was experienced, Em was feeling healthier than she had in the past, and while he didn't have much truck with the Lord or His church, it just might be that if God was all that good, He'd give old John Sumner Blake a birthday present. Yes, sir, fifty years old today, February 7, 1883. Maybe too old to take care of a young one, but he had a good job and he'd been on it for years. Nine dollars a week if it didn't rain. Of course stevedores didn't work if it rained. Not that the crew he was in charge of would mind, but the rain wasn't too good for some of the stuff that came off those boats. Em was a long time upstairs with this one. They had married right after emancipation and started trying for a family right away, but they never had any luck. One child, a boy, had lived almost two months.

When he was still with old master Blake and being used as a stud and taking care of two women at a time, he had sired twenty-seven youngsters that he knew about and God only knew how many more. But with Em. . . .

Meanwhile, in the front room on the second floor Emily Johnston Blake was suffering in the time-honored manner of women in labor everywhere, but she didn't let the pangs interfere with her prayers. Emily Johnston Blake never let anything interfere with her prayers. She had always been a good Christian woman and she never let anybody forget it, least of all her husband. Emily felt guilty for a while because she suspected she wasn't suffering enough. On the other hand, she reasoned, that could be the Lord's way of rewarding her for her unremitting devotion. Ever since she herself had been born back in Mathews County, Virginia, in 1850, she and her sainted mother before her had never shirked their duty to do His work. She wrestled with the effort of trying to make her humility overcome her pride. During this struggle curtain time arrived and the offspring made its entrance. The mistress of ceremonies billed it a boy, and the sound of applause resounded below. Absolutely nobody could have predicted how long a run this boy would have.

John Sumner Blake accepted the sincere congratulations of the ladies and ascended to view the most recent of his progeny. He poked the clump of blankets tentatively and growled, "Bully, you're a real boy!"

Em kept her eyes shut and did what she could to keep from smiling. It had to be sinful to parade your joy. Not the slightest show of tenderness passed between husband and wife. It just wasn't their way.

And so was born Master James Hubert Blake on February 7, 1883, a tiny infant—he might even have been described as frail. Actuarial tables of Baltimore Life would have pegged his life expectancy at about fifty-one, but given his in some ways insalubrious environment, his wispy physique, and the family history of mortality, that would have seemed to be too optimistic a forecast. Though he was baptized James Hubert Blake, the "James" vanished early through atrophy. When she was well disposed, his mother called him Wally. He was never sure why, but he suspected that was the name of an earlier, less successful offspring. When Emily was angered by his real or fancied misdeeds, he became "Mr. Blake."

John called his son Bully, a nickname in tune with the hyper-masculine qualities so highly valued in that frontier-oriented era. Friends and relatives called him Hubie, with laborious emphasis on the "H". The kids on the block named him Mouse, with the remorseless capacity of youngsters to create apt appellations. As Eubie tells it, "I stood by and watched this big kid tie a rope with a rock on the end of it and throw it so he could catch the electric line goin' to this man's house, and then he pulls the line down. It looked like the Fourth of July when the wire broke. When the policeman came, a lady in the window of another place pointed at me and yelled. 'He done it!' she says, 'that mouse-faced boy done it.'

"And that's how I happened to get the name Mouse, see."

When Eubie speaks of his parents, he does so with admiration for their honesty and strength. His mother he recalls as a pillar of virtue.

"I'll never forget the time," he says, "when my father started to wash his hands in the kitchen sink and she tells him not to use the soap. He asks her why not and she says, 'It's not our soap. It's left over from Mrs. So-and-so's wash and it's hers. She paid for it, not us.'"

Eubie's father, born in Virginia like his mother, used to say, "Everything I ever knew I learned from reading." He was strong in his insistence that Eubie become educated—and especially that he learn to read. He'd come home from work after Eubie started to school and make him read the Baltimore *Sun*. It was important to keep up with what was going on in the world. His nightly demand when he walked into the house was "Bully, tell me what the white folks are doin' today."

"The old man never had leather shoes until he went into the army," Eubie relates. "Those slaves were really kept poor. But after the war nobody had anyplace to go, so lots of them went back to where they came from. The ol' massa, you know, would give him a little money every day to live on—like a quarter or fifty cents. Course *he* didn't have anything either and he didn't *have* to do that."

The old man never stopped preaching to his son the evils of race hatred. Even though he'd been a slave, he insisted there were good and bad white people just as there were good and bad Negroes. Eubie's sharpest recollection of this lies in his recall of cold winter nights when the stories of slave days used to come out. John would come home from work bearing a ten-cent bag of walnuts. Telling about this, Eubie shows how big a bag of walnuts you could get for a dime. It must have been about five pounds. John would remove his shirt—Eubie recalls vividly the stripes left by the whip on his father's back—and sit with his back to the kitchen stove that burned wood or coal, depending on availability. He enjoyed the warmth on his back. Then he'd put a flatiron between his knees, bottom up, and, with a hammer, proceed with the business of cracking walnuts. As he broke the shells, he'd tell his son of the days of slavery. He told how he had once seen President Lincoln—"Ugliest man I ever saw!" He told of picking cotton from dawn to dusk and of unjust whipping by a sadistic overseer. He told how the master had discovered this, chastised the straw boss, and put a stop to the torment.

"All white folks aren't alike, Bully" was his oft-repeated lesson, though the youngster could barely contain his rage against the people and the system that had made the "peculiar institution" possible.

"And another thing," John would continue. "A smart man never bites the hand that feeds him. It's the white man supplies the work that keeps food on the table, and don't ever forget it. A white man paid for this house that we're living in, and he lets us rent it. It was a white man—even a foreigner, Lord Baltimore—that gave us this land. Don't you ever let me hear you say you hate white people. When you hate anybody, you suffer more than the people you hate."

Em never failed to object to John's telling his son about slavery, but he'd insist. "I *want* him to know about it, Em. Everybody, especially every colored child, *needs* to know."

Emily always insisted she'd never been a slave, but then John would ask her, "Em, did you pick cotton?" and she would answer, "Yes." Then he'd press on. "Did you get paid for it?" She'd admit she was never paid. Then he would turn to any third party and execute a broad and knowing wink.

Irrespective of the philosophical merits of John Sumner Blake's attitudes, Eubie never shook them. In later years they helped him to control his inevitable rage at obvious inequity and injustice. It's doubtful that he could have had all of the success in show business that he ultimately achieved had some of his father's guidance not remained in his personality.

Domestic appointments in the Blake cottage seem to have been at about the standard for their time and economic class. The outdoor privy was a good twenty yards from the kitchen door. Eubie remembers his father would go out there in the dead of winter, zero weather, clad only in a cotton robe.

"He'd sit out there and read the *whole* paper. Then he'd come in frozen and sit by the fire. And of course in my mother's house there was no such thing as taking a drink to warm yourself up. You just sat by the stove."

Emily Blake didn't have very much time to take proper care of her little family. Besides the mandatory hours in the church, she did her share to supplement the meager family income by doing other people's wash, either in her own home or theirs. Among her unquestionable virtues was not included any mastery of the culinary arts.

"Oh, she was a *terrible* cook." Eubie grimaces. "We got *enough* food, but half the time I couldn't eat it, the way she made it. The old man didn't go for it either. The quality was okay, but what she did to it! It didn't make any difference, beef, pork, chitlins, vegetables, chicken, it was really bad.

"But anyhow," he continues, "all *I* ever liked was sweet stuff. Anything with lots and lots of sugar. Any kind of dessert."

In this he has not changed, and watching him at age ninety-six as he dispatches four commercial-grade sugar doughnuts and a king-size 7-Up before retiring at 3 A.M. in the full knowledge that this has been representative of his regular diet all through the years, makes one wonder if the nutritionists really have anything to offer us.

"There was this bakery—Ulrich's bakery—on one of the corners by my house," Eubie remembers. "In this place you could buy a bag like this"—hands held to illustrate a sack two feet high—"of broken cake and cookies for two cents. It seems like I'd *sometimes* have a penny, but you'd never believe what I'd go through to get that *other* cent. That was the hard one. But when I'd get the two cents, I'd go right down to Ulrich's bakery and get this bag of broken cake. Then I'd eat every crumb of it. I mean *all* of it. I'd come in for supper, and of course I wouldn't be able to eat. She worried about me not eatin'. If she knew about that cake, she'd have killed me. But even if I was hungry, it wasn't easy to eat her cookin'. I don't see how my father did. She was a fine, honest woman—but she couldn't cook."

This wasn't all about Emily that was disadvantageous to Eubie. When she got angry at him, she would suddenly strike him about the head, frequently creating bruises visible enough to embarrass him about being seen in public. She'd say, as Eubie reports, "I'm not questioning God, but of all my children, why did he let *you* stay? I don't know why you're still here. You ain't no good. You ain't goin' to be *nothin'*."

Eubie says, "If she's mad with my father, she tells me, 'You're your father's son. He's no good, you're no good!' When she was pleased with me—that don't happen often—she'd say she didn't know *who* I took after."

He appraises the family's situation like this:

"Life was hard. Not like it is now. You had to come up tough or you wouldn't make it. She always treated me like she thought was best. My father rarely actually whipped me, but he'd give me these plucks on the head. Oh, boy! That hurt." He demonstrates by flicking his middle finger off his thumb. "He added a couple of commandments to the ones Moses brought down from the mountain. One of them was 'Don't mess in the white folks' business!' The other was 'Never run away. Stand up and fight!'"

It was the plucks on the head, Eubie insists, that taught him to read, instilled in him his sense of ethics and morality, and established the basis for whatever good conduct he could claim.

The old man made him take on any adversary, win or lose. It wasn't by any means necessary to fight fairly. The object was to win. Naturally, if your enemy was down, you kicked him. It was no game. It was directly from the survival handbook. Eubie learned his lesson well enough to be among those present today. But not by nature of a bellicose disposition and increasingly apprehensive about his piano-playing hands, Eubie did what he could to avoid trouble. He understood very well that he was primarily a musician—and, by the way, that playing made him a center of attention among the girls of the neighborhood.

Eubie's music making had begun when he was just four or five years old. The Blakes habitually did their produce shopping at night. "You could get everything cheaper because the vendors wanted to get rid of it before they went home. I was shopping with my mother in the market at night, and I must have got away from her. I wandered across this wide street and I found a music store. I climbed up on the bench of an organ and I fooled around with it until it made a sound. That's what I was doing when my mother found me.

"The manager of the store says, 'The child is a genius! It would be criminal to deprive him of the chance to make use of such a sublime, God-given talent.'"

Emily's resistance held up well until the man came to the part about the God-given talent. Who was she to stand in the way of the will of the Lord? That's how the Blakes found themselves making quarter-a-week payments on a seventy-five-dollar pump organ.

It was early understood in the household that music was justified only if it was doing the Lord's work, and Em had a sixth sense that communicated instantly when the rhythmic line between sacred and secular was crossed. Always suspicious of a musical instrument as a potential tool of the devil, she had her ear sharpened to detect any hint of Satan's syncopation and stood ready to exorcise it.

But there were those sounds of a working-class Negro environment that were too strong for an incipient virtuoso to resist. Why, even the gospel singers in Emily's very own church vocalized with a suspect beat, Eubie was quick to note. And there were houses of ill repute in the immediate area where the sounds of hot piano players drifted out through open doors and windows on balmy evenings. Very early, Eubie found himself a musical convert to the rhythmic preachments of a pair of the finest of them, Jack the Bear Wilson and the aging Jesse Pickett. Eubie noticed, by the way, that these worthies wore lots of diamonds and never worked, and even then he realized that they were primarily pimps who performed mainly to have an excuse to hang around the brothels where their women were employed.

One day Eubie found out what their kind of music was called. His mother caught him playing it and, her sensibilities offended by what she considered "the devil's music," ordered in firm and deliberate tones,

"Take that ragtime out of my house!"

That's how James Hubert Blake discovered he was a ragtime pianist.

A young next-door neighbor, Mrs. Margaret Marshall, organist at a Methodist Church, provided rudimentary instruction from the time Eubie was about seven. She carefully tried to work around Em's prejudices by avoiding the devil's music insofar as that was possible. Eubie, remarkably, remembers that he worked from a book prepared by a man named Kublick. But the exciting, nondescript sounds that emanated from the tonks and bawdy houses remained magnetic. And small wonder, for they consitututed most of the pool of existing American popular music. That pool was still shallow indeed. "Sweet Adeline," "Moonlight Bay," "Put on Your Old Gray Bonnet," and "Row, Row, Row," for instance, had yet to be written, and no classic rags had yet been published. The ragtime songs of Ben Harney were not yet on paper—no "Mr. Johnson Turn Me Loose" or "You've Been a Good Old Wagon"—and these predated the first instrumental rag published, W. H. Krell's "Mississippi Rag" of 1897.

"It's hard to say when I first started hearing this syncopated kind of music," Eubie says. "Of course, I remember the singing in my mother's church like it was yesterday—and then let me tell you about the funerals! You know, some big shot would die, some big-time guy—especially if the guy had been in the army before, a Negro, I mean—well, the people would sing and the band would play, you know, funeral music, dirges. Now on the way back, see, they play the very same melodies—he's buried now, see—in ragtime. Oh, how they'd swing! Now there just isn't any way I could stay away from this music.

"Well, I knew the band route—how they'd go to the grave-yard—and I'd hear them comin', and my mother would tell me, 'Don't you follow that band,' and I'd say, 'No, ma'am.' Well, they'd go on until she couldn't hear them anymore, and I'd ask her if I could go out and play. She'd tell me again, 'Don't you follow that band.' And I'd tell her, 'That band is gone now.'

"Then I'd run, all up hill too, and catch that band at Jefferson and Ann and stay right with it for the whole funeral, all the way to the cemetery gate. They didn't let the kids into the graveyard. Then before they bury this fellow, they shoot the guns over him. Wham! Hup-hup! Fire! Wham! Hup-hup! Fire! Wham! Now when I hear that first gun go off, I hear my mother yellin' in the shot—I don't really hear her, she's three miles away—'Hu-*bert!*' Now she can't yell *that* loud. It's only my imagination, but Hup-hup! Fire! Wham! 'Hu-*bert!*' Now she *told* me not to follow that parade, and I'm *sure* I hear her.

"Man, I come out of that graveyard like a shot! Down Gay Street. I know she's gonna kill me. Now I'm all by myself. On the way to the graveyard I'm safe, see, with all those colored people, but hoppin' cars alone all the way back—it's over two miles and the white kids threw rocks at you. But I jumped off the car at MacElder Street. Now I'm almost there and I really *hear* her calling me. She calls, 'Hu-*bert.*' I say, 'Ma'am?' She says, 'I thought you was followin' that parade after I told you not to.' I say, 'No, ma'am. I was right around the block.' I *swear* I heard her out at the graveyard. Still, you know that couldn't be."

How hard it is now to conceive of life without phonograph records, without TV, without radio or sound movies, without even *silent* movies, if you please! One wonders how songs ever became hits. They'd have to be disseminated slowly through live performance and sheet music. Eubie and three young friends formed a vocal quartet that could offer renditions of "In the Gloaming," "Camptown Races," "Beautiful Dreamer," and "Two Little Girls in Blue." These the boys rendered well enough to satisfy the neighborhood saloon trade. That's where their pocket money, such as it was, began to come from.

There were also songs to be heard and learned at the burlesque show. Eubie's father used to take him regularly on Saturdays, using some makeshift pretext about "taking the boy downtown." Eubie gives a shudder as he contemplates the domestic consequences that might have developed had they been discovered.

Eubie's father inadvertently caused many of Eubie's early troubles. "On the Christmas morning when I was twelve, my father gave me twenty-five cents. You know, in my whole life I never had twenty-five cents all to myself at one time. So I get a bottle and rinse it out with water and ashes until it's clean, see—that's how we used to do that stuff, see. I show the money to all my friends in the street, and I go down to the barrelhouse with them all following after me sayin', 'What you gonna do, Mouse? What you gonna buy, Mouse?'

"You could go to the back of the barrelhouse and get a bottle filled. It was Orleans Street and Central Avenue. They had shiny copper funnels, and they poured it into your bottle. 'Gimme ten cents of Overholt whisky for my father,' I tell him. That's a lot of whisky. More than a pint. He gives me a stogie for my father. It's Christmas, see. He says, 'Tell your father Merry Christmas.'

"I go in the alley and gulp down damn near the whole pint of whisky—*more* then a pint. Then I start to walk home and all the kids are still followin', see, because I still got money left. They didn't want me to buy 'em anything. They just wanted to see how I spent that fifteen cents. Those kids never saw anybody spendin' that much money. They want to drink some of that whisky, but I tell 'em they ain't big enough. Then I see my father, but not too clear, and I see the houses twistin' around and meltin', and I fall right down drunk. He picks me up and takes me home. Now my mother could smell whisky on your breath if she was in the market and you were home in bed. That night she prayed all night over me so I wouldn't die. Of course she's ready to kill me when I sober up. She'd rather kill me than let the whisky do it. She tells my father, 'This boy ain't dead, but *I'm* gonna kill him.' That was my first drink."

"When I was twelve I learned how to play a cornet. Did you know I once played the cornet? It made my neck swell up. There was a young white boy, I forget his name, he showed me how. He played in a city band. Then I played for a while in Cap Harris'—

Charlie Harris, they called him Cap—I played in his band. We'd go in furniture wagons to the beach and they'd have picnics. Sometimes we'd go on train excursions and play. The churches used to have these all the time. They'd have torchlight parades on down to the train stations or the boat docks on a Friday night. Then we'd play on the train or boat to Washington, Gettysburg, Philadelphia—all historic places. Then when you get there you play again. All together you play three times. The man come around and give me fifty cents. Some of the musicians got a dollar or two dollars. I got fifty cents.

"Now we're playin' these *arrangements*, see, and they're *white* arrangements. They weren't done by no Gershwin, see. And they're full of holes—the chords don't get filled up—and *I* filled 'em up with my own ideas.

"The leader says, 'Cut that stuff, Mouse. You don't play that ragtime in my band!' So I quit. Besides, it made my neck swell up. I figured I worked as hard as the other guys and that I *played* as much as they did, but Cap Harris just didn't care for the kind of music *I* cared about. Still, I think if I was the same color as those other guys, I'd have gotten more than fifty cents."

A photograph of Eubie taken at this stage of his life shows him with his boyhood buddy and next-door neighbor Hop Johns. It may be assumed that he dressed like this for mandatory Sunday church attendance. Both lads are "dressed to kill" in high-button shoes, neatly starched collars, neckties, and store suits with knickers. No ragamuffins these! We may reasonably assume their regular daily wear was less formal, but Emily demanded cleanliness, and Eubie learned that habit early, both from her and from the professional demands of show business. He remains immaculate at ninety-six just as though Em still stood over his shoulder with her scrub brush and laundry soap. His ensemble is always tasteful and carefully color-coordinated. Every item of apparel is flawless down to the fashionable folds of the handkerchief in his breast pocket.

Among the activities young Eubie cared least for were all those that involved physical exercise. Physical exertion was one of the evils of existence. Fortunately, as he could see, the piano might save him from it. Competitive sports were anathema to him because of the importance of protecting those delicate but powerful hands, and he had a militant disinterest in who won and who lost.

There was, however, one exception. He learned quite early to be an expert buck dancer.

"Back in those days," he explains, not without a hint of nostalgia, "we had open gutters—no sewers yet, you know. Then at each corner there'd be a big piece of slate, see, like a little bridge, so you could walk across the gutter without getting your shoes dirty. And right there on those slates I practiced buck dancing. You take a handful of sand, see, and you sprinkle it on the slate, and then you dance and it makes that little sound—but *you* know what it sounds like."

And so, since it was clear to him very early on where lay the direction of his life, and since neither the society nor the school system had prepared a curriculum leading to the achievement of his goals, the young man ingeniously improvised his own schooling, snatching out of the very air, as it seemed, the things he needed to become what he wanted to be. None of it was in pursuit of an academic degree. None of it promised to supply economic security. But there was a little music in the air. There was a little laughter in every heart waiting for the special kind of genius that could trigger it.

Baltimore Rag

Seeing His Chance
  A Word About Hookshops
    Nights at Aggie's, Days of Young Love
     Mama Finds Out
      Under the Crust

Eubie's fellow Baltimorean Henry L. Mencken characterized the 1890s as a period of intellectual war, "essentially a revolt against academic authority." Eubie's piano articulated the same message from the time he got his spidery fingers on his first keyboard. By the time he was thirteen years old, in 1896, those fingers were skilled enough to mirror the technique of Jesse Pickett, from whom he learned "The Dream Rag." Pickett, who had performed this piece of his at the Chicago World's Fair, the Columbian Exposition, in 1893, played it in one of Baltimore's innumerable brothels. Eubie could see the old man through the open window and study his fingering. He gaped in fascination at this extraordinary ragtime maestro weaving his minor-key magic. Eubie wondered at the effect of the tango beat. The worldly old pimp and gambler noticed him and for his benefit threw in a few sophisticated flourishes. Pickett also talked to Eubie and encouraged him, but Eubie needed no pep talks. He had already made music his lifetime commitment. Pickett had probably been playing that same music during the Civil War, but then and for a long time thereafter it was music current only in the social underground.

In '96, Sadie Koninsky of upstate New York brought out "Eli Green's Cake Walk." There was a spate of "coon songs," among them "Mammy's Little Pickaninny Boy" by Bert Williams and George Walker and "My Black Baby, Mine." by Thomas LeMack. Leslie Stuart, who hadn't yet composed the light opera "Florodora" and become Eubie's musical idol, had a sentimental entry that year in "The Willow Pattern Plate." The big hit was Geible and Buck's barbershop-quartet item "Go to Sleep, Kentucky Babe." The American musical establishment, however, welcomed Mac-Dowell's "To a Wild Rose" with greater enthusiasm. Thirty-four years later Eubie was to "build on" MacDowell's work what became one of his biggest hits and a permanent standard, "Memories of You."

Eubie was listening to all of it as it filtered through the turgid communications patterns of the era. It was all played in bordellos, saloons, and burlesque shows. When he attacked the more conventional numbers, he would add his own distinctive syncopation and turn them out as ragtime. He wasn't lacking in respect for the great names of the music world, but felt free to add his personal touch.

While white people were agitated about free silver and William Jennings Bryan, Eubie was honing his skills. Most Negroes, alienated from the political system and economically concerned more with coins than coinage, were living in a depressed jungle where opportunities for self-advancement and fulfillment were limited to very few lines of endeavor. One of these was entertainment, and Eubie was quick to grasp the point. Had he known about the race of the Cunard liner *Laconia* and the *St. Louis* for the trans-Atlantic speed record that year, he'd have known that any Negroes aboard were either busboys or musicians.

Eubie Blake never says "whorehouse." (He doesn't even say "hell" in mixed company—and says it only with apologies among the boys.) Not that he hasn't had a comfortable familiarity with these dens of iniquity. In the period in which his talents blossomed, the great hot pianists served their apprenticeships under the auspices of madams—most of whom were tone deaf, incidentally—and Eubie was no exception. But how to name such a place?

In pursuit of reasonable gentility, Eubie has tried "bawdy house" (too archaic), "house of ill repute" (too stilted), and ultimately, as a bowdlerized compromise, "hookshop."

Around the turn of the century every city had its greater and lesser hookshops, some of which had reputations that resounded through the civilized world, and each boasted one or more piano wizards who were considered indispensable to its gaiety. Chicago had a brothel operated by the notorious and talented Babe Connors from which the music world derived "There'll Be a Hot Time in the Old Town Tonight" and "Ta Ra Ra Boomderay." Tom Turpin operated his Rosebud Cafe down in the Chestnut Valley sporting district of St. Louis where Scott Joplin would take his occasional turn at the keyboard. Around the corner was where Frankie had shot Johnny and established a permanent place in urban folklore. Fabulous Storyville flourished in New Orleans. At Gipsy Schaefer's "house," for instance, the great ragtime-to-classical pianist Tony Jackson played to accompany "Naked Dances." Ferdinand Le Menthe, who would later be known as Jelly Roll Morton, only two years Eubie's junior, was soon to make his own debut in a Storyville bordello.

In Baltimore, Aggie Shelton kept one of the city's more aesthetic bordellos and there gave employment to a long line of illustrious virtuosi, including Eubie Blake, who was fifteen in 1898 when he went to work there.

It may be assumed that many readers of this biography have never seen the interior of an old-fashioned hookshop, and it might be helpful to have the details of this environment sketched in, including the interaction between the place and the performer. First and foremost, a hookshop is a business—cash flow is its sine qua non—so the music has to be what the customers like or what an adroit manipulator of the ivories can teach them to like. Though no salaries were attached to these musical assignments, the piano masters properly expected to make enough in tips to make the occupation worth while, apart from any pleasant personal relations they might establish with occupants of the house.

Prices charged to customers for hookshop services were related directly to the youth and attractiveness of the girls on duty and the luxury of the ambiance. Music helped create the ambiance, along with upholstered brocaded sofas, ornate chandeliers, the costumes of the inhabitants, and the "policy" of the house.

Policy was established by the landlady herself, who, if she ran a "respectable" house, would deploy bouncers at strategic locations as an aid to decorum. Beverages would be poured into glasses by efficient servants so that bottles were not potential blunt instruments. In a good hookshop, policy demanded that no patron's pocket be picked without the specific sanction of the madam, that the booze remain uncut except for the champagne in the late hours, when ginger ale would serve as well, and that the music be continuous. This last requirement might be met by either the employment of a second musician or the purchase of an auxiliary coin-operated piano.

In the halcyon days of hookshops a patron might expect the price of admission to entitle him to thirty minutes to an hour of undisturbed dalliance with the wench of his choice, preceded by an equal period of convivial activities in the parlor, where he might enjoy companionship, in some cases dancing, and the music. Drinks extra.

At Aggie Shelton's all this could be experienced by any white male with five dollars plus the cost of drinks. As might have been expected in those days, with no television, no movies, no radio, and the ministry raging over the evils of billiards, there were few places where a man might pass an entertaining evening. After all, there wasn't even night baseball then!

Shadowy figures out of the past had established a style in which an upright piano in a hookshop was to be played. Men like Jesse Pickett and Big Head Wilbur, Jack the Bear and One Leg Willie Joseph had been beating syncopated rhythms on such keyboards at least since General Lee conceded at Appomattox. Some amateur musicologists of the time, trying to identify and classify this peculiar musical form and lacking later, more sophisticated terminology such as "blues," "jazz," and "ragtime," called it "nigger music." In the known semantics of the era, it should be noted, that term was not considered necessarily negative in many circles.

If in 1979 an enterprising madam were to be permitted to erect a replica of Aggie Shelton's hookshop on its original site, employ a hot pianist, and recruit a covey of ladies of easy virtue prepared to play for pay, the operation would be looked upon with horror by an appalled few, as a quaint and colorful curiosity by many more. But in 1898 it was a fact of life, accepted by society as a "necessary evil," depraved but ineradicable. Nobody at that time could have conceived of a metropolis without hookshops.

By the standards of 1898, Aggie Shelton's "five-dollar house" was pretty classy. And the place had a relaxed atmosphere that patrons enjoyed. Six or eight assorted belles were always on hand to keep a marathon party going, and the atmosphere just wouldn't have been the same without music.

By this time Eubie's neighborhood reputation had bloomed and he was in the process of achieving "shark" status as a piano player despite his tender years. Now it's easy to say that a fifteen-year-old boy has no business playing piano in a whorehouse, but Eubie's economic situation and his extraordinary talent, combined with his demonstrated incompatibility with the school system, practically funneled him directly into Aggie's parlor. "I giff you," she promised in her thick Teutonic accent, "three dollar a night guarantee if you don't make so much in tips." But she never had to make good on her guarantee.

Eubie, once embarked on a career, never looked back. Quickly he became a favorite with the the girls and their customers. Because there weren't many popular tunes written yet, he'd drift easily into classics and semiclassics like "Rustle of Spring" and "The Beautiful Blue Danube," but beneath his left hand's spidery digits his "wobble" bass would develop that syncopated African sound that was to make him famous.

It is nowhere recorded that Eubie's piano playing generated higher levels of eroticism among the frolicsome couples that spent the nights in Aggie's or that he was a conscious subversive agent of Satan who had bartered his soul for power and pelf. But he did play then, as now, as though the demon were in him, defying exorcism. The wobble bass was heard abroad in East Street and the young maestro's future was assured.

At fifteen, if you were going to be an entertainer in a brothel, where you started your work stint at the unconventional hour of

10 P.M., and if you were going to manage this operation without the knowledge of the strict matriarch of your household, your mama, you had to create ingenious ways of getting out of the house while she thought you were tucked safely into bed. And there was another problem: At work you couldn't *look* like fifteen. That was solved by Mr. Rabb Walker, proprietor of the pool room on the corner, who maintained a rental pair of long pants in Eubie's approximate size. Eubie would sneak out of the house as soon as his hard-working parents went to bed, run to the pool room, give Rabb a quarter for the pants and head right over to Aggie Shelton's.

"Aggie Shelton's was a high class place," Eubie recalls, "a five-dollar house. That was a lot of money in those days. It was a place where you went upstairs, then there would be four or five sitting rooms all with nice, soft furniture. The girls were all *white*, and of course so were the customers.

"You know, those fellows and those girls used to just sit and talk together like a church social or something, no rough stuff at all. Of course the scagmo"—sexual intercourse—"happened one more flight up. I made a lot of tips. The more tunes you'd know, the more money you'd make.

"I picked up 'Hello, Ma Ragtime Gal,' and 'Any Rags' was popular, and so was 'After the Ball.' Those people mostly liked real sentimental songs like 'You Made Me What I Am Today, I Hope You're Satisfied," or they liked ragtime. You never heard any *dirty* songs in Aggie Shelton's. It was high class.

"I never did drink no water—*never*—and I never knew all the time I worked at Aggie's that champagne had alcohol in it. I never knew you could get drunk from it, and I used to drink at least a couple of bottles a night. Years later, when I worked in the Goldfield Hotel, people told me it was alcohol and not like ginger ale. It goes up your nose the same way, but I never got drunk from it."

In the late nineties, while the white world was celebrating a multitude of whites engaged in the arts and show business, on the other side of the tracks the achievements of the great black innovators in these fields continued to be anonymous. The whites' favorite author, Mark Twain, was still in production, and their kids were making a best seller out of Kipling's *Second Jungle Book*. Only a few, a very few, blacks had ever heard of Paul Laurence Dunbar, though his poetry had started being published.

There were other contrasts. In 1898, Caucasians were much occupied with the war in Cuba that Mr. Hearst had managed to stir up, but to many Negroes war was just more of the "white folks' business" you stayed out of if you could. Charles Hoyt's traveling show "A Trip to Chinatown"—featuring Charles K. Harris's overwhelmingly successful "After the Ball," sung by the tenor of the century, J. Aldrich Libby—didn't satisfy the darker citizens as much as did the Cole and Johnson travesty "A Trip to Coontown." The dramatic heroes were too light of tone for Negroes to identify with that year, which saw the footlight debut of Sherlock Holmes and Richard Mansfield's "Cyrano de Bergerac" as well as Mrs. Fiske's creation of the role of Nora in Ibsen's "Doll's House." It seemed to be a world of pale protagonists. Even though the actor DeWolf Hopper didn't come right out and say so, you just knew, as you listened to his stirring recital of "Casey at the Bat," that the mighty Casey wasn't a Negro, and most young ladies of the duskier hues didn't look very much like Charles Dana Gibson's meticulously drawn ideal girl.

So, over on the black side of town, if you were going to have any models, they couldn't very well come from among the elite of the world of show business or the arts—or even sports or the more stable professions, for that matter. You pretty much had to find your own way. Eubie found his by gaping at Jesse Pickett's hands to steal his fingering and absorbing the many tricks of which Jack the Bear was a master. There was also the friendly competition against his contemporary, Hughie Wolford, reportedly a giant among Eastern keyboard prodigies.

At fifteen, Eubie filled the adult working role at night, but he also had plenty of adolescent business to attend to. His extraordinary ability to produce those syncopated sounds from the pump organ caused flutters in the hearts of young girls, and he was surrounded by them at the many parties to which he was invited. This, he says flatly, is the main reason why he stayed with the music in the first place. For a while he was undisputed king of the social hill, and then one of his favorite girl friends, Miss Teeny

Pritchett, gave a party to which a young out-of-town fellow, Edgar Dowell, was invited. Dowell had apparently advanced beyond Eubie as a musician at this stage, and Eubie says he was cut to ribbons by Dowell's keyboard performance on this fateful afternoon. Not only was his ego frayed, but he lost his girl friend.

A lesser personality might have surrendered, but our young hero gritted his teeth and went back to the keyboard more determined than ever to make his mark on the music world.

And here he *was*, making it at Aggie Shelton's, and loving every minute of it. Between his mother's Calvinistic heaven and Aggie Shelton's funnel to hell there was just no contest.

Because of the eventfulness of the period in his life between 1895 and 1898, Eubie gets his chronology scrambled from time to time. He recalls well his bouts with schooling, highlighted by a classic antagonism between himself and a teacher he hated enough so that he hasn't yet forgotten her name was Mary McDermott. In school—Primary School No. 2, at 200 East Street—he first met Avis Lee, whom he was to wed some fifteen years later and who called him Dummy because of his notoriously undistinguished academic performance. Avis was his senior by two years, herself a pianist, and a mathematical genius. "She did what she could to help me, but it was no use."

The nineties were a happy time for Eubie Blake, if only for the girls. At fifteen the youngster had well-established assets that the girls found fascinating. First, he shared in the aura that always surrounds professional musicians, and second, he had plenty of spending money honestly earned as tips from Aggie Shelton's. Fortified by these enticements, he didn't find it difficult to arrange an endless succession of picnics in the meadows. The young ladies put up elaborate wicker baskets full of fried chicken, pork chops, ham, hard-boiled eggs, and fruit. The consumption of these feasts rarely took as much as an hour. After that, with long afternoons ahead and no portable TV to distract them, Eubie and the girl of the moment would rediscover the ancient and ever-popular amusements and pastimes of young lovers everywhere.

There was no way little Eubie could reasonably expect to continue indefinitely his employment with Aggie Shelton without his mother, sooner or later, discovering what he was doing. The conduit for this information was the minister's wife, who paid Emily Blake a visit and asked a leading question.

"Sister Blake, did you have any idea that little Hubie"—heavy on the "H"—"is playing the piano at night in Aggie Shelton's bawdy house?"

Not possible, Emily insisted, explaining that her youngster was in bed nightly by nine.

"Maybe in bed by nine," said the informant, "but out of it by ten and off to Aggie Shelton's."

"Well, sister, I know *you* haven't been in Aggie Shelton's. How do *you* know it's my Eubie playin' in there?"

"Just walkin' by, sister! Nobody plays with that wobble-wobble bass but little Hubie. Anybody can tell it."

Challenged at last by his mother, Eubie never got beyond "Well-er—a" in his reply. She pronounced that when his father got home, the incipient virtuoso would receive the whipping of his life. Apprehensively he waited for the hour of his father's arrival and no sooner had John come in the door than Emily blurted out in a single sentence that "Mr. Blake" of whom no good would ever come and who had abandoned himself to the devil and whose sins had already assured him a reservation in hell had been playing ragtime music in Aggie Shelton's "body" house.

John reflected briefly, concluded this was not a matter for general family discussion, but one better served by "man to man" talk, and ordered the boy upstairs.

"You been workin' at Aggie Shelton's?" John demanded.

"Well, I ain't gonna lie to you, Papa," Eubie answered, "I been workin' there every night. I've been leavin' the house when you go to sleep."

"What have you been doing with the money?" John wanted to know.

Eubie showed him where it was carefully hidden under the oilcloth floor covering, carefully spaced around to avoid bulges. There were fives, tens, twenties—maybe more money than the elder Blake had ever seen. "Mind if I take one of these?" he asked.

Downstairs, Emily met the descending pair with aggressive anticipation, still ready to denounce and to see that fitting retribution was effected. "You took care of him?" she wanted to know of her husband.

"Now Em," he stated flatly, "this boy is doing nothing wrong. He's gonna have to work, and this is good work with good pay. You just better leave him alone to do his work as he sees it."

Emily never did come to terms with Eubie's calling, though she couldn't fail to note a consistently improving standard of living in the Blake household from that day on. Eubie contributed substantially to the family coffers and kept his father in whisky and cigarettes until the old man died. But many years later during one of the peaks of Eubie's success in show business, she was asked how she felt about his celebrity and his renowned achievements as composer and conductor. Her answer was, "He could have been using his talent to do the Lord's work."

As the century drew to a close, a skilled social observer might have become aware that smoldering beneath the crust of popular culture, especially in urban black communities, there rumbled certain creative musical phenomena that would alter the life styles of all of society. A music publisher in Kansas City marketed Scott Joplin's "Original Rags," in 1898, and in 1899 John W. Stark issued Joplin's "Maple Leaf Rag," which would awaken a nation to a new and exciting concept in music. And in Baltimore in that year young Eubie Blake completed the composition of a piece that would establish a basis for the Eastern "stride" style of piano playing. At the time it had no name, but it was eventually sold to M. Witmark & Co. as "The Charleston Rag." Eubie is quick to explain that he didn't *write* "Charleston Rag" in 1899. That's when he *composed* it. "I didn't learn how to *write*," he explains, "until 1915."

At the end of the century there were many touring Negro shows, some of them vestigial remains of stylized tours of "Uncle Tom's Cabin," others traditional minstrel shows with actual colored performers in blackface. Among these were "The Black Patti [Sissieretta Jones] Troubadors," the "South before the War" troupe, Billy Kersands' "Wide Mouth Minstrels," Sam T. Jack's "Creole Company," Bert Williams and George Walker's reviews, and various outfits featuring superb Negro comics like Sam Lucas and the team of Bailey and Fletcher. One of the most popular was a plantation-style review called "In Old Kentucky" in which Eubie was to make his New York bow in 1902. Eubie recalls having seen many of these productions, but mostly later and in New York or elsewhere, though some of them played Baltimore from time to time. From Baltimore he does recall the Richard K. Fox Championship Cake Walk Medals competition and the music that accompanied it, though he never competed or participated.

The whites were closing out the century with some remarkable though not always innovative songs. Probably the best was Paul Dresser's "On the Banks of the Wabash." Other white composers like Harry Von Tilzer sensed a new vitality creeping into the music world but missed the point entirely with titles like "Mammy's Little Kinky Headed Coon." This was a gentle little ditty intended to show sympathy for Negroes.

Eubie himself played out the century happily coaxing a new music out of any pianos he could reach. And he prospered in his modest way, really spectacularly for a barely grown colored kid in that day and age, and looked to the day—and he just knew it had to come—when the whole world would sing his songs.

Finding His Way in an Unfamiliar Century

A Job Here, a Job There
Bert Williams: A Subtle Shift of Tone
Composer in the Bud

Throughout the countryside at the turn of the century there still existed an almost universal confidence in the efficacy of snake oil, and even the few budding scientists who were skeptical of its medicinal values maintained an abiding affection for it. If it didn't actually cure lumbago, rheumatism, the grippe, and sick headache in ladies, it did bring fast temporary relief from minor boredom and the cultural effects of chronic isolation. And the "medicine shows" put on to boost its sales were memorable events in many of America's small towns and villages.

Nestled in among the hills of southeastern Pennsylvania lay the hamlet of Fairfield. World renown persistently eluded this lonely village, and time passed there in the most pedestrian of ways. Yet Fairfield did have a gloriously different day at least once. For on one sunny spring day in 1901 there arrived, with its accustomed pomp and circumstance and in full panoply, the opulent caravan of Dr. Frazier not only to offer balm for Fairfield's physical ills but also to regale the burghers with the newest songs and dances from the wide world outside, having journeyed from far-off Baltimore, thirty-five miles distant.

And the seal of history was impressed on Fairfield that day—by the display on the boards, for the very first time anywhere, of the prodigious talent of James Hubert Blake, in person.

The massed humanity, possibly as many as fifty souls, crowded about the tailgate of Dr. Frazier's wagon, which let down to form an effective portable stage. The young Blake demonstrated the most recent breakthroughs in buck dancing and, as though that weren't sufficient, wrung impassioned melodies from the melodeon. With the rest of the company he harmonized selections from Bland and Foster and generally performed all the chores expected of a show-business trouper. Then, as the evening sun went down, the people of Fairfield, well fortified inside now with Dr. Frazier's all-purpose nostrum and sufficiently stocked up on it to face more confidently a full season of dyspepsia and ingrown toenails, wended their way home, to regale each other for days with the recollection of the knee-slapping witticisms and musical artistry of Dr. Frazier's production.

It's not likely that the citizenry took the trouble to separate one young Negro performer from another in its collective memory, and there was no local press to review the extravaganza, so we are deprived of contemporaneous evaluations of Eubie's buck dancing or keyboard wizardry on "All Coons Look Alike to Me" or Jesse Pickett's composition "The Dream Rag." Let history note, however, that there in Fairfield, Pennsylvania, in the spring of 1901, is where the legend of Eubie Blake, master showman, actually starts.

But Eubie and his fellow troupers Preston Jackson (not the celebrated New Orleans trombonist of a later era) and one Knot-Head, a more experienced young entertainer, were enchanted neither by their reception in the community of Fairfield nor by Dr. Frazier and his operation, so in a body they tendered their resignations, giving the customary twenty minutes notice, and, facing southwest, began making their way back to Baltimore on foot, doing a little entertaining at a wayside tavern or two en route to earn eating money.

Knot-Head, stating he had previously traversed this path, pointed out a shortcut over a mountain that led, he assured his companions, straight to Baltimore, but Eubie and Preston, momentarily surfeited with heady adventure, decided to trust their fortunes to the regularly traveled road. They arranged to meet Knot-Head in Baltimore, but, Eubie relates with a certain continuing curiosity, "That's the last we ever heard of him. We never saw him again. Never did find out what became of him. Man, could he dance!"

With this kind of experience to put in his resumé, by 1902 Eubie Blake, age nineteen, was ready for the big time, and he found himself, excitingly, part of the company "In Old Kentucky," a well-known traveling show, and on his way, for the first time, to New York. He doesn't recall who got him the job. His association with the big city on that occasion lasted but three days. He never got to see Broadway.

"The way they did," he recalls, "they backed the truck up to the stage door and we went into the theater and did the show. Then we got back in the truck and they took us to this little boarding house on Bleecker Street. I've looked all up and down Bleecker Street for that house, but I never could *find* it. Then we go to bed, and the next day the same thing. I only stayed three days. My mother made me go home."

The theater was the Academy of Music on Fourteenth Street. It belonged to Colonel Mapleson.

"You asked me could I dance. Well, in 'In Old Kentucky' you sang or you buck danced, and I wasn't no singer! I went to New York with the show so I could see Broadway. Hell, I never even got to see Fourteenth Street."

"In Old Kentucky" was a distinguished production. It had three companies touring the country simultaneously. In the one he performed his brief stint in, Eubie had the chance to see some of the greatest Negro dancers, including Clarence Bowens, Bert Grant, and Harry Swington.

The year 1902 marked the end of Eubie's own career as a buck dancer; all that happened later involved his compositions, theatrical productions, and piano playing. On leaving "In Old Kentucky," he returned to Baltimore and got a job as a relief pianist to one Big Head Wilbur for a dollar and a quarter a night. He started at 4 P.M. and worked to midnight. He wrote a piece called "Corner of Chestnut and Low" to celebrate the place, Alfred Greenfeld's saloon, which was at that address. It seems to have been the prototype for all those stage and movie sets with the pimps and whores, the sawdust on the floor, the bartenders with handlebar mustaches, the beer kegs to sit on, and that ragtime piano with the wobble-wobble bass.

Eubie was impressed by the appearance of the classic pimps of that day. What if the diamonds *were* a little yellow? They were enormous. Box-back coats and Stetson hats were the latest style, and of course, those St. Louis flats—long, pointed shoes with ten-dollar gold pieces set in the tips. His admiration for this grandeur lingers in his voice as he describes the scene.

"You know, I was only the piano player, but I'd look at all of these fine people and I'd know that somewhere people had those diamonds and those high-class clothes, and I wanted some day to be like that. I'm not saying I wanted to be a pimp or nothin' like that, but I wanted to be somebody who could *live* like that."

"My mother! She just had to learn to put up with all that what I was doing. She used to stay up till I got home at night so to make sure I'd get all the sawdust off of my shoes before I came into the house. The old man never said anything more about it. He knew when he had a good thing going. I'm glad I was able to make their lives easier. They worked hard for me and they deserved it."

Eubie's composing career was largely experimental during the first years of the twentieth century, evolving what can best be described as an urban-oriented sound, as opposed to the rural-flavored products in the Stark catalogue. The characteristics of his bass, his relatively complex harmonies, and the dynamics of his concepts would later be heard in the pianistics of James P. Johnson, Fats Waller, and Art Tatum. It's difficult to keep in mind that so much of what he was doing then is what is now regarded as modern. "The Charleston Rag" was invented two years before corn flakes!

The life of a piano player is inherently itinerant. Either the musician and the regular patrons at the place of employment get tired of each other or there are personality conflicts between the talent and management. Sometimes a disagreement rises centering on satisfactory emolument. Places go bankrupt and other places open. A player goes away and takes up some other kind of work for a while, or finds what seems to be a better piano-playing job. In

1903 Eubie left Greenfeld's saloon and found regular employment in Annie Gilly's rowdy sporting house. This place was a huge hall where the girls and the "johns" whooped it up so that you could hardly hear the piano. It was at 319 East Street, very near the old homestead.

Eubie learned an important lesson at Gilly's. Never sit with your back to the door. If trouble walks in, you've got to see it quickly enough to duck. Today, whether in his own home or in a plush hotel restaurant, he still demands to be seated facing the doorway.

The people at Annie Gilly's danced wildly to "Good Morning, Carrie," a new hit by Tim Brymn and Cecil Mack. If Eubie tried "Bird in a Gilded Cage," it would be drowned out in the melee. Everybody would join in the chorus, though, of "Down Where the Wurzburger Flows" or "Under the Anheuser Busch."

Now Eubie sees a certain humor in the cultural qualities of this bawdy bagnio as it operated in 1903, but as he tells of it, working there was a grim experience.

"All hookshops ain't alike," he observes. "Aggie Shelton's, like I told you, was a high-class house, but Annie Gilly's wasn't *nothin'* like Aggie Shelton's, see? Annie Gilly's was just a big, big room, like a dance hall. That place was so noisy I used to think nobody in there could hear the piano. But there was always a lot of people just like to hang around by me and listen.

"They had all kinds of fights in there. Customers came in with brass knuckles and knives and sharp razors—just *lookin'* for fight, see?

"I don't remember where the girls took the men for the scagmo. They must have had little bedrooms attached somewhere. That was a dollar house—a dollar an hour. She did a big business.

"Those girls were really tough! Sometimes I thought the customers needed to be protected from *them* more than the other way. I don't think Annie Gilly had no bouncer. The men had to watch their wallets, too.

"It was a big, wild party all night long. I used to be so *tired* when I'd get home. You keep one eye on the piano and the other lookin' out for flyin' bottles."

The end of slavery hadn't, of course, been an "open sesame" to equality of opportunity for the American Negro. The taboos, prejudices, and fears of white society proscribed most avenues to success, leaving only certain areas of entertainment and sports available to any substantial number of blacks.

Upward mobility in the world of pugilism made it possible for Joe Gans, Jack Johnson, and Peter Jackson to achieve high levels of fame and fortune during the early part of the twentieth century, at least in comparison with their brethren, and since their success was in open competition with white prize fighters, they became folk heroes to the black world—models for the more robust among Negro youth. At the same time these gladiators felt the fierce racial antagonism every time they stepped into the ring against a white opponent.

For the most part, black entertainers in the late nineteenth century didn't threaten the white ego. In fact, their demeanors and routines achieved the opposite effect, since they accepted the role of the comic and ignorant semisavage that the whites demanded they be. The talented were able to develop white as well as black followings. The prime show-business geniuses of the race like Ernest R. Hogan and Billy Kersands made their successes by presenting this stereotype of the Negro. In the 1880s and 1890s the Negro self-image was of so low an order that blacks no less than whites responded to the crude and primitive caricature that black performers of the times presented.

But by the turn of the century, only thirty-five years—barely a generation—from the close of the Civil War—the seeds of a more assertive and radical attitude were becoming manifest among the blacks of the stage and the music world. On the boards the comedian Bert Williams, master of his art, broke the ice in subtle ways by almost imperceptibly altering the focus of his humor. Though he continued to undergo the indignity of blackening his handsome features with burnt cork—he was light-skinned and could easily have passed for white—his presentation shifted emphasis from slapstick to satire. He did this so deftly that his audiences barely noticed the transition. Deliberately and sardonically he developed a footlight personality that could mock white bigotry before white audiences and get away with it.

Today, people listening to his records or viewing the single film he made might comment "Uncle Tom" to each other, but that would be because they failed to grasp the essence of his historical situation. Among vaudeville performers, what Bert Williams was doing was not only socially innovative but revolutionary. His role was crucial to black progress in theater.

On the other hand, it never crossed Eubie Blake's mind to blacken his physiognomy, even when he was buck dancing for a living. He appears to have been acceptable without that to his audiences of either color from the beginning. He learned to play what audiences wanted to hear. It was the simplest of formulas and it worked.

His listeners reacted to his vivacity and were amazed by his seemingly endless improvisational capacity. He remains acutely aware that other Negroes had to resort to countless demeaning theatrical devices to get a place before American audiences for themselves, and his sympathy for their plight remains profound, his memory of it green. Yet because he took his own talent for granted and concentrated on such matters as polishing his technique and broadening his theoretical grasp of his idiom, he was competent to supply a kind of cultural leadership that, like what Bert Williams did, was essential in black efforts to achieve equality in the world of show business.

During the pre–World War I era Eubie and Bert Williams lived just a few doors from each other on 137th Street near Seventh Avenue in Harlem.

"Bert Williams," Eubie says, "was only seven or eight years older than me, but he was a star when I was a kid. He *still* died very young. He was only about forty-five, I think. Big, handsome man. Come from big, *strong* people. I met his father and mother in 1915. They were both very big. Very strong. He opened a saloon for his father in his later years.

"I think if Bert Williams had lived, I might sometime have done a show with him. It would have been a good show and a great honor. He was a great artist and a great man.

"Me and him were friends, but we didn't visit back and forth. His wife was *fierce*, and it seemed like she never liked him to have *any* friends. He was a man liked to keep to himself anyway, except down to the corner at Matheney's. That was a saloon—135th Street and Seventh.

"One morning—it was just gettin' light—I'm comin' home, see, and Bert, he's comin' out of Matheney's at the same time. You know sometimes that man would drink *too* much and he would get *drunk*. Well, he *was* drunk, and he puts his arm around me—I don't like nobody to do that—but he don't know too much what he's doin', see? Now he's carryin' a loaf of bread. He's holdin' it like this, like a football player, and he says he's bringin' it home to Lottie because he loves her and she's such a good woman. He says to me, 'Come on home with me, Eubie. Lottie won't be mad if she sees me with you. She knows you're a respectable man.'

"I didn't want to go, but what you gonna do? That Lottie, she really made him toe the line, see, and when we come up the outside steps I see she's watchin' through the window. You know, waitin' up the whole night for him to come home, see?

"Now, I'm helpin' him, see? *I* ain't been out with him. I don't know who he got drunk with. He could get drunk with anybody. I'm just bringin' him home. She opens the door and she says to me, 'What happened to my husband? What did you do to him?'

"Poor Bert, he tried to kiss her, you know, to make up, but I didn't wait to see how *that* came out. I just got out of there as fast as I could.

"He was a man liked to see *everybody* do good. When our show was such a big hit, he just as happy as if it was *his* show."

Eubie tells of Bert Williams—who died in 1922, the year after the show "Shuffle Along" opened and became a great hit—as though it were only yesterday. His expression shows his continuing respect for the memory of this titan of comedy.

"Now Bert Williams was a big star in the Ziegfeld Follies—the *only* Negro to play in the Follies up to that time—but when he wasn't on the stage, he didn't act like other show people. He spent his time sittin' in Matheney's watchin' people. He never seemed to be interested in havin' company. He'd just sit there and drink. But he wasn't mean. Don't get the idea he was mean. He was *very* kind.

"I was with him one time in Matheney's when a guy comes in to the place. I see the guy talk to a couple of the men in there, and I see they give him some money. Then he comes to where *we're* sittin', see, and he says, 'You know, so-and-so just died.' I knew who he was talkin' about. I don't remember his name, but he was a musician. He says, 'I'm takin' up a collection to help his wife pay for the funeral.' I give him a couple of dollars, but Bert didn't. He just shakes his head no and the guy leaves.

"So then Bert gives the bartender—we knew him good—he gives the bartender fifty bucks to give to the widow. But the bartender ain't supposed to tell where the money came from.

"That's the way he always did things. Some people thought he was mean, but he was soft-hearted. He did a lot for our people. If it wasn't for him and Jim Europe"—the distinguished black conductor and composer who did so much to make the world treat black musicians like the professionals they are—"I don't know *where* Negroes in show business would be today. I wish everybody would understand that."

Like life for so many talented Negroes in show business, much of Bert Williams's life was less than felicitous. His enormous popular success notwithstanding, he, more than most, was sensitive to the snubs and slurs of white society. It seems not unlikely that his very genius as a performer was rooted in a heroic effort to find a way to neutralize the effects of that oppression. He made himself a renowned, even a beloved, figure in black and white society alike, and he made a great contribution to his own race—it's unlikely that he was aware how great when he died.

Eubie, by contrast, has lived on into a new social order in which barriers of bigotry have receded. He isn't morbidly introspective and is thoroughly equipped to enjoy his life. It's doubtful that Williams knew joy on a single day of his life that matched the routine joys of any one of Eubie's.

Bert Williams's success began late in the nineteenth century on the vaudeville stage. He and his partner, George Walker, one of the great dancer-comics, were billed as "Two Real Coons" in vaudeville, and the shows in which they appeared bore such billings as "In Bandanaland," "Williams and Walker in Abyssinia," and "Williams and Walker in Dahomey" (all of 1902).

Many songs from black productions of the years around the turn of the century were less than edifying, though much of the music was superb. Consider such titles as "All I Wants Is My Chickens," "The Warmest Coon in Darktown," and simply "Coon, Coon, Coon." Society was not ready to accept even the musical achievements of classically trained Negro composers, conductors, or virtuosi—such giants as James Reese Europe, with music degrees from Columbia University, who led the gigantic Clef Club Orchestra, or Leipzig-trained Will Marion Cook, conductor of the New York Symphony Orchestra, later on tour in Europe as the American Symphony Orchestra. Some breaks in musical stereotyping were beginning to show, leading to anomalies on stage. In 1905, dusky Tom Lemonier wrote the classic emotional song "Just One Word of Consolation," and it was sung by a superb black tenor, Henry Troy. But the show in which it was introduced was Ernest R. Hogan's "Rufus Rastus" of that year.

Meanwhile Eubie Blake pursued his career as a professional musician strangely untouched by the sometimes overt, sometimes subtle social pressures of the early years of this century, learning his instrument, becoming a genuine master of his musical art. In his brain there was no "white music," no "black music." His prime musical idol was Thomas Barrett, who, as Leslie Stuart, composed "Florodora" and brought the Florodora Girls to the world. Stuart was a white Englishman. As Robert Kimball and Bill Bolcomb put it in *Reminiscing with Sissle and Blake*, Eubie got from Stuart "an angular but flowing melodic sense, full of surprising leaps and turns."

Eubie also learned from Victor Herbert and Edgar MacDowell. He studied their songs and a couple of times, at least, used them as a basis for his own pieces. One of Eubie's most successful numbers, for instance, was "Gypsy Blues," a minor variation on Herbert's "Gypsy Love Call."

"Just wait until the Old Man"—Victor Herbert—"sees you," he remembers people telling him. "You'll catch some hell. He's really mad that you stole his song!"

"I didn't steal *nothin'*," Eubie insists. "Not one note is the same. But I did build it on his chords because I admired him. You can play the two tunes together and they fit."

Soon after, he approached the great maestro while both were working at a benefit. Eubie told Herbert he had stolen nothing from him and Herbert, in his almost stage-German dialect, asked, "But you *used* mein zong?" Eubie acknowledged that, to the extent described, he had.

"Then," said the old man, smiling, "I must be ein pretty goot composer, hah?"

One of the incidents that stands out brilliantly in Eubie's memory, and one of those that he tells about most frequently, is Baltimore's Lyric Theater fire, which took place very early in the century. He had a date with a girl named Edith Buchanan, he remembers. He remarks on her long, beautiful hair, and says that as he left her house and walked down Pennsylvania Avenue, that long, beautiful hair was occupying his mind almost exclusively.

"On my way home I stop by at this bar and get a milk punch. Now remember, you can't get drunk on one milk punch. Anyway I can't. I get down to Mount Royal Avenue where the Lyric is. There's a little grass that grows along the curb there and I see zebras grazing! Now I see the theater is on *fire*, see? Right over here is the B&O station and there's more zebras eatin' grass in the little park. Then I'm thinkin' about the milk punch. Could it do that? The next thing I notice is elephants. Elephants! But when I saw the lions, that's when I left. No way to catch me. I could really run, but I never knew how fast before.

"I get to Calvert Street and there's a white man walking. I fell right down on the ground in front of him. 'What's the matter with you, boy?' he asks me. I point back to the Lyric. 'There's lions there. I saw 'em,' I tell him. I had to repeat it. He says, 'Good God A'mighty! The zoo is on fire.'

"He picked me up off the ground and I went on down Calvert Street. Somebody told me later that Frank Barstock's circus was playin' there then. They told me the watchman was asleep and a chimpanzee that had been watchin' him had learned to open the gate, and the monkey opened it to let the animals get saved. That's the most scared I've ever been in my life."

Another fire affected Eubie's life—the great Baltimore fire of 1904, which on Eubie's twenty-first birthday burned down a large part of the city. In the ashes were a number of places that had been supplying him with employment. By this time, though, the quality of his playing was so outstanding that there never was a question of being able to find a good job.

He had become prosperous enough to make the biggest expenditure of his life—for a Jacobs piano, on which he arranged a hymn authored by his mother. He also developed a musical piece of unique character which remained nameless for many years and was eventually published as "Eubie's Boogie." It's really the formalization of his highly identifiable wobble-wobble bass.

While the smoke of the conflagration cleared away, he spent a little time in New York, where he performed at Edmund's Cafe on Twenty-eighth Street. He had a room above a store, and though it was noisy enough around there to inhibit sleep, some of the excitement of the metropolis entered his consciousness and the city started to exercise a lure that it has never lost.

Returning to Baltimore, he spent most of 1905 working at the Middle Section Assembly Club. As was his custom, he kept bringing most of his pay home to his mother. He kept tips for himself, and these he began to learn to lose in the third-floor gambling room of the club. One of his fellow losers was a pugilist friend who very soon was to become the world's lightweight boxing champion, Joe Gans.

"One day," Eubie recall's, "there was this little fellow we used to call Jew Abie. He was only this big—could have been a jockey—but he's a gambler, see. He liked me. So he says to me one day, 'Hey, Eubie, why the hell do *you* gamble?'"

Eubie answered that he gambled because he wanted to win some money; then he asked Abie why *he* gambled.

"Because," Abie assured him, "that's my business. I'm a gambler. A professional gambler. I *win*. You're a professional musician. You don't know how to gamble. It's dopes like you that put my two daughters through college."

With his rare capacity to derive lessons from the knowledge and experience of others, Eubie Blake right then swore off gambling and hasn't gambled since—even on the horse races—which is quite a feat in view of the fact that Baltimore's race track, Pimlico, features an annual race called the Eubie Blake Purse.

Because of the fact that it gets very hot in Baltimore during the summer and there was always a lull in entertainment during those pre-air-conditioning days, Eubie took to working summers in Atlantic City, New Jersey, where lucrative jobs and balmy sea breezes were strong inducements. Even though, as Eubie remembers, the competition was the stiffest in the world, employers thought of him as the pick of the pack. Besides Eubie's lifelong buddy Hughie Wolford, there were such luminaries as the classically trained One Leg Willie Joseph (who, Eubie assures, could play anything perfectly, from the most difficult concert pieces to ragtime), Slew Foot Nelson, Jack the Bear Wilson, No Legs Cagey, Willie the Lion Smith, and Luckey Roberts. Eubie stood in awe of a sixteen-year-old kid who wandered into a place where he was working, heard Eubie play one of his most difficult numbers, "Troublesome Ivories," and then, sitting down at the piano while Eubie was taking a break, executed this test piece flawlessly. The kid was James P. Johnson.

The boardwalk was a world of its own. Atlantic City already had its own little ghetto centered about Baltic and Mediterranean Avenues. Most of the Negro clubs were clustered there—places like the Bucket of Blood, the Belmont, Allen's, and the Boathouse. In 1906 this was the world to Eubie. Washington could be alive with Teddy Roosevelt's trust-busting program, Chicago on its ear with the impact on its packing plants of Upton Sinclair's *The Jungle*, but here on the oceanfront nothing counted but those eighty-eight keys and the myriad melodies they could engender.

Back in Baltimore when the summer had passed, big excitement was created by Joe Gans winning the lightweight championship and starting to build the Goldfield Hotel, which promised to be the plushest spot in town, and where Eubie was to preside at the keyboard for three years. Meanwhile, it was business as usual at the Middle Section Club.

The Middle Section Club itself was a musically lively place for Eubie. He recalls, "You know, in 1910, I believe, there was a big hit published called 'Raggin' the Scale.' Ed Claypoole had his name on it—a fine musician. Now I'm not sayin' he *didn't* write it. But let me tell you this.

"Hughie Wolford and I are workin' in the Middle Section Club, see—now this is about 1905 or '06 because I ain't in the Goldfield Hotel yet, see. Now on Sundays there's a lot of church people sneak in there for a little drink—women too—they went on the second floor. Hughie's playin', and I hear a lady ask him to play 'Holy City.' Now he plays it, you see, but he *rags* it—and Hughie is a hell of a piano player. He puts in so many variations that she don't recognize it. So when he gets finished, she asks him again to play 'Holy City.' She ain't bein' smart now. She really doesn't know *that* was 'Holy City.' So I say, 'I'll play it for you, ma'am,' and I sit down at the piano and play it straight so she knows what I played, and she gives me twenty-five cents.

"Now later I say to Hughie, 'Why didn't you *play* it for the lady?' He tells me, 'She didn't say how she wanted me to play it.' So I say, 'If somebody asked you to play the scale, you'd rag it too.' Now he don't say nothin'.

"The next day he comes in and he plays the scale for me, only now it's a rag, see. He went home and he made a rag out of it. He says, 'You give me an idea yesterday.'

"Well, now I want to play a joke on him. I go home and put the scale in five keys, and the next day I come in where Hughie is shootin' pool. They got a piano in there. So I go and sit at the piano and rag the scale in five keys. He says, 'Hey, you copped that from me!'

"I say, 'I copped it from *you?* I didn't have to cop that from *nobody*. Don't you understand? That's the scale. Nobody owns the scale.' Then I show him that I put it in five keys and he only got it in one.

"After that we both played it all the time in five keys. Never thought to copyright it or anything, but *everybody* come into the club asked for it all the time. Still I'd have felt foolish tryin' to copyright the scale.

"But Ed Claypoole copyrighted it—in five keys like I had it. And you know that was a *big* hit. The scale!"

Eubie never made a concerted effort to get his rags published in his early years. For one thing, he didn't really view them as publishable. In common with most of his Eastern colleagues, he considered most of what he composed a mere point of departure for his personal improvisations. The music on the paper wasn't designed to be played literally; in fact it would change in each rendition. The John W. Stark list of composers included Scott Joplin, Joseph F. Lamb, and James Scott, who conceived their rags as set pieces to be performed as written. But Eubie never took ragtime compositions seriously.

"In my time," he points out, "it was all very competitive. You always looked to compose things to be built on tricks that nobody else but you could do. That's why so many things that I composed didn't even have names until much later. 'Charleston Rag' was first named 'Sounds of Africa' by Will Marion Cook when he heard it. It ain't until modern times that I ever really looked at it as a piece of music.

"I was always up against *real* piano players, so I had to depend on my tricks if I was gonna cut *them*. Those *tricks* became my rags."

Certainly one of Eubie's highlights of 1905-06 was the evening Will Marion Cook walked into the Middle Section Club and listened to Eubie performing his own work on the piano. Cook was to become his mentor and tutor. Much of what he has become he owes, he says, to "Pop" Cook.

The celebrated musician listened to the composition, as yet untitled, and inquired what its name was. Eubie confessed he hadn't yet given it a title. Cook listened awhile and intoned, in his well-known theatrical voice, "Sounds of Africa." He was amazed to learn that Eubie hadn't yet learned to write his music down.

"*That's* the man who taught me to conduct," Eubie relates. "I believe he was reincarnation of Richard Wagner—looked like him too. Very proud! He studied in Leipzig. Cook never wore a hat because he was proud of his bushy hair. That was all that give him away so you could know he was a Negro. Most eccentric man I ever met."

Eubie gives an example of this.

"I go to New York—Cook is already there, see—and he takes me down to Schirmer. That's the biggest publishing house in New York at that time. He introduces me to one of the finest gentlemen I ever met. His name was Curt Schindler—manager down there. He treated me like a real artist—not like a lot of other people—you know how it was for colored people back then. Now he takes me into a big room. There's four pianos in there, all tuned to perfection. He tells me to pick out any one I wanted to play on, which is good because I don't like a piano with stiff action. So I played my piece, and he raved about it. Then he called in three men who worked around there, and he asked me to play it again, so I did.

'Sounds of Africa.' Now Mr. Schindler *really* likes it. He tells his secretary to make me out a check for $100 advance royalties. Now I never saw that much money to be my own at one time in my entire life. I'm gonna give $25 to Cook and keep the rest, see?

"Then Schindler says to me, very friendly—he bought the number already, remember. He says, 'I see you go from G flat to E flat without any preparation or modulation.' Now he don't mean nothin' at all. He *bought* the tune. He's just curious. Then suddenly Cook gets very indignant. He says, 'How dare you criticize Mr. Blake? He's a great artist. What do *you* know about genuine African music? *That's* genuine African music'—he's lyin' now. 'I insist that you apologize to him.'

"That crazy Cook! We had the song sold. So of course Mr. Schindler changed his mind. He never gave me the check, and I didn't have the number published or the money. So we walked out of there. I didn't know *what* to say to Cook."

Will Marion Cook was one of the most important musical figures of his time. He attended Oberlin College in Ohio, from which he was graduated at fifteen. He won a scholarship to continue his studies at the University of Berlin and became a student and protégé of the world-famous violinist Joseph Joachim, a friend of Brahms. After his 1895 Carnegie Hall concert debut Cook was reviewed by music critics as "the greatest colored violinist in the world." The race reference galled him so badly that he swore never to pick up his violin again. The polished pleas of Jim Europe persuaded him to play in the Clef Club Symphony's Carnegie Hall concert of 1912. The symphony of some 150 musicians was to play Cook's compositions "Exhortation," "Rain Song," and "Swing Along." He agreed to play on condition that his name not be advertised and that he not be introduced when these numbers were played. However, he was generally recognized, and the tumultuous applause with which the packed house responded to his compositions forced Europe to go back on his word. He introduced Cook, and the great virtuoso tearfully took his bows.

Toward the Big Time

The Years of the Goldfield Hotel
Eubie Marries Avis Lee
Marking Time

The *Lusitania* was making her maiden voyage. She would shatter the world speed record by making it to New York from the port of Queenstown, Ireland, in five days and fifty-four minutes. She was the largest ship afloat. Her Edwardian splendor reflected the lifestyle aspirations of the Western world. Gilded and mirrored, wood-paneled and chandeliered, this aquatic princes' palace was a very synonym for golden-age luxury. Deep and soft were her rugs and carpets, swirling and graceful her staircases. Eight years later a German U-boat would send the *Lusitania* to the bottom of the sea. Meanwhile, there she sailed, the flagship of an era.

And as the *Lusitania* sheared her way smoothly over a calm Atlantic, her stationary counterpart, the Goldfield Hotel in Baltimore, opened its doors to the public for the first time on a rainy September night in 1907.

Exactly a year earlier, in Goldfield, Nevada, under a scorching desert sun, the young Baltimore Negro Joe Gans had contended for forty-two grueling, strength-sapping rounds to outlast one Battling Nelson and wrest from him the world's lightweight boxing championship. Superficially this event might seem to be of more interest to sports fans than to the devotees of ragtime and native American music, but there is more than a passing relationship. Joe

Above left: Emily Johnston Blake, Eubie's mother.

Above right: John Sumner Blake, Eubie's father, a stevedore.

Eubie and his friend Howard (Hop) Johns (left) on Baltimore stoop.

Joe Gans (Joseph Saifuss Butts). A Baltimore marble shooter for whom Eubie and Hop Johns used to run errands, Gans won the lightweight boxing championship in 1906 in forty-two rounds against Battling Nelson. With his winnings he built the Goldfield Hotel in Baltimore, where Eubie was hired in 1907 at fifty-five dollars a week to play piano, along with One Leg Willie Joseph.

Avis Lee married Eubie in July 1910. To Eubie, "she was one of the ten most beautiful girls in Baltimore." A pianist and schoolmate, she helped Eubie with his homework during Eubie's brief formal education. She died childless in 1939.

Eubie in 1919, not long before his big success with "Shuffle Along" (1921).

Eubie in his raccoon coat, a product of being part owner of the highly successful "Shuffle Along."

Eubie Blake in mid-life.

Eubie with his mother, when he was just back from his 1925-26 stay in England.

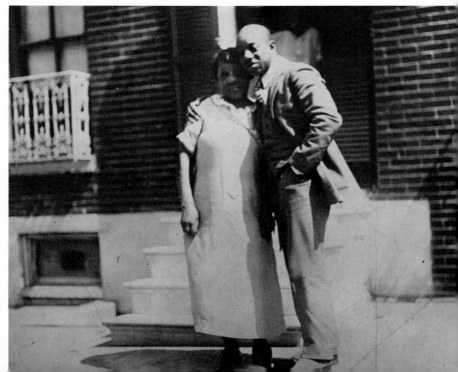

Marion Tyler married Eubie on December 27, 1945. A showgirl in black musicals of the late 1920s, she is the granddaughter of Hiram S. Thomas, the famous chef and inventor of potato chips.

Leonard Bernstein and Marc Blitzstein (in background) watch Eubie play piano at Music Inn at Tanglewood, Lenox, Massachusetts, in 1953.

Eubie and his wife Marion.

Maxine Sullivan dances with Eubie at his eighty-ninth birthday party at the Overseas Club, New York, in 1972. In background from left to right are Billy Taylor, Max Kaminsky (both partially obscured), Tyree Glenn, Tony Parenti, Charles McGee (partially obscured), Roger Glenn, and Joe Jones.

Gans returned to Baltimore and with his winnings proceeded to erect in the heart of Baltimore's red-light district, at the corner of Lexington and Chestnut, a pleasure palace that would have attracted Kubla Khan himself. In honor of his scene of glory, he named it the Goldfield Hotel.

"The very highest class of people came to the Goldfield," Eubie Blake remembers with a proprietary pride, "every race, every color. Nothing but the finest food, liquor, and champagne. Baltimore never *saw* anything like that. Joe Gans hired me to play the piano for him. Two piano players. Me and Boots Butler. Poor Boots died just a few weeks later.

"I was twenty-four years old, and Gans was thirty-three. He used to work in a market cleanin' fish when I was little. He was a good fighter then, already. Me an' Hop [Johns] used to run errands for him because we admired how tough he was and still a real gentleman.

"Joe Gans was very impressive. Of course, everybody *knew* he was a great fighter—maybe pound for pound the best there ever was. But besides, Gans did things in a big way. He *spent* his money. The first Negro in Baltimore to own an automobile. So naturally, everybody in the *world* came to the Goldfield. All the sport stars, people like John L. Sullivan and Jack Johnson. Famous entertainers, opera stars, and stage actors. We saw them all.

"Now I ain't braggin', but this was some great music. By this time I could really *play*, and then when Boots died, Gans brought in One Leg Willie. *Nobody* could copy him. He knew everything, the heaviest classics and any kind of rags. I learned plenty from just watchin' him."

Many old timers stood in awe of the pianistic feats of One Leg Willie Joseph. James P. Johnson said Willie was "the only piano player I'd pay to watch." Luckey Roberts never failed to name him among the all-time greats. Moody and volatile, he mesmerized patrons and musicians alike. Thwarted in his dreams of achieving stardom on the concert stage by reason of his color, he strove to perform ragtime so stupendously that it would rise above the importance and quality of concert music. Joseph had lost a leg in an accident at an ice-skating rink as a youngster; he felt this as just one of a string of misfortunes of which his life was composed.

Willie worked for Joe Gans through most of 1908, then tried his luck, with indifferent success, in New York. Had not his bitterness and cynicism always vied with his virtuosity, his abilities might have brought him immortality as a great performer. Eubie saw him again in Atlantic City, probably in the summer of 1909. Shortly thereafter, in his mid-forties, One Leg Willie died somewhere in Virginia, shattered by the effects of whisky and narcotics.

During the three years he worked in the Goldfield, Eubie's creativity bloomed. He wrote "The Baltimore Todolo" to support the big 1908 dance fad. "Kitchen Tom" was a nod to a popular Atlantic City chef. The tour de force "Tricky Fingers" was designed to display Eubie's dazzling skill, especially to his pal and competitor—"and when I say competitor I *mean* competitor!"—Hughie Wolford. It remains a staggering test piece with high musical quality. He still performs it. "I play it allegro, but I *used* to play it vivace."

"Novelty Rag" and "Poor Katie Redd" followed. Sixty-six years later Eubie performed the latter flawlessly to a full house accompanied by the New Orleans Ragtime Orchestra.

Much of Eubie's facility with composition during these years developed under the expert tutelage of the well-known Baltimore conductor Llewellyn Wilson. This association followed appropriate recommendations to both parties by Will Marion Cook. Wilson demanded that Eubie compose away from the piano.

Because of Gans's status as lightweight champion—it's hard for young people of the later twentieth century to understand the importance society granted to boxing idols—his hotel became a rendezvous not only for the wealthier Baltimoreans but for sports and entertainment celebrities from the entire world. Inevitably, Eubie, given this opportunity to hobnob with the famous and powerful, expanded not only his musical but his social horizons. His easy manner, his confidence, and his worldly polish began to evolve dramatically through the Goldfield experience. Eubie's ready entree into the homes of the mighty in later years couldn't have been effected with as much grace as it was without his schooling at the hotel piano. He played with facility what the people asked for, but with his own inimitable touch. In 1907, the year the hotel opened, they were asking for "Heart of My Heart" and "Cheyenne" and by the time his stint ran out in 1910, Eubie had had lots of requests for "I've Got Rings on My Fingers" and the epic saga of "Casey Jones," which took the world of 1909 by storm—the same year that Percy Wenrich brought out "Put on Your Old Gray Bonnet" and Harry Von Tilzer intrigued the ballroom crowds with his "Cubanola Glide." Irving Berlin scored with "My Wife Has Gone to the Country, Hurrah! Hurrah!" at about the same time.

Eubie smiled and chased those now renowned fingers over the keyboard night after night with his versions of these sensational hits. Already he understood that people of all kinds just natually loved him. It was a good feeling. It still is.

As part of his profession he had the opportunity, both in Baltimore and in Atlantic City, to accompany many of the great singing stars of the era too, including Mary Stafford, who sang the first recorded vocal of "Tin Roof Blues." Others were Lottie Dempsey, Alberta Hunter, Madison Reed, Big Lizzie, and Alabama Blossom, all featured in places he worked.

Many white theatrical stars came through Baltimore during 1908, and a visit to the Goldfield became automatic. George M. Cohan, touring with "The Yankee Prince," and Eddie Foy, in "The Orchid," showed up that year. Eubie knew them both, and they came in to hear him play. Other piano players would stop by to marvel at Eubie's uncannily developed accenting techniques and the complexity of his musical concepts.

Nostalgia was already box office in 1908. Broadway had "The Old Homestead" on the boards, complete with live oxen and real haystacks. The newspapers ads proudly announced that "not a thing . . . has been changed or brought up to date" since an earlier production. "Take me back" songs could be heard anywhere popular music was heard. "Take Me Back to I-O-Way," "Back, Back, Back to Baltimore"—to the sunny South, to silver-haired mothers and dear old dads, to the scenes of your childhood or your first love, to various states, cities, hamlets, lakes, rivers, and even school days. Even though the economic catastrophe of 1907 hung on as the depression of 1908, competent composers and musicians could stay alive by reminding their audiences that there had been better times, and the more optimistic ones suggested that there would be better times again.

In Baltimore and in Atlantic City during the summers Eubie capitalized on the nostalgia of the era, but nevertheless continued to develop an instrumental style that must have been considered modern. And watching and wondering at his skills were figures from the long, long ago. In the process of interviewing Eubie, I frequently brought up the names of well-known Negro composers of bygone days just to see how he would relate to them. One day I brought up the name of James A. Bland, composer of "Carry Me Back to Old Virginny," "In the Evening by the Moonlight," and "Oh, Dem Golden Slippers," expecting Eubie to relate what he had *heard* of him. The big surprise was seeing Eubie's face brighten as he pointed his finger in his frequently didactic way and said, "Let me tell you about Jimmy Bland!"

"He didn't seem to me to be so old when he was around Atlantic City. I suppose he must have been workin' in some joint around there. Anyway I meet him on the Boardwalk and he says to me, 'Hey, Eubie! Lemme buy you a drink.' Then he took me for a walk *past* all the places the colored people could go in safely, to this real high-class place. Now there's no colored people in here. Even the bartender is white, see. Well, he orders his drink. I get my Old Overholt. That's all I ever drank, 100 proof, in those days. We talk a while, and he tells me how much he enjoys hearin' me play. Then we have another one. Now I got to get to work pretty soon, see, and I suppose he does too. Now he goes to the men's room and he never comes back. I got a dollar in my pocket, see. I never liked to carry money around with me. I still don't. Anyway, this bad-lookin' bartender gives me a tab for two dollars and twenty cents. Now I ain't got two dollars and twenty cents, so we argue and I tell him I'll pay for my own but I got nothin' to do with that other fellow. I was still a dime short, but he let me go. I don't know whether Jimmy Bland ever paid his tab or not, but I know *I* never saw him again. But I guess he didn't live too long after that. Poor Jimmy was another drinkin' man. I guess that's why he was unreliable."

Atlantic City in the early 1900s was a combination of Brighton, Ostend, and the St. Louis Fair. On the world-famous Boardwalk you could buy anything from Armenian lace to Dunlop hats. Affluent families from Philadelphia and Baltimore headquartered at the Savoy or at Green's Hotel, right on the Boardwalk. Green's, entitled to a gold star in any gourmet's memory, produced a steamed bluefish fit for Zeus himself. The hotel adjoined Ye Olde Mill, which in a few years would spotlight popular dance bands like Art Hickman's. The biggest attractions worked at the Million Dollar Pier. But during the first decade of the century, these hedonistic meccas were reserved for whites. As fans of the game called Monopoly, know, the board shows the properties on Baltic and Mediterranean Avenues, where the Negro hot spots were, as the cheapest.

A big happy event happened in Eubie's life during the long, hot summer of 1910. He married Avis Lee in July. "She was so beautiful," Eubie recalls. "I never saw anybody so beautiful as Avis."

"I told you before that I met Avis Lee in school, but don't get the idea that we were sweethearts or goin' with each other or anything like that, because we weren't. She was too high class and she was too smart for me to even *think* about that, and she was older than me. Besides, Avis was a very conservative person, you know. There wasn't nothin' wild about Avis. Her grandfather is Firpo Lee, and her father used to sing with the Black Patti company. But now it's 1910, see, maybe fifteen years later, and I took Avis on an excursion in Baltimore. Then I made a date with her. I really liked her. Of course I'm still workin' at the Goldfield Hotel now, and I get my friend Eddie Myers to lend me a car and a chauffeur. I still can't drive a car in 1910. So anyway we go out and we have a real good time, and then later on when it's time to take her home, I pop the scagmo question"—that iş, Eubie propositioned her.

"Now I told you Avis is a very smart girl, and she says, 'I know all about you, Eubie Blake, and I know all about all your women. You better understand right now that that's not what I want out of life.'

"So what could I do? The next month I married the girl!"

He took his bride to Atlantic City for a working honeymoon, but it had its problems. He had to carry her birth certificate and their marriage license in his pocket as ready evidence that she was not underage and that they were in fact legally wed.

Avis was Negro high society in Baltimore, not only because she was beautiful and talented but also because her grandfather Firpo Lee had established himself in the upper economic echelons by accumulating a fleet of oyster boats that supplied the city's leading restaurants with the specialties for which they were so famous. Avis was classically trained as a pianist, but was so much the product of a sheltered upbringing that it would have been hard to imagine her supporting herself out in the world. She found her existence with Eubie to be merely an extension of her family life. He was always a good provider, and he didn't get married until he was confident that he could support a wife in some ease and comfort. It was part of Eubie's good fortune that she got along well with his father and mother.

Just a month after the wedding, Joe Gans succumbed to tuberculosis brought on by the exigencies of making the weight for his encounters in the prize ring. Not only did Eubie lose a good friend, but Joe's demise was the beginning of the end for the fabulous Goldfield Hotel, which, without Gans as a catalyst, deteriorated badly and became an unfit place for Eubie to sharpen his skills. There is now a federal housing project on the site.

Back in Atlantic City with his new bride, though, Eubie felt that the world was his. He enjoyed introducing Avis to *his* world, and took the conventional amount of joshing from his fellow entertainers. Hughie Wolford reminded him of the time Edgar Dowell had lured his girl away with his keyboard magic and issued the mock threat "If you get me mad, I'm gonna bring Edgar Dowell down here and introduce him to Avis."

"You know," says Eubie in a philosophical vein, "the world goes on no matter what *you* do. If somethin' good happens to you, you just enjoy it. If you lose somebody, you don't go to pieces over it. You can see *they're* gone and the world is still here. If it was you that was gone, it would still be here too. But you got to get up and go out and live your life."

The light dances in Eubie's eyes. "Avis used to call me Dummy," he says. "I never went to college and I never was no good at school learning. But I got college degrees Avis never had."

And it's true. Both Brooklyn College and Dartmouth have presented Eubie with sheepskins testifying that he is a Doctor of Humane Letters. Rutgers University and the University of Maryland have made him a Doctor of Fine Arts, and he has so far received three doctorates in music: from the New England Conservatory of Music, Pratt Institute in Brooklyn, and Morgan State University.

Asked how he feels now, at the age of ninety-six, about the wreath of academic laurels, he says, "I guess now I won't have any trouble getting a job."

"In 1910—I was just married to Avis—and I'm workin' in Atlantic City at the Boathouse. Now, that's a night club, see. A big night club with a lot of different singing acts. My partner at that time was Madison Reed. God, he could sing! The publishers used to send around professional copies of new tunes, and I always had a stack this thick"—two inches—"of bran' new music. Madison goes through the stack and picks out the ones he wants to sing, and one of 'em is 'Alexander's Ragtime Band.' Now I already knew Izzy"—Irving Berlin—"because he used to hang around the Boathouse asking me to play his songs, and I always did because they were very good. You know he could only play in one key. Well, he always used to like the way I play. He used to come by the place wearing his little derby hat and his yellow—I don't mean tan, I mean *yellow*—pointed shoes, and he'd say in his raggedy voice, 'Hey, Eubie, play my tune, play my tune!'

"Of course we *did* play 'Alexander's Ragtime Band' and Madison really liked to sing it, about twenty times a night. There was no question it would be one of the greatest hits of all time. Funny thing about it, there's no ragtime *in* it. No syncopation at all! Still it's a great tune, and it sure was what the public wanted.

"I've seen him a couple of times in recent years at ASCAP dinners, things like that, and I tell him, 'I'm still playin' your tune.' You know it's hard to go through a program of popular music without playing *some* tune of his."

In Eubie's recollection, his career from the end of 1910 to May of 1915 is a succession of jobs—good jobs. The money was good, and Baltimore provided ample work opportunities. To a great degree

Eubie and Avis got used to each other's ways. For her it wasn't easy to adjust to the irregular hours and the geographical mobility of the life of a musician's spouse, but she held up well.

The good times are reflected in the fact that from his pen in 1911 came two outstanding rags, "Chevy Chase" and "Fizz Water." A qualification as to musical form: the world calls "Fizz Water" a rag; Eubie, with his customary meticulousness, classifies it as a one-step. These two pieces, when they were sold to Joseph W. Stern & Co., were sold without "mechanical rights," that is, reproduction rights for phonographs and piano rolls. Eubie failed to read the fine print and signed a contract that cost him several thousand dollars in royalties.

"It wasn't because I'm Negro," he hastens to say. "They try to get away with that with any inexperienced person. That's just the publishing business. Anyway, that's why I never played those two numbers anymore. Well, I did play 'Chevy Chase' in the last few years, but not 'Fizz Water.' I can't play that because I don't remember it."

"Troublesome Ivories" was completed that year and so was "Brittwood Rag."

"One day in the thirties I walked into the Brittwood Club in Harlem just to say hello to Willie Gant. Fine piano player. A man I know for years. Now before I talk to him, I hear a piece he's playin' and I know it and I don't know it. I'm tryin' to think and it's so familiar, but I just can't place it. So he gets finished playin' it and we say 'Hello' and I ask him, 'What's the name of that piece you just played?' He gives me a funny look. He says, 'I never *did* know the name of it. *You* wrote it. In fact you taught it to me almost twenty years ago.' Now it didn't come back to me right away that I wrote it, but then when I *knew* I wrote it, then it *did* come back to me. I never did give it a name, but then in honor of the place where Willie Gant was workin' I named it the 'Brittwood Rag.'"

Through the summer of 1914 Eubie spent the hottest months in Atlantic City. His popularity had grown to such an extent that the musicians were outnumbered by the customers around his piano. It was never slow at Ben Allen's or at the Belmont, where James P. Johnson "caught" "Troublesome Ivories." In Eubie's final summer he was working at Kelly's, fully expecting to be back in 1915, but he went on to even bigger and better things, and Kelly's opened its next summer season with Willie the Lion at the keyboard.

All of this that Eubie had been doing with such success in the past decade was considered the big time among Negroes in the entertainment world, but as succeeding events were about to show, they hadn't seen the big time yet, and James Hubert Blake of Baltimore, Maryland, a thirty-two-year-old "old pro," though he didn't know it himself right then, was about to show it to them.

Enter Noble Sissle

Ham and Egg Team Up
James Europe: Society Entertainers
Home Front and After
The Road
"Crazy Blues"
No Cork

The egg is a compact unit that is complete in and of itself. It has been a widely appreciated entity throughout recorded history. Only an egg is an egg, and its versatility is universally acknowledged. It has utility boiled, fried, scrambled, coddled, shirred, deviled, or metamorphosed into omelettes and soufflés. More importantly, the world accepts the egg as it is for what it is. It stands alone, noble and unique, and mankind is grateful for it.

Ham, despite Semitic demurrers, has been from the beginning of time a staple sustenant for Homo sapiens. Today, sugar-cured or hickory-smoked, it starts the New Year right. It has had a distinguished history, celebrated in song and story—for instance the beloved Charles Lamb's "Dissertation on Roast Pig." It is savory, nutritious, and somehow luxurious. It too stands alone.

Now it's also a fact that, for reasons not easy to elucidate, the ham and the egg served up in tandem assume a joint identity and and existence transcending the clearly demonstrated ability of each to survive on its own merits.

All of this is to suggest what it was that happened on the day, May 16, 1915, when Eubie Blake and Noble Sissle met for the first time. In short, the ham met the egg. One look at Eubie's hairless pate and it was easy to see which was which.

The job that day was at Riverview Park in Baltimore. Joe Porter's band was booked, with Eubie Blake at the piano. Singer Noble Sissle was coming in from out of town. The musicians waited for him on the steps of Eubie's house on Argyle Street until the last possible moment, then started for the job. Eubie, sixty-three years later, can state firmly and without fear of contradiction that "Sissle was *always* late." But on that afternoon Eubie had no way of knowing that a lifetime of allowances would have to be made for this fact.

"He was never on time for *anything*," as Eubie tells it, "but *this* time it really wasn't his fault, because the train was *very* late."

Finally Sissle caught up with the group, and "Porter—no, his brother, Arthur—does the introductions, only he doesn't introduce *me*, see. Just overlooked it. Then he remembers and says, 'I almost missed our pianist. This is Eubie Blake, Noble Sissle.'

"That rang a bell with me. I knew I heard that name before. I said, 'Do you write lyrics?' He says he writes lyrics. I said, 'I thought I saw your name on something.' But I was wrong. He only did a little writing in college. I said, '*I* need a lyricist. I've been looking for one.' Their long partnership began right there.

It began to seem there might be a conspiracy to insure the success of this partnership. Sissle and Blake produced a song within a few days of their first meeting, and as fortune would have it, it was a week when the celebrated Sophie Tucker was doing her SRO act at the Maryland Theater in downtown Baltimore. It was a Keith theater—big-time vaudeville.

"Now Sissle is educated. He's talented. He's a good businessman—and he's all brass. He says, 'We should get Sophie Tucker to sing the song.' Fellow named Eddie Nelson helped a little with the lyrics. I says, 'Who do we know that can bring it to Sophie Tucker?' Sissle never had no patience with me about things like that. He says, 'We don't need anybody. It's a good song. Let's take it down ourselves.'" Though this may sound like Mickey Rooney saying to Judy Garland, "Gee whiz, let's give a *show!*" substantially the same story was told independently by Sissle.

"I said, 'She ain't going to see *us. We* ain't nobody.' He says, 'What have *we* got to lose? Let's go.' As usual, we're late. I write a piano score in a hurry. In those days I don't even know there's such a thing as music ink that doesn't run. Not like regular fountain-pen ink—a special ink.

"Now we get backstage with Sissle's fast talk, and we see her come off stage and Sissle is talkin' to her. I don't remember what he said, but I hear her say, 'Yes, yes,' in her very harsh voice, and the first thing I know I'm sittin' at the piano and playin' and Sissle is singin' 'It's All Your Fault.' That's the first thing we ever wrote together. Now the music all ran but you could still see where the notes were, and she says, 'Do you have an arrangement written?' I guess I had a dumb look on my face. But she just smiled, bless her, and she says—voice like a man—she says, 'Yes, I'll take it.' That was a Monday matinee. I didn't make the orchestration. Somebody in her band did it. She introduced it on Thursday and it was an instant hit, at least in Baltimore. Everybody whistled it in the street. But after that it didn't go nowhere. But we still performed it sometimes."

Noble Sissle was born in Indianapolis, Indiana, on July 10, 1889. In common with Eubie Blake he had a clearly defined musical talent and a pair of rigidly religious parents. But here their similarities ended. Sissle's family was well-to-do. Both his parents had been school teachers until his father was ordained. He was unaware of any personally directed race prejudice either in his neighborhood or at school. He was the lone Negro in the Central High School Glee Club in Cleveland, Ohio, after his family resettled. He also sang in the school quartet, besides functioning as a cheerleader. His strict adherence to the Protestant work ethic and his parents' values almost made him a Methodist minister.

"Sissle," recalls Eubie fondly, "was a real square. A goody-goody. He never wanted to do *nothin.'* He didn't drink, he didn't smoke, he didn't cuss, he didn't gamble. Of course he was a handsome fellow and he could have had all the girls he wanted, but I always thought all he needed was that audience out there, and when he heard that applause. . . . "

Educated at De Pauw University in Greencastle, Indiana, and

Butler University in Indianapolis, he worked as a waiter in the Severin Hotel there to pay his expenses until the manager asked him to organize an orchestra to play in the hotel. In the spring of 1915 he was invited to join Joe Porter's Serenaders at Riverview Park in Baltimore.

"He was really a fine actor," Eubie explains. "He could put a song over. He couldn't really play, though. He *held* a banjo. But he *did* know music enough to look over my shoulder when I was writin' and say, 'Eubie, that's wrong'—and it would be, too."

Before the year 1915 was out, the pair published one other ditty, a patriotic piece entitled "See America First." Also, Sissle began at once to work toward getting Eubie and himself permanently out of Baltimore and to New York. By the time the job ended in Riverview Park that fall, he already had his plans made.

Sissle had spent summers working in Palm Beach in support of Nora Bayes's appearances and had even played the Palace on Broadway in her act, as a member of the band. It was his practice to cultivate the good will of the rich and the powerful; he was full of the practical conviction that this couldn't do his career any harm. Armed with a letter of introduction from a Palm Beach socialite, he contacted James Reese Europe, a monumental figure in the Negro music world, and quickly found himself working regularly in one of Europe's units. Noble and Jim Europe became close friends, and through Noble's intercession Eubie found himself, in 1916, working in Long Island as a full-time pianist. It didn't take long for Sissle, Blake, and Europe to become close, and Eubie's admiration for Europe never flagged. He venerates Europe's memory profoundly.

"To colored musicians he was as important—he did as much for them as Martin Luther King did for the rest of the Negro people. He set up a way to get them jobs—the Clef Club—and he made them get paid more. He tried to get as much for them as whites, and sometimes he could and sometimes he couldn't. And all the rich white people loved him. He used to get *all* the jobs for those millionaire parties, and of course we went along."

The pre–World War I era was a time in American social history when, with competition glorified in every area of human activity, the compulsion among the very rich to outdo one another in lavish and extravagant social functions reached a peak. Vernon and Irene Castle danced their way to immortality as they taught the world Jim Europe's Castle Walk and the variety of ballroom steps his music accompanied. It was inevitable that his young buddies Sissle and Blake should become well-known society entertainers along the Eastern seaboard. They played for Goulds, Dodges, Schwabs, Wanamakers—anybody who was anybody in the *haut monde*. Eubie learned to live in tuxedos and swallowtail coats. Of the three friends he was the only one not carried away by the grandeur of the mansions and their appointments. Europe and Sissle always maintained a caste consciousness and hauteur they thought appropriate to the society with which they mingled, but Emily's boy retained the common touch—always gentlemanly and considerate of the feelings of others, always conscious of the fact that he was a Negro and knowing that no matter how these white people acted, their relationships could just go so far. He never failed to take note of the fact that when the Negro musicians were fed in these grand palaces, it was always out of sight of the guests—and other Negroes did the serving.

"I remember one night we were playin' for John Wanamaker. I mean the *old* man Wanamaker. We didn't have anything to eat since two o'clock in the afternoon, and we're all starvin' to death, see, and the help is too busy with the people—the guests—to take care of the musicians. Now Jim, after it was late enough to be unreasonable, Jim complained to the Negro butler about us bein' hungry.

"Now, the butler, see—because he's workin' for the great John Wanamaker, see—he thinks he ain't like *other* Negroes. He don't like it when Jim complains. But anyway, in a little while they tell us to sit down at a table in this big room, and a waiter brings in this big china thing they use for soup, and he serves us all. I can't wait now, see—we're all dyin' from hunger. Now we grab our spoons and as soon as I tasted this stuff, I had to spit it out. And I see everybody else is doin' the same thing. This stuff, I'm still sure, is the water they washed the dishes in—soap, everything. And it's because the butler is mad, see. He don't like no colored people to complain. But Europe—I see Europe is eatin' the stuff just like it's soup, he don't pay it no mind, just keeps eatin'. My God, I thought, that Europe will eat anything. Now everybody else is watchin' him too, see. It ain't just me.

"I realize Jim Europe didn't get where he is with the white folks by complainin'."

Eubie played big dance jobs with Europe. Mainly, Europe was booked into the best hotels and they'd have two bands. One might be a twenty-piece white dance orchestra. They'd set up on a stage at one end of the room. Then Europe's ten-piece outfit would be at the other end of the room, and that way the dancers would have the benefit of continuous music.

Europe's orchestras always featured two pianos. "This guy, Carpenter, that played the other piano," Eubie recalls, "boy, he could play! I was the assistant conductor, and Jim used to hand me the baton almost every number after he started it off, then *he'd* go and mingle with the people.

"Now the *white* bands all had their music stands, see, but the people wanted to believe that Negros couldn't learn to read music but had a natural talent for it. So we never played with no music. Now this is the truth. Europe's orchestra was filled with readin' *sharks*. That cornet player, Russell Smith! If a fly landed on the music, he'd *play* it, see, like *that*. But we weren't supposed to read music!

"I'd get all the latest Broadway music from the publisher, and we'd learn the tunes and rehearse 'em until we had 'em all down pat. *Never* made no mistakes. Of course I'd always leave room for a *little* fakin', and them guys that *could* fake, they did it. Then we'd go on a job and naturally we'd play all those tunes perfectly.

"All the high-tone, big-time folks would say, 'Isn't it wonderful how these untrained, primitive musicians can pick up all the latest songs instantly without being able to read music?' That William Grant Still who played oboe with us—I wonder if he could read music when he was arrangin' for Paul Whiteman.

"Europe was a big, tall man, very commanding. Stood up straight like a West Point soldier. *He* knew his music—studied arranging and conducting at Columbia. Play? Well, he used to *sit* at a piano and *hold* a violin. We all called him Jim. None of the musicians called him Mr. Europe. He was very flexible. At home or in the White House, it was all the same to him. You couldn't *make*

him mad. And he had a brain! My God, he could see around corners. He could always figure out what was going to happen and be
prepared for it. And he knew how to make a plan and *stick* to it.
"We all owe so *much* to Jim Europe."

Europe had about fifteen bands working with more or less
regularity, using the Clef Club, of which he was the president, as
a sort of musicians' social club and booking agency. He had an ambition to put an all-colored show on Broadway. Along with Sissle,
he enlisted in the army at the time the United States entered World
War I.

"They'd have some fun with me after they're in uniform. Europe
is a lieutenant now, see. And everybody knows they're goin' to the
war, but they're just gonna be musicians. Ain't none of us was a
fighter, you know. But they'd introduce me to girls and they'd say,
'This is Eubie Blake, the slacker.' Now they don't tell the girls I'm
thirty-five years old, see, way over the age for the army.

"Then they give Europe the 369th Infantry Band and him and
Sissle go overseas. They wrote some music over there too. They
wrote 'On Patrol in No Man's Land' and 'All of No Man's Land Is
Ours.' Now I didn't have nothin' to do with those tunes. I did not
write any part of them. But they put my name on 'em right along-
side of theirs, because that's the kind of partners they were. I've
been lucky to have such friends in my life.

"One thing he [Europe] wanted to do, when he got back to the
U.S.A. and into civilian life, was for the three of us to do a Broadway show. Then he got killed in 1919. This crazy drummer killed
him at the auditorium in Boston. I don't think he *meant* to kill
anybody. I wasn't there. I was in New York. Sissle was with him.
At first nobody thought the cut in his neck was serious. Then,
bang! All of a sudden he's dead." The drummer, angry over what
he saw as an unfairness to him, fatally knifed Europe during a concert intermission.

"People don't realize yet today what we lost when we lost Jim
Europe. He was the savior of Negro musicians. He was in a class
with Booker T. Washington and Martin Luther King. I met all
three of them. Before Europe, Negro musicians were just like
wandering minstrels. Play in a saloon and pass the hat and that's
it. Before Jim, they weren't even supposed to be human beings. Jim

Europe changed all that. He made a profession for us out of music. All of that we owe to Jim. If only people would realize it."

It is impossible to overestimate the role played by Europe's Clef Club in the legitimization of music performed by Negroes in America. Through the club, the best of the colored conductors found assignments in New York's leading hotels and virtually monopolized the lucrative private-party business in the mansions of the rich as far north as Newport, Rhode Island.

With Europe and Sissle off making the world safe for democracy, Eubie Blake did a vaudeville tour with an extraordinary entertainer, Broadway Jones, who seems to have derived his name from an early song hit by George M. Cohan.

Broadway Jones had a phenomenally effective baritone voice. It was for him that Jerome Kern and Oscar Hammerstein wrote "Old Man River," but then they couldn't meet his price for singing it in "Showboat," 600 dollars a week. "I can make more than that just scufflin' around," he boasted. He wasn't exactly a show-business tyro. Many a winter season he had produced the show and led the orchestra at the hoity-toity Royal Poinciana Hotel in Palm Beach, Florida. During the summer seasons he had built substantial followings around New York resorts such as Sheepshead Bay and City Island. At the time the war broke out, he was operating a prosperous night club called Bamville at 129th Street and Lenox Avenue.

With his partners overseas, Blake joined Jones and organized an act which was very well received on the vaudeville circuit operated by Benjamin Franklin Keith. Eubie found his new partner amusing. "I don't think I ever saw him wear the same suit twice. He had so many clothes. Big, fat guy, but so clean and neat! Everything spotless. Now he could *really* sing. He was real show business. You couldn't follow him. But it was funny how he worked.

"He come on stage, and you know, they got chalk marks on the floor, so you got to stand by the chalk marks. Now Broadway comes out smilin', see. Now he looks perfect. He's right on the chalk where he's supposed to be, see. Well, if you move the piano ten feet away, he still stays on his mark—like either he's afraid to leave it or he doesn't see that the piano is moved.

"Every move he makes is studied and polished. Every smile, every expression. Broadway don't improvise at *all*. His concentration is complete. You yell anything to him from on or off stage while he's workin', he don't hear nothin'. The place is on fire, your grandmother died, you just won a million dollars. Nothin'. That's how he is until he goes off stage. His whole act is like in a trance. But a great entertainer. Later on he had an act with my old pal Hughie Wolford."

With Sissle out of the service, he and Eubie worked up a musical vaudeville routine and in 1919 found themselves on the Keith circuit as the Dixie Duo. They strode toward each other at stage center singing "Gee! I'm Glad That I'm from Dixie" to open their act. They opened in Bridgeport, Connecticut, from which they moved on to the Harlem Opera House and right into the Palace. They stopped the show there, which meant they were in business.

It was a tough business to be in. Those were days when Negro performers worked under heavy pressure. They got the worst dressing rooms in the worst locations. They performed, as they knew, for far less pay than white entertainers received. They were expected to black up and do low "darky" comedy. And they always were second on the program. That was because the representatives of the press—the all-powerful critics—didn't arrive until the third act. It was policy not only on the Keith circuit but also on the Pantages circuit for there never to be more than one colored act on a bill. As a result, black artists never got to know their soul brothers and sisters except at benefits.

Another side of the professional life of Sissle and Blake was smoother. They signed with M. Witmark & Sons as a songwriting team. Acting for the firm was Julius Witmark, youngest of the illustrious family, who had already made a name for himself as a vaudeville singer. Eubie remembers that Julie had a wooden leg. Sissle and Blake coudn't have been associated with a more prestigious and ethical firm than that of the Witmarks. Their list of composers was far more imposing than any boasted by their competitors. Victor Herbert, Sigmund Romberg, and Ernest R. Ball were in print under the Witmark aegis, and the firm was never reluctant, as were some, to produce and encourage the work of Negro artists. Among these were Paul Laurence Dunbar, James

Weldon Johnson, J. Rosamund Johnson, and Harry Thacker Burleigh.

Isidore Witmark even composed the verse for Ernest R. Hogan's biggest hit, "All Coons Look Alike to Me." Brother Julius was a founding member of the American Society of Composers, Authors and Publishers (ASCAP) despite the fact that most music publishers looked upon it as a threat. He proposed Sissle and Blake for membership in 1922 and they were admitted, which meant financial support through royalties for the performance of their compositions.

The contribution of the Witmarks to the development of black musical talent in America cannot be overestimated. It was they who produced, in 1898, the landmark Will Marion Cook show "Clorindy, or the Origin of the Cake Walk," which ran for a full season on the Casino Roof in New York.

Eubie appreciated them. "So for ten years we were with Witmark. They're fine people. They paid us each twenty-five a week, and we got two cents a copy on all the sheet music *and* our part of the mechanicals. The Witmarks always did right by us. We stayed with them until we went with Warner Brothers, the movie people, who bought them out in 1929."

Jim Europe met his tragic and wasteful end on May 9, 1919. He was mourned not only by his best friends, Sissle and Blake, but by the entire Negro community, especially show folks and musicians. A large section of affluent white society missed him, too. Professionally, Sissle and Blake filled much of the gap his death left. More than ever they trekked back and forth to the Long Island oceanfront, bringing original and animated entertainment at constantly advancing rates.

Avis held up beautifully through the neglect built into the life of a jazzman's wife, but Harriet Sissle was showing the strain. Bored, lonely, and lacking in inner resources, she began to seek solace in bootleg alcohol. Noble was unaffected, though. His good spirits, good health, and ambition kept him dynamic and alert to any promising opportunity.

Eubie Blake, phlegmatic and dedicated to the magic of the keyboard, went along in his detached way, confident that other people were taking care of the less important requirements of living. Avis was completely competent to deal with his domestc needs, and with Sissle in his life he didn't need to handle money, read contracts, or make minor decisions—Sissle took care of those things.

"I never been homesick," Eubie asserts. "I always knew when I was well off. When I was a kid, the house I lived in wasn't the kind of a place you want to come back to. Yeah, I wanted to see my *mother* and my *father*, but that *house* was nothin'. You get in a good hotel room with your own bathtub and your own toilet, it's not easy to go back and stay in the kind of a place I grew up in.

"No matter where we played, Sissle *always* complained. The food, the water. Nothing suited him. The room was never clean enough. He was a guy wiped a doorknob before he went in anyplace. And he always carried twice as much baggage as me.

"He'd always be writin' letters home, and in the early days he always got homesick. Now, you know, Sissle grew up in a nicer place than I did and maybe these hotels were not as nice as *his* house, but they were nicer than *my* house.

"You understand, Joneses couldn't *stay* anywhere they wanted. They found ways to keep you out of the highest-class hotels and restaurants even in the North. You go into a restaurant that don't want any Negro trade, they put so much salt in your food you can't eat it. If you show up at a hotel where you got a reservation, they see you're colored and find out that 'there must be some mistake, we haven't got a record of that. All our rooms are taken.' I don't blame *all* white people for them things. That's just the way things were. You don't know—well maybe *you* know—but a lot of white people don't know what we went through.

"Of course it wasn't like that in Canada or in Europe. Color don't make any difference to *them* people, and I can understand why a lot of Negroes stayed over there to live, like your New Orleans friend, Sidney Bechet.

"But me, I *love* this country. I wouldn't want to live anywhere else. *This* is home to me. I feel like George M. Cohan about Broadway. It's just in my blood. It's my world."

Even though Eubie has been so many places in the world, he

continues to maintain provincial attitudes. There's nothing of the cosmopolite in his conversation.

"Japanese keyboards look the same as the ones in Baltimore," he observes. "Most of my travelin' I was no tourist. People take me to a hall, show me a piano, and after that, all I see are the keys and the audience. I see the inside of a lot of buildings, and I am invited to some wonderful homes—but I never get to stay long enough to see the whole place, see. So now I got friends all over the world and I know *them*, but I don't know their cities even though I been there.

"In the early days with Sissle or Broadway Jones, or in the USO, it was mostly split weeks and one-nighters. In vaudeville most of the day you spend in the theater. You got to show up ten or eleven o'clock in the morning to rehearse your act with the pit band. Sometimes you got to time it and stretch it or cut it to meet a time schedule.

"It even takes longer to *dress* for the stage. Everything got to be just right. Sissle always took longer than me because he had to comb his hair." Eubie wipes his hand across his bare cranium. "This here is all *I* have to do. Then we look ourselves over in the dressing-room mirrors, then we look each *other* over to see that we didn't miss anything. We brush each other off with the whisk broom—all that kind of stuff.

"I was always comfortable on the road. I missed my wife when I was away from her, but if show business is your life, it's not the same as other people's lives. You just got to know that's how it is. Avis learned how to work them things out for herself.

"To tell the truth, I wasn't no angel on the road. Sissle neither, but he'd be able to hide it. If you didn't know Sissle, you'd think he always behaved himself, but he never got tired of the women. You'd be standin' on a corner or in front of the theater talkin' to him and a girl comes by and his head turns just like a piano stool, and he keeps lookin' till he can't see her no more.

"Show people always *complained* so much about livin' on the road. *I* never saw nothin' wrong with it. Maybe that's why I never got worn out with it like so many of 'em did. Every actor you talked to wanted to buy a chicken farm somewhere or a little hotel or go into some other business. But you know, the only ones who ever did those things were the ones who were not succeeding on the stage. People *stay* on the stage as long as they can. It must not be so bad."

"You know how it came that the blues were first recorded? It was 'Crazy Blues.' Now I want you to understand that other colored people were fightin' for the race too. Mule [Perry] Bradford used to bother the record companies to record his blues all the time"—that is, Bradford's "Crazy Blues." "Poor Mule couldn't play, but he could play *that*. Oh, he pestered them and pestered them. At last Okeh agreed to record Mamie Smith singing Mule's blues.

"At that time they didn't let any colored artists on records yet. After that they made *plenty* of them. They used to Jim Crow the records in those days. Did you know that? They called 'em race records. White people didn't know *nothin'* about the blues.

"Now there's a street in Baltimore where colored people shop, on one side where the good stores were. Pennsylvania Avenue. There's this record shop. A guy, Al Delaney is his name, he was the first one to play the horn from the phonograph out of the door of the shop, right out into the street, see. Well, people come in and say, 'I want that record.' They didn't know what it was. 'I want that record.' Okeh would only sell him twenty-five records at a time. They didn't have any confidence in it. He kept sellin' out, and he couldn't get records fast enough. But that record put Okeh back on its feet. It was almost bankrupt and it kept them from goin' out of business.

"Now it's months later, early in 1920, I meet Mule on 135th Street. Me and Sissle are on our way downtown. Mule says, 'Hey, Cuz'—he called *everybody* Cuz—'can you lend me a quarter?' See, Mule has got his own publishing company. He's got an office in the Handy building. All the Negro songwriters had offices there—we used to call it Uncle Tom's Cabin. He's got records sold, but he's got no money. He ain't got paid yet. So I give him a quarter. I tell him to remember to buy a return ticket. No tokens in them days—ticket. So that's a dime for a round-trip ticket downtown and fifteen cents to eat, right? So me and Sissle go on.

"Now it's later that afternoon. I'm gettin' ready to go home and there's Mule, sittin' on the curbstone, holdin' a piece of paper in his hand. I go over to him—he's got a dazed look—and I see he's holdin' a check. I say, 'Hey, Mule, you all right?' He hands me the check. It's for $100,001.01. I'll never forget it. That's for his first three-months royalty for 'Crazy Blues.' See, Mule never had *nothin'*. Now he's a millionaire. A hundred thousand dollars! That's a *colored* millionaire. Now he asks me for another quarter. He's got a hundred thousand and he's askin' me for a quarter. It's a *shock*, you know. From broke in the morning to a millionaire in the afternoon.

"I tell him to take a cab and go home. He ain't never been in a cab in his whole life. This time I give him a dollar and a quarter, and you know, till this day he never paid me back. When I asked him for it, he always told me, 'You got plenty money. You don't need it.' And this is all true. He told it himself."

Mule Bradford is gone now, but Eubie always likes to get everything straight and make sure that credit is given where it's due. And I myself heard Mule tell it that way.

"I remember Jolson," says Eubie, "before he put on cork."

During the early days of the Sissle and Blake act the use of cork became a fundamental and symbolic issue among colored entertainers and among white ones who did darky acts in blackface. Burnt cork was used to blacken the faces of entertainers. Blacks used it too, no matter how dark their natural skin color. They participated in creating the coon stereotype. It wasn't merely a matter of altering the skin tone—it was a full make-up job as thorough as that of a circus clown. It called for simulating a wide mouth and exaggerated eyes. Up to the advent of Sissle and Blake, all popular Negro entertainers performed in cork. They had grounds for believing that had they not pursued the stereotype, they would have created resentment at best, violence at worst, in the white audience. Some blacks found white blackface acts odious, but Eubie says there was a stage in the careers of Al Jolson and Eddie Cantor when they had to put on cork or vanish into show-business obscurity.

Jolson and Eubie were friends. This didn't have anything to do with the theater, because they never worked together. Rather, they both had a love of prize fighting and used to go to boxing matches together, engaging in jocose discussion of the relative merits of Negro and Jewish pugilists. They would occasionally wager a bottle of whisky on these bouts.

"Sissle and I were in Chicago about 1916 playing at an Erlanger theater and Jolson was playing at another theater, and that's when he put on cork. We didn't know Miller and Lyles yet, but *they* put on cork. When Jolson left town, Eddie Cantor came into the theater and *he* had to start puttin' on cork. That's how he came to be in the Ziegfeld Follies doing an act with Bert Williams. He played Bert Williams's son in the Follies."

Long before the Dixie Duo, young Negroes had begun to recognize the contradiction between cork and racial dignity, but Sissle and Blake were the first Negro act in history to succeed in show business, playing to white audiences, without cork. Before them the white public would never take seriously colored actors pretending to the same creativity and the same emotional capacities as whites. They felt uncomfortable seeing Negroes whose manners and morals were the same as their own—sometimes better. The precedent of Sissle and Blake prepared the ground for black artists who followed to explore the full spectrum of ther own creative potential. Thus modern theatrical and cinema stars like Sidney Poitier and James Earl Jones owe a lot to the then revolutionary idea that blacks could come on without cork and to this pair who implemented it.

Surveying the entertainment world of the final quarter of the twentieth century, one sees no remaining vestige of cork. As far as human dignity is concerned, this is a giant forward step in American culture, and a major achievement for the American theater.

"Shuffle Along"

Entr'acte

Sissle and Blake and Miller and Lyles

Problems to Start With

Getting It Together

The Show Itself

Love-Life Reprise

What Came Out of the Show

It was six degrees above zero in New York on the night of January 16, 1920. A Minnesota congressman with a face like a dyspeptic bloodhound heard on his crystal set that the saloons were closing in New York. This legislator, Andrew Volstead, was about to have a profound effect on the entertainment business. Eubie Blake had never met Volstead, whose legislative initiative put the teeth in the prohibition amendment, but he watched the effects of the new law with interest.

In Eubie's case this could be a detached interest: he was one of the few entertainers whose career was not affected by the event. The Dixie Duo, Sissle and Blake, weren't a night-club act. Firmly established as a star vaudeville attraction, the team also had other sources of wealth and fame. Though Jim Europe was deceased, his program for his friends' advancement remained in effect. Eubie and his partner were the darlings of the idle rich. Eubie didn't know much about political science, but he did know that the poor folks might have some trouble getting their liquor. Also, he noticed that he and Sissle kept getting invited to the mansions of the mighty but Mr. Volstead didn't. The hosts didn't like his act.

In 1920 the pair toured for Keith through Canada and the Northeast. Eubie wrote "Florodora Girls" for a Shubert Brothers review. Together, he and Sissle found time to author "Oriental Blues." That was also the year they wrote "Pickaninny Shoes," which was destined to be Sissle's show stopper for many, many years.

"He stands there on the stage in the amber spot, see, and he's got his hands in front of him like he's holdin' a pair of baby shoes in them. Now he got no shoes in his hand, nothin', see, but the audience, they *see* them shoes—he was a great actor—and he sings 'Pickaninny Shoes.' There's no way to follow him. He can't follow *himself*."

"My Vision Girl," quite successful, was out in 1920 too. The boys were doing, now, a well-developed act with songs and sophisticated patter. It was built on a series of set pieces with a few openings to accommodate the leading popular songs of the moment or any improvisations that seemed appropriate. The finale, with Sissle singing "On Patrol in No Man's Land" and Eubie providing the bombardment on the piano, was almost too much for an audience to stand without cheering and stomping. They became a major theatrical attraction.

Eubie Blake is a firm believer in fate, which, he says, guided Sissle and himself to the new Paul Laurence Dunbar Theater in Philadelphia one night in early 1920. This theater, dedicated appropriately to the black lyricist and poet, was that night the scene of an NAACP benefit. Sissle and Blake performed, and on the bill too was the very successful comedy team of Miller and Lyles. Each team had heard of the other, but they'd never met. Each was impressed with the other's routines, and noted that they had not a thing in common stylistically.

Alumni of Fisk University, Flournoy E. Miller and Aubrey Lyles had been the life of the campus in their student days, working up hilarious routines for university productions. They had been in vaudeville for several years in cork, doing traditional blackface humor. There was a little dancing and lots of beautifully executed pantomime. Miller was able to design, even choreograph, their movements in a manner that bespoke true genius.

"Those guys were not improvising," Eubie recalls, "but they looked like they were. That Miller, he worked out every move, and they'd practice it over and over. Lyles had complete confidence in him, and he really knew how to follow orders. In the *act*, that is. Outside the act, he was the most irresponsible man I ever saw. Me and Sissle never did *anything* like that. Oh, sure, we'd rehearse *songs*, but Miller and Lyles, *that* was old-fashioned colored comedy."

That night at the benefit, Sissle responded to requests to sing the big hits of 1920, "Margie" and "Apple Blossom Time," and Eubie had no trouble improvising the accompaniments. But Lyles told Sissle, "You guys are so good with your *own* stuff, you ought to leave those songs to Frank Crumit and Julia Sanderson."

Sissle, in turn, was high in his praise of Lyles's act.

To Eubie it still remains a demonstration of the mystic manipulations of the infinite that these four met again, without having planned it, on the sidewalks of New York and Flournoy Miller unfolded there his grand plan for a shoestring Broadway show based on small-town politics, to be called "The Mayor of Jimtown." They stood on the sidewalk listening to Flournoy's glib exposition until it began to seem real. With much arm waving and gesturing he developed the vision. An agreement to go ahead with the project was made more or less on the spot.

Not long thereafter, in 1921, the project matured into the historic "Shuffle Along."

There exists a most remarkable book by Daniel Blum, which has gone through several editions and multiple printings, entitled *A Pictorial History of the American Theater*. The fourth edition (Crown, 1977), enlarged and revised by John Willis, covers the years from 1860 to 1976. It takes a couple of long evenings to look carefully at all the interesting and rare photographs in it. Eight pages of this large-format volume, with text and seventy-six photographs, constitute the entry for the year 1921. It is easy to see that 1921 was a big year on the street, including what was going on on the musical stage. The musicals represented in this opulent volume include "Blossom Time," "Tangerine" with Frank Crumit and Julia Sanderson, and "Two Little Girls in Blue" with Oscar Shaw. We note that Doris Eaton was featured in the Ziegfeld Follies. In the impressive photo gallery of 1921 we see Al Jolson in blackface for "Bombo" and Bert Williams corked for the Follies. There is no photo from the most successful, significant, and socially influential production of the year, "Shuffle Along," and the text gives it only a six-word phrase in the middle of a long sentence covering six musicals: "Other musicals included . . . 'Shuffle Along' with Sissle and Blake. . . . "

David Ewen's *Life and Death of Tin Pan Alley* (Funk & Wagnalls, 1964) is a comprehensive survey of American popular music. In the index we find John D. Blake, who turns out to have written the lyrics for one song, but the *big* Blake, Eubie, creator of songs in the hundreds and hit after hit, is missing.

There's no conspiracy here. It's just that quality art and entertainment executed by Negroes have been psychologically invisible, or nearly so, to many American scholars and authors unless they were covered with cork. Negroes could always make it with the deplorable darky stereotypes, but whites found it difficult to swallow the concept that there was a *real* Negro somewhere who could do anything the white man could do.

Performers of course know all about this problem—and the practical problems Negroes have had getting themselves and their work up on stage in the first place. Sidney Bechet, in his autobiography *Treat It Gentle* (Hill & Wang, 1960), zeroed in on practical problem number one, money, and used "Shuffle Along" as an example of a show that "had troubles you wouldn't have in the regular kind of production." As Bechet saw, Noble and Eubie, in writing the songs for the show, weren't free to do it as they wanted, but had to turn out songs that could be produced well on virtually no money—and then changes had to be made to save money; good things had to be left out and ideas couldn't be made to work because of expense.

It must not be assumed, however, that "Shuffle Along" had only race prejudice and short funds as obstacles to its success. It took a considerable amount of courage to offer *any* kind of a show on Broadway considering the caliber of the competition that year. *Playbill* shows what went on during the time "Shuffle Along" was on the boards.

Doris Keane was starring in "The Czarina" at the Empire. Marilyn Miller and Leon Erroll had a hit in "Sally" at the New Amsterdam. The original version of "Bulldog Drummond" thrilled audiences at the Knickerbocker. On Forty-fourth Street Lenore Ulric was becoming a major star in "Kiki"; the celebrated Laurette Taylor was working at the Henry Miller in "The National Anthem." As if these weren't enough, superstar George M. Cohan and his sister Georgette packed 'em in with "Madeleine and the Movies," and "The Perfect Fool," an Ed Wynn tour de force, was at the Cohan. The Earl Carroll Theater and the Globe were both showing musical comedies, and comedian Ernest Truex appeared in "Six-Cylinder Love" at the Sam Harris. At the Liberty, "To the Ladies" offered Helen Hayes. And on Wednesday nights, when "Shuffle Along" did a special midnight show, it had to buck Flo Ziegfeld's scandalously extravagant "Midnight Frolic" on the New Amsterdam roof.

Fast company.

Back in the days when there were still minstrel shows, there was Eddie Leonard, and very likely he was the biggest name in that branch of show business. For a generation his name on a marquee was a guarantee of standing room only. The American theater-going public so loved his blackface presentation of "Ida, Sweet as Apple Cider" that to this day there are still imitators doing impressions of him singing it—and also singing the number possibly even more personally identified with him, "Roll Those Roly Boly Eyes." His valedictory vehicle, not surprisingly, had been a theatrical production entitled "Roly Boly Eyes." It was a hit through World War I, then closed after a long and profitable run, and Eddie Leonard retired.

The sweat stains on the costumes of the chorus girls of Leonard's show, after several hundred performances, would have gotten this former finery rejected by the Salvation Army. But somehow Sissle got his hands on the "Roly Boly Eyes" bag of rags—plantation costumes, they'd once been—and persuaded a platoon of fresh, attractive, and talented young girls to mend these scraps and put them on. If you weren't sitting too close, you might be deluded into seeing them as costumes.

And so, since they now had enough costumes for one production number plus a chorus line and a cast, all Sissle and Blake had to do was to write the number. It was called "Bandana Days," and it became one of the big hits of the show.

Frank Fay appeared in the original stage version of "Harvey" and that made him very famous, but before that he was already a prime vaudeville attraction—a stand-up comic who very nearly may be said to have invented the style. He got ambitious and starred himself in a musical revue of his own entitled "Frank Fay's Fables." It was an elaborate production, but it didn't do well. The scavengers of "Shuffle Along" recycled its costumes and some of its scenery.

It isn't easy to do a Broadway show with no money. In those days of miracles, you might try to do it with very little money, but not with *no* money. Undaunted, the principals and the Corts, who owned the theater, did it with *no* money. The entire show was financed out of the weekly vaudeville salaries of Miller and Lyles and Sissle and Blake. The girls in the line were satisfied to wait for their pay until the enterprise got rolling.

"It was an inspiration," Eubie remembers. "Just a few professional theater girls, the rest just nice girls from good homes. Oh, how they worked!"

Still in awe of the achievement of getting "Shuffle Along" on stage, he avows, "I still don't know how we did it. We didn't have money for *nothin'*—not for train fare when we needed it, not for scenery. It just seemed that we *found* everything just when we needed it. I believe if something is *meant* to happen, it's *going* to happen. That's how we *all* felt! It was like watchin' new miracles every day."

No money for scenery and no money for costumes. There was no money, either, for big-name stars. Without money you just have to make *them*, too. A look at the roster of show-business luminaries who were started on their ways or, if already started, given a boost in "Shuffle Along" tends to make one share Eubie's "miracle" thesis. Florence Mills became the very top black show-business star. Paul Robeson, who was delighted to sing bass in the show's Harmony Kings, became a monumental figure in the music world. Josephine Baker, who made an overnight sensation when she joined the chorus line in Boston in 1922, went on to become one of the great ladies of the international entertainment world. Adelaide Hall, Eva Taylor, and Lucille Hegamin each became a well-known recording star. Adelaide Hall's phenomenal vocal musicianship won her the admiration of show-business insiders.

As for the songs themselves, Eubie and Noble had only three numbers to write. They were "Bandana Days," "Love Will Find a Way," and "I'm Just Wild about Harry." The composers had had the rest of the tunes in their portfolios for years, unable to convince Tin Pan Alley publishers to buy them. At last Witmark discovered that anything from Eubie's pen was profitable.

Flournoy Miller could think of much to write about, including much to satirize. Miller's small-time politicians illustrated the same venality as their nonfiction counterparts in the Teapot Dome. A burlesque prize fight mirrored the recent Dempsey–Willard championship match. The show dealt with small-town Negro life just as the year's best seller, "Main Street," dealt with small-town white life.

There was enough hard-shelled, old-time religion in Miller, Lyles, and Sissle to insure that the show would rise above any suggestion of prurience. Miller probably even disapproved of the fact that the state of Iowa was in the process of legalizing the sale of cigarettes to adult males. Reviewers would report that "Shuffle Along" was the cleanest show in New York.

When difficulties arose, Eubie listened to Miller's "Dad blame it" and Sissle's "The Lord willing" without comment. His conviction remained that it was all meant to be; nothing could change it, "nothin' could go wrong."

In his important popular historical work *Black Manhattan* (Knopf, 1930), the distinguished Negro intellectual leader James Weldon Johnson characterized "Shuffle Along" as "a record-breaking, epoch-making musical comedy" with more song hits than most, dances that furnished new material for hundreds of performers, and up-to-the-minute music. He also recounted the trials and triumphs of the show's trip to Broadway. Organized in New York, it was taken on a short out-of-town tryout tour. When the company assembled at Pennsylvania Station, they did not have quite enough money to pay for tickets, and some funds had to be raised quickly. This seemed an ominous sign, and "there were misgivings and mutterings among the company," as Johnson put it, but the doubters were persuaded to go ahead.

The tour included two successful weeks at the Howard Theater, a black theater in Washington, which provided enough money for the company to move to Philadelphia to play the Dunbar Theater, also a black house. As Johnson recalled, the company managers, seeking to make sure of getting the company to New York, suggested to the Dunbar's owner that it would be a good investment for him to buy a half-interest in the show for 1,000 dollars, but he refused. They played "two smashing weeks" at the Dunbar and brought the company intact into New York—but on a shoestring.

"Shuffle Along" opens with an exterior scene showing the front of the run-down Jimtown Hotel. The entire company appears on stage. The audience observes that bobbed hair is really in style because all the girls in the chorus and among the principals display the full range of treatments of the new coiffure.

Miller and Lyles are cast as partners in a grocery store. Each, correctly, suspects the other of stealing from the cash box, and each engages a private detective to catch the other in the act. True to the time-honored tradition of farce, he turns out to be the same detective.

These two are also rival candidates for mayor of Jimtown. The first act is largely occupied with establishing the premises of the plot through the comedy lines and action of Miller and Lyles. The soubrette, Gertrude Saunders in the opening cast, is introduced with "I'm Just Simply Full of Jazz," supported by the male chorus—the Syncopation Steppers, according to the program. The love interest comes in next as Lottie Gee and Roger Matthews take the spotlight to sing "Love Will Find a Way."

This latter number was viewed as the crtical element in the show as far as audience acceptance went. Some felt that a seriously romantic scene between Negroes that featured a "straight" conventional love song would be rejected by white audiences, among whom resentment and bigotry would flare, and possibly cause the failure of the production. The relationship among the principals in the show and the white people who had financial interests in it left the decision whether to drop or keep the number essentially to coproducer John Cort.

"Leave it in," he ruled. "Love Will Find a Way"made it with audience and critics alike. It went on to become a substantial hit.

The duet is followed by the production number "Bandana Days," sung by Arthur Porter and the company, with Adelaide Hall featured. It was Porter who had introduced Sissle to Blake in 1915. The plot advances in a barbershop-quartet sequence with Matthews and the Board of Aldermen rendering "Sing Me to Sleep, Dear Mammy." Roger has also announced for the mayoralty race.

Noble Sissle, in the role of Tom Sharper, Miller's campaign manager and a master of Watergate-style dirty tricks, makes his bow with the melodic "In Honeysuckle Time." Then, preceding the first-act finale, Matthews, Lottie Gee, and Gertrude Saunders sing some impressive harmony in "Gypsy Blues." Miss Saunders was later replaced in her role by Florence Mills.

Act two begins with a busy scene focused on a traffic policeman in a rush-hour crowd. The company introduces the title song. Then Miss Gee, the leading lady, announces her affection for Matthews, whose character's name is Harry Walton, by singing and dancing, with the chorus, the timeless hit of the show, "I'm Just Wild about Harry."

This melody was originally composed as a Viennese waltz, and that's how it was planned for the show. Miss Gee, an experienced and skilled trouper, insisted that for *her* to get anything out of the song, it would have to be a one-step. Eubie was enchanted with his pet waltz and also with Miss Gee. Sissle's enthusiastic agreement with Lottie's concept carried the day, and the alteration was effected. Hearing Eubie perform his original waltz version makes it clear that the number was headed for success either way.

Sharper's crooked manipulation elects his candidate, Miller, who thereupon appoints Lyles to be chief of police. Lyles might have won the election himself except for the activities of his militant suffragette wife, Mattie Wilkes, who alienates the voters. All this builds to a conflict between these two great comics, Miller and Lyles, which culminates in their celebrated fight sequence, already honed and polished through many Keith vaudeville seasons. It never failed to stop the show.

There's a sort of intermezzo featuring the mayor's staff and the Board of Aldermen which supplies the modulation into the raucous "If You've Never Been Vamped by a Brownskin, You've Never Been Vamped at All." This one features Miller and Lyles and the chorus. Miller's mastery of show-business devices makes it a hit.

Charles Davis and Billy Williams perform a song-and-dance piece entitled "Uncle Tom and Old Black Joe," a kind of editorial on racial stereotypes. Meanwhile the plot moves along with Harry mounting a political clean-up campaign that effectively sweeps Miller and Lyles out of office, bringing clean government to Jimtown—and of course he wins the girl. In the process he and Lottie get to sing a beautiful ballad, "Everything Reminds Me of You."

Sissle and the chorus then present "Oriental Blues," incorporated in the show to accommodate costumes left over from "Frank Fay's Fables." They already had the song, and Fay's outfits were Oriental. Miss Saunders then offers two numbers, "I'm Craving for That Kind of Love" and "Daddy."

"I'm Craving for That Kind of Love" is a song that Eubie says "should have been a bigger sheet-music hit than it was. That's because people went in the stores and asked for 'Kiss Me, Kiss Me.' That's how the song starts, see—'Kiss me, kiss me.' But when Gertrude Saunders or Florence Mills got down to the end, why, nobody ever got to hear the title, that's the *last* line, because there's so much clappin' and stompin' and whistlin'. The audience goes crazy, see. The audience never *did* hear the name of that tune."

Now just before the last number and the finale, Eubie relinquishes the baton, hops up on the stage, and, together with Sissle, goes through the Dixie Duo vaudeville act, already familiar but cherished by most of the audience. It never failed to bring down the house.

Eubie then gets back into the orchestra pit and conducts the big number, "Baltimore Buzz," in which some of the show's catchy melodies are heard. There follows a brief interlude, "African Dip," a comedy bit with Miller and Lyles. And then the finale—filled with excitement, flag waving, reprises, sing-alongs, and audience participation. The crowd is delighted and exhausted.

It took several performances before most of the reviews came out, since the show opened without either advance advertising or publicity, but the excitement of the crowds was so intense that during the week the critics began to show up. By the end of the week the Sixty-third Street Theater was mobbed, and traffic became so thick that the city had to make Sixty-third Street one way.

"Shuffle Along" was officially staged by Walter Brooks, a white man of substantial Broadway credentials, but according to Eubie, "This fellow really didn't do *anything*. He might move an ashtray from there to here or turn a lamp around. But Sissle kept sayin' we needed him for 'the Broadway touch.' The only thing he touched was a percentage of the profits. We got all the Broadway touch we needed from Larry Deas. *He* did the choreography. He took care of the props *and* the scenery."

Deas appeared in "Shuffle Along" too, as Jack Penrose, the detective Miller and Lyles hire to spy on each other. He also danced in the production.

Eubie handled the writing of the music, but the arrangements are by Will Vodery, a distinguished figure in the world of American music. In the shadows immediately beyond the glare of the footlights of the musical theater, arrangers go about their professional business with feverish and purposeful zeal. Audiences rarely, if ever, know their names, but those names are uttered with respect and sometimes awe and reverence among composers and performing musicians. Vodery was pre-eminent among the black arrangers of the first quarter of the twentieth century.

After his successes with the Bert Williams and George Walker productions beginning around the turn of the century, he was in constant demand right into the thirties. He had a hand in not only "Shuffle Along" but every subsequent spin-off including "Chocolate Dandies," "Runnin' Wild," "Hot Chocolates," "Brown Buddies," and the Lew Leslie "Blackbirds" series. Hearing the old records of the "Shuffle Along" Orchestra playing numbers like "Baltimore Buzz" and "Bandana Days" can only increase the high regard in which his music is held. It was clearly the *liveliest* music yet played on the Broadway stage.

What impressed the critics more than anything else, it seems, were the verve and enthusiasm of the entire company and the general wholesomeness of the characters and dialogue. They were unanimous in their praise.

"Sure!" says Eubie. "Those kids really *kicked*. It was like they learned from George Walker!"

Eubie at this point rises from his easy chair and says, "Here's how a *regular* chorus line kicks." Then with a sudden move that in a flash brings back a whole world of glorious show-business tradition, he snaps to attention, military style, and executes a real precision kick, so sharp and vigorous that suddenly you see the entire contrast between the "languid efforts of ordinary Broadway musical affairs . . . and 'Shuffle Along'" *(Billboard)*.

"That," says Eubie, resuming his seat, "is how George Walker kicked, and that's how *our* kids did it."

The world of show business, as everyone understands, is not like other worlds. There is indeed no business like show business. Within it there exist a youthful esprit and camaraderie that generate intense excitement and emotion and at times, not always for the best, romance.

Eubie's marriage to Avis was a happy one. They loved each other and had a workable relationship. She never envied his fame and success but was delighted to share in it. Eubie has been lucky that way with his wives.

He admits there were women in his life besides his legal spouses, yet it's clear that he never thought of himself as a ladies' man. In fact, he is quick to accord that distinction to his friends and associates Sissle and William Grant Still.

He discusses his amours with an unerotic detachment that gives the impression that he went through them without ever taking any initiative at all. "It's like livin' in a flower garden," Eubie reminisces. "You might pluck one, but that doesn't mean you're gonna remember it." His personality was never organized to resist the temptations of sex—especially as represented by the seductive and exciting gals of "Shuffle Along."

But when he talks of Lottie Gee, his whole attitude changes. In 1921 he "took up" with her, and for ten years he remained her lover of record. He set her up in an apartment and divided his time between Lottie and his legal spouse, Avis. He can't say—doesn't know—whether he was in love with Lottie, but it's clear that she brought out tenderness and compassion in him. He worried about her comfort, her safety, her general well-being.

Lottie had been the junior partner in an act called King and Gee, the Two Indian Girls. "Indians!" Eubie says. "The things we had to do to get in show business!" Eubie met her when the act played a benefit in the Ford Theater in Baltimore in 1911. Ford Dabney—who married Martha Lee, a high school friend of Avis—was conducting the orchestra and Eubie was in the audience. Later Dabney introduced Lottie and Eubie backstage. When Effie King broke up the act to get married, Lottie went on to greater success alone. Eubie didn't start going with her until rehearsals for "Shuffle Along" began.

With the luster it added to her name, Lottie got innumerable theatrical offers after "Shuffle Along" closed. Her position in show business could have made her an instant headliner, making really big money, as Florence Mills did. She preferred to go into the new Sissle and Blake show "In Bamville," which became "The Chocolate Dandies," at a relatively nominal salary just to be near her man.

The apartment Eubie kept her in was comfortable but not elaborate. Lottie didn't feel a compulsion for more luxury as long as Eubie came around regularly.

Emile Coué fascinated Americans when he told them, "Day by day in every way I am getting better and better."

The statement applied to "Shuffle Along," too. From the day it opened, May 23, 1921, through its 504 New York performances, it developed into a polished and ever more exciting production. Ready at last to end their New York stay, the company headed for a two-week run in Boston. They were able to rent the Selwyn Theater there for two weeks only, because of the scheduled opening of a Shakespearean presentation by E. H. Sothern and Julia Marlowe, two of the great names in the American theater. These patient folk held off their opening for fifteen weeks so that "Shuffle Along" might run its course in Boston—and at last had to threaten to sue in order to get the bard on the boards. Edith Spencer had replaced Florence Mills in the cast before the show left New York. Florence went directly into Lew Leslie's "Plantation Club Revue." She was an international sensation when Leslie took her to Paris and London. Later she appeared in "Dixie to Broadway." She was starring in Leslie's "Blackbirds" when she died in 1927 of acute appendicitis. Florence had worked in vaudeville with her husband, Ulysses S. Thompson, better known as Slow Kid, in an act called the Tennessee Ten, and was singing in the Baron Wilkins Club in New York when she was discovered by Harriet Sissle. Slow Kid survives and Eubie sees him from time to time. Sadly, the much-loved, birdlike voice of Florence Mills was never recorded.

It's hard to establish a fixed date for the closing of "Shuffle Along." After leaving New York, it bloomed into three companies touring the United States. Everywhere it went, it played to packed houses and upbeat reviews. The companies played themselves out in the summer of 1923, but there were revivals later.

"Shuffle Along" made all the original owners affluent, and it established a pattern for any number of successors that made it possible for colored show people to keep working on a higher level than they'd ever known before. "Shuffle Along, Jr." went into vaudeville eventually as a one-hour-and-twenty-minute "tab show" with Eubie and Broadway Jones. Miller and Lyles brought out "Keep Shufflin'" and "Runnin' Wild" successfully, the former with music by James P. Johnson. Miller's brother Irving and Spencer Williams toured in "Chocolate Brown." "Hot Chocolates" made it with the aid of lyrics by Andy Razaf and music by Fats Waller.

"Shuffle Along" grossed close to 8 million dollars. For the world of entertainment it changed everything. Its sponsors and the quartet that conceived it are true folk heroes.

"It was the first Negro show on Broadway," Eubie asserts. "But it wasn't the first Negro show to play on Broadway. Now that sounds funny, so I better explain it.

"You see, Williams and Walker, Cole and Johnson, Ernest R. Hogan—they played on Broadway, too. But they played in dark theaters. Now I mean theaters that were closed, where no shows ever go in, only meetings, political conventions, and that kind, and then these shows would come in out of season. They never got five dollars for a ticket. It was a dollar, top.

"See, it's the price that makes Broadway. That's what makes a Broadway show. Otherwise you can put a flea circus next to a theater and call it a Broadway show. I don't mean Williams and Walker and the rest of those people weren't high-class shows. But they could never get into a real Broadway theater in Broadway *season* at Broadway *prices*. When it comes to *quality*, there was nobody could touch Bert Williams and George Walker. Bob Cole and J. Rosamund Johnson were musical *geniuses*. Great! But they could never bring even their greatest shows to Broadway. Of course Bert Williams could bring *himself* to the Ziegfeld Follies, but that's a white show. Even there he was in cork."

Stage and Screen

Backstage Rhapsody
Talking Pictures

"You always find plenty of geniuses around the musical theater," Eubie notes. "People who have the urge to create are always around you. But only very few have the talent. By the time you get into the big time, usually only the really talented ones make it that far.

"So I always get excited when I go in a theater—backstage, I mean. That's why I like to rehearse either an orchestra or a chorus line."

He admits that his fascination with the chorus line has frequently exceeded his enthusiasm for the baton.

"Why not?" he asks. "I always *did* like pretty girls! That's another thing I like about backstage in a theater. Men always liked dancin' girls, even back in Bible days. You can look it up. I'm not gonna tell you I didn't do my share of playin' around—in fact almost every time I ever got the chance—but I really wasn't no ladies' man like Still and Sissle. The girls would just hang around them. And remember, when I made it to Broadway I was a lot older than those guys.

"But I'll tell you, see. The minute my hands hit the piano those girls become *machines* to me. I want to see those precision kicks. I want to see the snap more than I want to see the legs. And I'll play all day to rehearse 'em, long as they keep doin' it better and better. Anytime I walk backstage I'm a new man.

"You know, yourself, no man can resist. You meet a Josephine Baker in her prime, you know she's a *girl*. That's the first thing you notice. If that *ain't* the first thing you notice, you need to see a doctor. Valada Snow, Adelaide Hall, Florence Mills. They got the whole city of New York excited, so how ain't they gonna get *me* excited? How can you resist 'em if you know 'em face to face?

"When you compose or when you work with a lyricist, well, that's not something you do in the theater. You do that at home. So the people you work with got to be good *people* too. I always been lucky about that. But when you see the lyricist in the *theater*, that's different. You ain't workin' with *him* then, so you don't pay him any mind. Razaf was different. He could write lyrics in the theater while everything else is goin' on. You play a melody and he makes a whole new thing out of it, and before you know it you hear it playin' with a full orchestra and somebody singin' it like Ethel Waters or Edith Wilson and it's a *thrill*. It ain't only *you*. It's a whole lot of geniuses get together and do something great and you know it's great and the people out front know it too—you can't fool 'em. They know they just saw somethin' great.

"You can walk out on Broadway in the crowd and nobody knows you. You sit in a restaurant you never been in before and they don't recognize you. You're just one in ten million people. Then you open the stage door and it's like you're home! *Everybody* knows you and you know they need you."

One doesn't think of Eubie as a sentimental person, and he isn't morbidly nostalgic. When he talks of the old days, they aren't necessarily the good old days. There are things to remember fondly and things to forget. At ninety-six he's more interested in the present and the future. He's a self-appointed cheerleader for every genuine talent he comes across. He takes a keen delight in even the slightest phenomena that indicate the traditions of show business will carry forward. But he remains shrewdly and knowledgeably critical.

In New Orleans in April 1978 he met with members of the press for an informal afternoon, and someone asked him if he'd seen the TV musical production of the life of Bert Williams with Ben

Vereen. Eubie was seated on the piano bench and a look came over his face as though he were eating an unripe persimmon. Then he began to state his view.

"Now don't get me wrong," he began, "I got nothin' *against* this young fellow. In fact he's a very talented man, *very* talented. But before anybody tries to do the life of a great man like Bert Williams—well, you need to do a little research. If you're gonna do his songs, well, he *did* make records, you know. You know how this fellow did 'Nobody'? I'll show you, see."

He turned to the piano and gave—playing and singing—a fast, highly rhythmic and syncopated rendition. Even had one not seen the show in question, Eubie's re-creation let you know eactly how it had been. You could see Ben Vereen in action.

Then he turned back to those present and said, "Now I'll show you Bert Williams."

With that, this irrepressible nonagenarian stood up and looked silently at his little audience just long enough to build their anticipation to the exact point where a master showman knows to begin. It's as though he had silently counted the beats. It was mid-afternoon, but houselights seemed to dim and an amber spot to fall on his frail figure. Eubie created this illusion by pure timing—a timed silence. Then in a slow, almost funeral tempo, subtly gesturing in ways that weren't his own and therefore must be those of his departed friend, he went through almost a chorus of the song. When he stopped abruptly and proceeded to discuss the matter further, the audience was jarred back into the present. That afternoon we all knew we had *seen* and *heard* Bert Williams.

I was aware of Eubie saying, "Now *that's* Bert Williams. And that young fellow could have—well, he wouldn't have to imitate, but he could have got the *feeling* of Bert Williams. But these days they don't really *care*. It's a shame. But this guy is brilliant. Great dancer! And it's talent like that that's always made show business so great to work in.

"You don't know what excitement is like until you're in the middle of gettin' a musical stage show ready for production. Especially you know everybody wants it to be a success as much as you do. The way those chorus girls *work*. It would kill a horse. People will sing and sing—the same song a hundred times—until they get it perfect. The patience! Actors giving each other suggestions and the other actors *taking* them. These are times when you *love* every-body. You *trust* everybody. You hope everybody's gonna come out of it a star. Nothing's too good for them.

"People say about somebody, 'Show business is his whole life.' I don't think there can *be* a better life than bein' with—workin' with—these people.

"When you leave the theater, it feels like you're leavin' the *real* world and the *fake* world is out here in the street where nobody knows anybody else. I'm sorry you couldn't know people like James Weldon Johnson and Rosamund Johnson and [Will Marion] Cook, and Jim Europe! You should have seen Abbie Mitchell"—the lovely trained vocalist who was Cook's wife. "Anybody would *have* to be happy in a world full of people like them!"

People born in the thirties or later tend to have distorted conception of what Broadway was like in the jazz age. While it's true that many, if not most, critics considered this the golden age of the American theater, marquees advertising the legitimate shows didn't dominate the scene on the Great White Way. If anything did, it was the electric Maxwell House billboard that dripped light bulbs into a Grand Canyon–size cup. At twilight one day late in 1922, for instance, the only display that compared with it was the visual extravaganza on the face of the Criterion Theater building heralding the presence within of the film "Scaramouche," starring Ramon Novarro. Nearby, the modest exterior of the Palace announced that Sophie Tucker was to be seen on stage in the company of seven other headline acts. In various side streets one might glimpse posters announcing performances by such stars as Jane Cowl, Ernest Truex, Marilyn Miller and Jeanne Eagles, but these were dimmed by the massive high-wattage declamations promoting silent films.

That day nobody except one individual suspected that some equipment he was working with was a cultural time bomb that would blow these mammoth silent-screen attractions to oblivion along with superior vaudeville and would effect drastic and fundamental changes in the legitimate theater. This man, Lee De Forest, while his original professional motivations had been purely scientific, did understand that he'd perfected a device that was to wreak fundamental and irreversible changes in the nature and patterns of world entertainment. He was using the device to produce what he called "De Forest Phonofilms" and "vaudeville pictures." Al Jolson's "The Jazz Singer" was still half a decade off in the future. There was as yet no "Vitaphone" in the Warner Brothers logo. It would be a long, hard struggle for De Forest before he'd get the film companies to take his invention seriously.

On the particular day in question, using charm and money, he had persuaded nine individuals to be the first entertainers to perform in this new medium. His cast was drawn from the top of show business. The roster included Weber and Fields, the "Dutch act" now in the dusk of an illustrious career; Eva Puck and Sammy White, the most successful boy-girl song-and-comedy act in show-business history; Ziegfeld Follies star Eddie Cantor; the laconic accordion-playing comedian Phil Baker, who brought the word "stooge" into the American vernacular; and Sissle and Blake, the talk of the town. Only one of the acts, Conchita Piquir, managed to elude immortality.

Eubie remembers it all as though it were only yesterday.

"Sissle always took care of the business. I never paid attention where we were workin' or how much we got paid. Sissle did all that. So this day we went to—I think it was the old Metropolitan Opera building, I don't exactly remember. And there's all these show people. If Sissle was still livin', he could tell you whether we went on first or last—all that stuff. The only way I know what we sang is because we saw the film recently. It was 'Affectionate Dan,' which used to be the opener of our act after our theme, 'Gee! I'm Glad That I'm from Dixie.' It's one of those snappy pieces that wakes an audience up.

"Now this was the first time we worked in front of a camera, and in those days they couldn't move the camera around on wheels or turn it every way, so naturally it couldn't follow you. That didn't bother me too much because I'm sittin' at the piano anyway, I ain't goin' nowhere.

"But Sissle, he's all over the stage, see. If he has to just stand still and sing, it's just real hard for him to do that. He's an *actor*, and that cramps his style. So when you see the film—and if you know how he is the rest of the time—you can see he's not up to his best.

"Another thing. If you play to a theater audience, you have to learn to do a stage smile. Now that means you show your teeth.

The audience is too far away to see if you're laughin' or cryin' or if you *really* look sad. But if those people out there see teeth, they're satisified.

"Now if you do the stage smile and the camera is eight feet away, then when the films come out your stage smile looks like a Hallowe'en mask. The audience can see you're not happy at all if you're not. You can't hide *nothin'* from that camera.

"So me and Sissle don't look natural in that film. We sound *real* good. There ain't nothin' fake about the sound. At the time I didn't think too much about the whole thing, but then as time went on I realized that we made show-business history that day. The first Negro act in talking pictures! The first film music!"

For vaudeville, this film that showed for a select audience at the Rivoli Theater on Broadway on April 15, 1923, was a preview of disaster. Doom was delayed for a few years while De Forest set about convincing the film companies that they were going to be forced into the new medium, that countless millions would have to be spent in wiring theaters across the country for sound, and that the entertainment industry was heading into a new era.

In 1927, when such things as camera angles, close-ups, dolly shots, and the full arsenal of talking-picture technical devices were available, Sissle and Blake were to get the full Warner Brothers treatment, complete with massive sets, full orchestration, and beautiful girls. I remember seeing the film. They did "All God's Chillun Got Shoes," which I don't remember at all, but I memorized, in two showings, the words of "My Dream of the Big Parade."

"These talking pictures are a strange thing," Eubie says, "I never would have believed it."

Eubie has been involved in other films. There was a full-length Bill Robinson opus entitled "Harlem Is Heaven" under the Blake baton, plus a one-reel short in which Eubie Blake and His Orchestra supplied the music behind the sensational taps of the Nicholas Brothers. These were in 1932.

In 1976, at the age of ninety-three, Eubie performed a bit part as a much younger man in the TV–film biography of Scott Joplin. He played the part of Will Williams, proprietor of the legendary Maple Leaf Club in Sedalia, Missouri. With the advent of videotape Eubie's playing has been widely documented, most notably by the Frenchman Jean-Cristophe Averty in 1974 for French TV. This has been edited into four one-hour shows. "Averty," Eubie says, "is one of the great men of television and one of the finest people I ever met, but he damn near worked me to death!"

Jazz-Age Variations

Some Golden Years
   Trans-Atlantic
      Home to Baltimore
         Nothing Stays the Same

One day you wake up and you suddenly realize you're a star! Surveying your own life, you remember where you came from and you see where you are now, and it seems you've reached, at forty, the summit of your career. You've got a wife and a mistress who both love you and stay out of each other's way. Your closet is full of good clothes, derbies for winter, caps and skimmers for summer. You're up to date in cold weather with your new raccoon coat and your pearl-gray spats. Parked outside is your rakish new Paige. Your name is in lights on Broadway and people keep asking you for your autograph. You turn on the radio and hear your own music, or you can go 'round to Sissle's Music Shop and buy your latest record. Your shoes are always shined and you can afford to buy genuine Old Overholt bottled-in-bond whisky—even at bootleg prices. You're buying your cigarettes by the carton instead of four for a penny, and if you feel like a good cigar, there are plenty of Corona Coronas in the humidor. You've provided a decent home for your parents and your little adopted sister, Trudy. Where could you possibly go from here?

Relax and enjoy it? The only way Eubie could enjoy it was to keep on working. For him, all the world's other rewards couldn't equal the thrill of the keyboard. Easily he adapted to the fine clothes, the sporty car, and the public adulation. At the same time, he never failed to remind himself that he was a Negro and this wasn't a Negro's normal station in life, and he did things from time to time to show himself that it was all true.

"I tried to get my mother to come to New York, but all her friends are in Baltimore, in the church," Eubie recalls. "Now I'm makin' money, see. I got a hit show. Biggest thing on Broadway! She won't come.

"My adopted sister is a young lady by that time. I call her up at night when I know my mother is in a church meetin', and I tell her I want to buy my mother a fur coat. Now you got to understand how it was for Baltimore colored people in the stores. You could go *in* to O'Neill's or Stewarts' "—department stores—"but if you try something *on*, you bought it, see? It don't make no difference if it cost a million dollars. If you put it on, it's yours. The white folks wouldn't put anything on if they thought it was ever on a Negro. It's true. That's how things were. I don't mean slavery days. I mean right then in the twenties and thirties.

"In Baltimore we had a fellow, Tom Smith. He was like an ambassador between the colored people and the powers that be. He could fix things. He could fix it so that Joe Gans' wife, for instance, could go in after six o'clock—that's when they closed the store—and buy whatever she wanted. You know, try things on and all that stuff. So I told Trudy I'd fix it for my mother to try on coats, and I did.

"I told Trudy first to go to the head saleslady and give her fifteen dollars and tell her I wanted to buy a beaver coat for my mother. I told her no matter what the coat cost to get the saleslady to make out a slip for seventy-five dollars. If my mother saw it cost any more than that, she wouldn't wear it, because she'd be *sure*, then, that I was doin' somethin' crooked. She suspected it anyway, but that would convince her.

"Now that coat, even in those times, cost 650 dollars, but she's got the sales slip—it says seventy-five dollars. Of course, she had to go in and try it on after six o'clock.

"So she's sittin' in the church, see, and she's got the coat on. One of the ladies says, 'Sister Blake, where did you get that beautiful fur coat?'

"She says, 'My son, my Eubie bought it. Seventy-five dollars.'

"See, she wouldn't have worn it if she knew how much it cost. I'd send her 500 dollars every couple of weeks, and she was afraid to take it. She says no colored people could make that much money. My sister, Trudy, would explain, 'But Ma, Eubie is rich. He's a Broadway producer. They *make* a lot of money.'

"My mother would just shake her head and say, 'He's doin' somethin' wrong. They goin' to *catch* him. He's doin' *somethin'* he shouldn't do. I don't want no tainted money.'

"That old lady died thinkin' I had sold my soul to the devil."

Eubie never cared much for jewelry for himself, but he showered it on Avis, who accepted it all with grace as a token of his affection. She'd have been perfectly contented without it and without the elaborate New York apartment. She enjoyed it, naturally, and she appreciated the car of her own and the chauffeur. But she really felt she had all she needed if she had Eubie. When she called him Dummy these days, there was no longer any derision in the tone. While she wasn't much at pitching into his business affairs and helping him professionally, she didn't need to. He had Sissle and a platoon of bookkeepers and detail people to take care of all that.

Eubie was contented just to admire her beauty, dress her up, and show her off in society. Just having her for his wife was enough. She certainly wasn't like other wives—like Sissle's, for instance, always nagging. "Where were *you* till three o'clock in the morning?" Nothing like that from Avis. She had a smile for Eubie when he left and when he got home, and she never interfered with anything he thought was necessary.

Professionally, there were limits for a Negro, as Will Marion Cook and One Leg Willie Joseph demonstrated. The serious concert field was the white man's preserve. The foreign kid, twenty-one, who got such great reviews at Carnegie Hall last week—funny name, Jascha Heifetz. He was probably very good, but if he were colored he wouldn't be there. Eubie had fame and fortune beyond anything he'd ever dreamed. But maybe it would be a good idea to go to school and learn some more music—when he got more time.

Avis always bought the magazine *Vanity Fair*. Looking through it Eubie saw pictures of all the people who were important, really important, in the theater. Some of them he'd heard about and some he hadn't. Everybody knew who Galli-Curci was, but who was this young girl Judith Anderson? He saw Gertrude Lawrence in a publicity pose, holding a guitar. It told how she was about to appear on Broadway in "Charlot's Revue," but it didn't say her big hit song "You Were Meant for Me" was by a couple of colored guys named Sissle and Blake. In England it was the first duet she ever sang with Noël Coward. She did it with Jack Buchanan in the states. Of course, there was Eubie's old friend Paul Whiteman, and he'd heard of Ring Lardner. Who in the hell was Marcel Proust? Anyway, there in *Vanity Fair* one thing he noticed was that none of these people was Negro. Maybe you don't notice things like that if you're white, but if you're black, you notice.

And how about the great colored stars? Here it is 1923. You're on top of the heap. But where are the others? Well, of course, Sissle's here, and Miller and Lyles. Poor Bert Williams died last year, only forty-five. You shudder when you do the arithmetic. Hogan's gone. George Walker—that's been a long time already. But then, right after "Shuffle Along" hit, lots of new ones popped out. That Spencer Williams wrote some good tunes. He's got his own show. Bill Robinson, he's lookin' good. And there are all those blues singers. It was Mule—Perry Bradford—who started all that. Mamie Smith. Then all those record companies fell in line. Bessie Smith, Ma Rainey, Trixie Smith, Clara Smith. Even old Mary Stafford is out on Columbia. But looking around, it's better to be Eubie Blake than any other Negro in America, because Eubie Blake is *the man* in colored show business.

For a couple of years the act of Sissle and Blake was hot in American vaudeville. With the triumphs of "Shuffle Along" and "The Chocolate Dandies" behind them, they found throngs across the nation eager to see them in person. The act didn't change.

"It ain't much of an act," says Eubie. "I play and Sissle sings. I mean we don't come on with scene changes and costumes or anything like that. We just come out and do songs. Of course, Sissle, he could really *sell* a song. We were havin' a good time."

In 1923, 1924, and 1925 show people had no reason yet to

suspect that within the decade the footlights for variety performers would be dimming down to off as the talkies matured. These were golden years for Sissle and Blake.

In September of 1925, one brisk morning in New York, Eubie and Avis and Noble and Harriet stood behind the rail of the luxury liner *Olympic* waving down to friends, relatives, and well-wishers on the dock below. Their fame preceded them to France, England, and Scotland, and the William Morris Agency, which represented them, had organized an eight-month itinerary.

Sissle and Blake's sensational tour on the European variety circuit achieved a thing or two unplanned by their agency. They shelved the tag line "Dixie Duo" and became "American Ambassadors of Syncopation." Charles B. Cochran, generally thought of as the Ziegfeld of England, engaged the team to write songs for his 1926 review. They included "Tahiti" and "Let's Get Married Right Away," which were sung by Basil Howes and Elizabeth Hines. A year earlier Sissle and Blake had written "Lady of the Moon" for this producer's "Still Dancing." So successful were these efforts that Cochran invited the team to stay on and write his entire 1927 show. They didn't.

Theaters weren't the only showcase for Eubie's talents.

"There was this famous night club. Oh, *everybody* showed up there. It was called the Kit Kat Club. One night the Prince of Wales—he was King Edward VIII later—was there. He wasn't a bad drummer.

"Now there's some way that they pick out one act from each one of the best theaters, then they send for the act, and then when the theaters close, why, *they've* got the *real* show. So we're playin' in this theater, and they've got a famous American band. It's led by Isham Jones and his girl friend is the singer in the band. She's *famous*, too, but I don't remember her name. But she gets mad when the Kit Kat Club picks *us* and not *her* to do the show. I mean she was really upset. Her boy friend had to buy her a new fur coat for that.

"Sissle really *loved* England—couldn't get enough of it—but I knew when I had enough. You know, they all treated us just fine. Avis liked it, Harriet liked it—well, *I* liked it too, but I had enough of it. That's what caused me and Sissle to have our first argument. Now you know we're partners for *sixty-one years* and we only had one fight. We just finished the tour, see, and we been in Europe eight months and now it's time to go home.

"Now I'm sittin' on the bed in the hotel and Sissle comes in and he's all smiles, see. Happy as can be, and he says, 'Hi, kid! Hi, kid! Well, I did it again.' I ask him what he did again and he tells me, 'I booked a return engagement for the tour. We're goin' around again.' Now he's really happy, see. But he had gone and booked us again for the whole tour we just been on, without even askin' me if I wanted to go. I suppose he liked England so much he couldn't imagine everybody wasn't so crazy about it. I says, 'No, Sissle!' I says, 'I ain't goin' on that tour again.' Well, he gets mad, see. I don't blame him, I guess. But he's mad. We have an argument. But that's not bad. One argument in *sixty-one years.*"

Eubie says, "I couldn't wait to get out of there. It wasn't that I had anything against England, but I wanted to get home so bad."

They came home by way of Paris, taking advantage of the opportunity to visit Josephine Baker, whose meteoric rise had brought her to the star's dressing room at the Folies-Bergère. They sailed for home on the *Paris*, another luxury liner, and arrived in New York in November of 1926.

"Sissle went back to Europe later," Eubie says. "I've gotta tell you a story about that. Now Sissle denies all of this, but the only way *I* know it is because he told me it himself years ago.

"Now Sissle's walkin' on that big, wide street in Paris"—the Champs Elysées—"and he sees Cole Porter, so he yells to him. Now Cole Porter idolized Sissle. He liked me too, but Sissle is from his home town. So he asks Sissle how he's doin' and Sissle says, 'I'm starvin' to death.'

"So Cole tells him, 'Why don't you get a band together? I think I can find a spot for you.' Sissle says he doesn't know any musicians in Paris—how is he going to get a band together? But Porter says there's lots of American Negro musicians around Paris, and Sissle goes out and sure enough gets together a band, and Cole gets them a job at Zelle's, which is this big, famous dance place.

"Now that's all there is to the story, see. That's the way Sissle *told* me the story. The last time I told it on him while he was there, he said, 'I never told Cole I was starvin' to death. I didn't even say I was lookin' for work.' He don't like me to tell that on him, but he told me it himself!"

As soon as Eubie planted his feet on U.S. terra firma, he turned them in the direction of Baltimore and went to see his mother. "I miss the smell of Johns Hopkins," he says. "You know I grew up—no matter what house I lived in, I grew up with the smell of the medical center here"—pointing to his nose. "Anytime I smell carbolic acid, it means home to me." The press noted the native son's return. The headline of the story in the *Sun* informed Baltimoreans, "EUBIE BLAKE BACK FROM FOREIGN TOUR." Interviewers solicited his views on a variety of subjects: ". . . says don't visit Europe . . . Bread Lines, Poverty, Poor housing, Queer English. . . ." The press told how he was home to visit his mother at 915 Rutland Avenue, and how he had scored a triumph in England. He expressed his dissatisfaction with things British, the traffic customs, the lack of baths and steam heat, the British accent. He acknowledged, however, that he had been treated with extreme courtesy and that the trip had been very rewarding financially.

Emily of course was pleased to see her son, though she tried not to show it, as was her habit. She remained suspicious of his activities, convinced that if the police didn't catch him and punish him for misdeeds, inevitably the devil would.

Eubie tried every way he could to make his mother comfortable and to convince her he was making an honest living. She never questioned the extent of his talent, but relentlessly she bemoaned the fact that it wasn't directed to doing the work of the Lord.

Baltimore was to welcome Eubie home many and many a time. He never forgot his old friends, many of whom still live there, and he now enjoys annual visits there.

Inevitably, a time was to come when, on his return to the city of his birth, his mother, born way back in 1850, would no longer be there to greet him. "It's 1927, now. I'm in Bridgeport, Connecticut, in the dressing room of the theater where we're workin', see, me and Sissle. Paul Whiteman—bless him in his grave—was in there with me. He's gettin' ready to go to Cleveland to open with his band. They just had a short vacation. He's sittin' there drinkin' my Old Overholt and he says, 'You know I got a thirty-two-piece band and I'll bet I don't open with more than eighteen or twenty.' He means they're still gonna be drunk from the vacation. I tell him they're all fine upstandin' young men, but he says 'I'll bet you a bottle of whisky I don't have more than twenty.' And I don't remember now whether we made that bet or not, but just that minute is when the telegram came to tell me my mother is dead. I don't know how I went on, but I did."

Eubie's father, John Sumner Blake, had died ten years before at the age of eighty-three. He was coming home on the streetcar from a meeting of the Grand Army of the Republic post to which he belonged and expired with dramatic suddenness.

"You can't stop livin' because those things happen. You *know* they got to happen. You pay your respects and turn around and go do whatever your work is in this world."

"One thing you always got to know is that nothing stays the same," Eubie admonishes."I don't remember what town we were in, but I'll tell you how the act finally broke up. My pal Romaine [Johns] was with me in the dressing room and Sissle comes in and sits down on the bed. Now he sits and looks at the floor. Romaine is sittin' in a chair. This is the summer of 1927. Sissle says, 'I'm goin' to the American Legion convention in Paris.' He was a soldier, remember. I say, 'When you comin' back?' He don't say nothin'. I ask him, 'You gonna stay over there?' No answer. I tell him, 'You know we still got eleven weeks of bookings left on our contracts.' He still don't say nothin'. So I say, 'Well, I guess this is the end of Sissle and Blake.' He never takes his eyes off the floor. In a minute he gets up and leaves. And that was the end of Sissle and Blake.

"A man will do anything for love of a woman. I'll tell you what I believe really happened. I can't prove nothin', of course. But what I *believe* is that Harriet started tellin' him, 'You don't need Blake. The people comin' to see you, not him. They wanna hear you sing. They don't care who's playin' for you.' Things like that, you know. And a man can't *take* that day after day, and she *was* like that. So that's what I think happened to Sissle and that's why I think the act broke up."

Sissle became a successful bandleader in Paris, and Eubie spent the rest of the year writing floor shows with the expert lyricist Henry Creamer ("Way Down Yonder in New Orleans," "Strut Miss Lizzie"). Together with Creamer, Eubie composed a long list of excellent songs.

"That Creamer talked like a Sunday-school teacher. It seems like I always run into them kind of partners. But he was good."

In September of 1927 Eubie organized a brand-new act with that talented and popular performer Broadway Jones, with whom he'd worked the Keith circuit in 1918 when Sissle and Europe were overseas. The act opened at the Lincoln Theater in Union City, New Jersey, on a contract that called for three or four shows daily, with rehearsals at 11 A.M. The pair received $162.50 for four days of this—not $162.50 each. It was clear that the suburbs of New York weren't going to bring much prosperity to this act even if they worked all the time. They played such metropolises as Patchogue and Lynbrook, Long Island, as well as New Britain, Connecticut, at an average income of $50 a day for the act. Through an entire winter season the pair suffered through split weeks and one-nighters. This may seem close to starvation pay today, but Eubie doesn't seem to have felt any pinch. He found the compensation reasonable, and neither of them had too much trouble getting along financially as long as the work kept up. Of course Eubie had his royalty checks coming in from ASCAP. And with Eubie money was never decisive. Audiences continued to thrill him.

In 1928, largely through the initiative of Broadway Jones, the two organized the tab-show version of "Shuffle Along" entitled "Shuffle Along, Jr." They went on tour with this hour-and-twenty-minute digest featuring themselves and a cast of eleven—Marion and Dade, Dewey Brown, Katie Crippen, and a chorus line of seven. This junket held together through 1929. The pay was a little better this time around, but by 1929 vaudeville itself was doomed. Talking pictures were everywhere. It had taken no time at all for almost every theater in the nation to equip itself for the wave of the future. As though that weren't devastating enough, there came the financial crash of '29 and it was suddenly time for everything to screech to a halt. The debacle wasn't only a matter of stockbrokers raining on Wall Street from atop its taller buildings. Banks were failing and the life savings of millions of people vanishing. Bankruptcies proliferated and the breadline was born. Show people had to adjust to new conditions. The fortunes of the footlight world collapsed along with the prices of securities. Theater orchestras melted away. Every marquee that read "100% ALL-TALKING" meant a platoon of unemployed performers. And Herbert Hoover's assurances that the free market would set the nation's ills right didn't feed anybody.

The Palace itself had barely eighteen months to go before it would have to close its doors. In the meantime the Broadway Joneses of the country were to fade into obscurity, becoming, at best, bartenders, cab drivers, waiters, and janitors. Hardly anyone but a superstar could survive in the stage world of the thirties. The plight of Negroes, as always, was worse. Talking pictures, for all practical purposes, were closed to them. Show business quickly became a jungle. But Eubie Blake *was* a superstar, and what was left of the entertainment industry could not ignore his vast talents.

In 1930 one ornament of the Broadway scene was a producer who had consolidated his gains with a successful formula that had been established by "Shuffle Along." Simple. Black entertainers doing what they did best. Lew Leslie could have been charitably described as "eccentric." A veteran of brighter vaudeville days, he struggled against paranoia and it eventually overcame him. But in 1930 he was stealing the Broadway musical audience that had once been the prime constituency of Messrs. Ziegfeld, Carroll, and White. His shows were called "Blackbirds," and for this new 1930 edition he had commissioned Flournoy Miller of "Shuffle Along" to do the book. Better than that, he'd had the good taste and judgment to engage Andy Razaf to write the lyrics.

Leslie nervously approached Eubie at his home knowing that the Blake touch might well be the difference between success and failure for "Blackbirds of 1930." He needn't have been nervous. Times were bad and might get bad enough so that even Eubie, normally oblivious to what was happening in the outside world, could have begun to notice.

Leslie was armed with a 3,000-dollar cash advance, high for that year, for which he got a commitment from Eubie to supply twenty-eight songs. As it turned out, a couple of these became permanent standards. Eubie found it very satisfying to work with Razaf.

"He never had to change *anything*," Eubie reports, not without awe. "His meter was always *perfect*, and he could write the words nearly as fast as I could whistle the tune. God, he was smart!"

Razaf, a native of Madagascar, was born an authentic tribal prince. His full name, Andreamenentania Paul Razafinkeriefo, was poorly adapted to theater marquees. He was one of America's greatest popular lyricists, with a credit list perhaps more distinguished than anyone else's among his contemporaries. He was a strange combination of intellectual and mystic. A master of languages, urbane and sophisticated, witty and charming, he was almost ludicrously superstitious. Andy believed in witchcraft, voodoo, astrology, numerology, and ouija boards, and nobody ate peanuts or whistled in *his* dressing room. And if you threw your hat on the bed, he'd carefully salt it and return it to you.

But with all of this, he also was acutely aware of the fundamental economic and political bases for what was called "the race question." He never ceased pointing out that there was no race problem, only a class problem that was rooted in the American economic system. His political attitudes were militant, and his spectacular personal success never altered his views. A born agitator, he attracted wide attention when young as a street-corner orator denouncing job discrimination and slumlords, two of his main targets. It was always an effort for him to keep political propaganda out of his Broadway lyrics.

With Razaf fabricating his skillful lines, Eubie's music took on a new dimension. Sophisticated songs such as "You're Lucky to Me" represented a new sound for Eubie. Sung in the show by Ethel Waters, this one was more chordally complex than other songs of its time, but became a genuine hit. The effective recorded version by Louis Armstrong was one of his best sellers of that year.

"Memories of You" was tailored for the full range of the voice of little Minto Cato, which was considerably beyond the vocal span of most popular singers. Its success was limited by its not being easy to sing. Even so it's one of the musical high spots of Eubie's career. Frequently played as an instrumental by Benny Goodman and His Orchestra during the palmy days of the swing era, it became a worldwide best seller in a version waxed by the Casa Loma Orchestra. Seventeen-year-old Sonny Dunham's sensational trumpet solo on the piece was the instrumental achievement of its year. When Dunham organized his own successful orchestra in 1947, he used it as his theme, thereby further expanding its popularity.

In the cast for "Blackbirds of 1930" were Buck (Washington) and (John) Bubbles. Flournoy Miller not only wrote the book but appeared as a comedian. Along with Ethel Waters, Eubie's vaudeville partner Broadway Jones found a spot and so did the incredibly disciplined dancers the (three) Berry Brothers. Mantan Moreland, better known later for his roles in Charlie Chan movies, was also featured.

Buck and Bubbles had a side-splitting piano-mover routine that kept them in show business for years. John Bubbles, a beautiful dancer and stimulating conversationalist, had something of a vogue on the TV talk shows of the sixties. Buck was not only a very funny comic and an accomplished dancer but also a very convincing and satisfying ragtime piano player.

Ethel Waters had by this time made a name for herself on phonograph records. In later years, says Eubie, "she got religion worse than my mother." She became, in the seventies, part of Billy Graham's road show.

"Blackbirds" was a beautiful show, and the critics loved it. It opened on September 1, 1930, in the Majestic Theater in Brooklyn. There couldn't have been a less auspicious time for its premiere. It toured for six weeks, then opened to raves on Broadway. It lasted ten weeks, then moved to Newark, New Jersey, where the unstable Leslie abandoned it and disappeared, leaving the performers and musicians to find their own ways home.

For Eubie—and for Razaf—"Blackbirds of 1930" was a success. Eubie got $250 dollars a week as conductor, big money for 1930. The great songs, especially "Memories of You" and "You're Lucky to Me," never stopped paying substantial royalties, and the team had the satisfaction of doing three more shows together later.

For Broadway, though, the big time was over.

Intermission:
Sissle and Razaf
Talk about Blake

The first time I met Noble Sissle was backstage at Nixon's Grand Theater in Philadelphia. It was 1936. Vaudeville was still hanging on and even prospering in some black theaters. Mainly the name bands like those of Cab Calloway, Duke Ellington, Chick Webb, and Fletcher Henderson were the headline attractions. There'd always be a comedian or two—typically someone like Pigmeat Markham who developed a very successful routine known as "Here Come de Judge." In that year Noble Sissle was waving a baton in front of a big band, doing the vocals and billing himself as "The Colored Rudy Vallee." I had some business with theater owner Sam Steifel and also wanted to talk with the clarinetist Buster Bailey, a friend of mine. He was performing with the Sissle band, and he introduced me to Sissle.

I had just returned from an interview in Kensington with Mr. and Mrs. Ben Harney in which Harney had claimed to be the "original creator of ragtime music," and I mentioned that to Sissle and Buster. Sissle in his mild and gentle manner said he doubted this assertion was to be taken seriously.

"My old partner Eubie Blake," he said, "who's about eight years older than I am, composed 'The Charleston Rag' in 1899, and he never claimed *he* invented ragtime. He can tell you about old men who were playing that music when he was a little boy. I'm sure that Mr. Harney, with all due respect to his musical and performing ability, couldn't be old enough to have invented ragtime."

At that time I was surprised to learn that Eubie had ever written any rags at all. As a jazz-record collector I had his early Victor "Shuffle Along" Orchestra records of "Bandana Days" and "Baltimore Buzz," but to me they were typical show-biz items. Eubie Blake meant nothing more or less than Broadway musical comedy. A genre he shared with Irving Berlin, George Gershwin, and Jerome Kern. The music of his that I knew had nothing distinguishably Negro about it, the rhythms were conventional Broadway beats in waltz or fox-trot time. Of course I was only twenty and had not yet spent a lifetime in the study of American popular music.

Furthermore, having seen and heard Sissle, I couldn't imagine his having had any kind of an association with ragtime or jazz. His music was reminiscent of Paul Whiteman, if anything, and he was so staid and prim in his personal appearance and manner that there seemed to be no way for him to have performed in any other style. And being young and brash, I said so—diplomatically, I thought.

"Young man," he told me politely, "I was and am a professional entertainer, and I've had a certain success at it for many years. Part of our art lies in being prepared to give the public what it wants. When they wanted ragtime, I sang ragtime." He turned to go tend to other business, looking back and adding as he left, "Not that I ever enjoyed it particularly."

The next time I talked with him was on New Years Eve, 1948. He was leading the orchestra at Billy Rose's Diamond Horseshoe. Again, I wasn't there especially to see Sissle, but to talk with W. C. Handy, blind, full of dignity, who was featured on the elaborate floor-show bill. By that time I already knew Eubie.

"Do you ever see Blake?" I asked Sissle. It was still early in the evening and the stars hadn't yet done the first show.

"Every so often," he said. "Sometimes I get lonesome for the old man. You know I've never had the same satisfaction in collaborating with anyone else. He's a real genius. Most people don't recognize it yet, but someday there'll be songs of his that nobody's even *heard* that everybody will know." His liquid eyes gazed past me for an instant and he said, more to himself than to me, "I wonder how it would have been if he hadn't left me high and dry in London twenty-five years ago.

"We did work together after that, but I don't think we really felt the same about it. I think he felt guilty. But now we're both older and wiser. I wonder if we ever could do anything together again—even for old times' sake."

By this time I had a clearer grasp of the scope of Eubie's work, and one way I'd gotten that was by discussing it with that other collaborator of his, Andy Razaf, some years before. We were in his room in a hotel in New York getting ready to go to a benefit at either Town Hall or Madison Square Garden. I was to do an hour of the M.C. chores, and he was booked to take a few bows. We were sharing the transportation.

I asked him about the differences in working with Eubie and Fats Waller. I made no notes, but I remember enough of what he said to put it down in his own terms.

"First, let me tell you, I love 'em both. They're wonderful people and I've enjoyed working with each of them. It's been a privilege.

"There's no way you can write for Waller without being aware all of the time that he's the one who's going to perform what you write. Writing for a specific performer is much easier, because if you know his style, you can almost hear how he's going to sing your words while you're still writing them down on the paper. You kind of get inside a singer and in your mind you're doing an imitation of him while you get the words down. That's a real advantage. Another thing, I knew Fats was a very *true* singer who didn't scoop his notes, so you'd always know everybody would understand every word he sang. Even his narrow vocal range helped. When Fats sang, the audience never missed a word.

"Now Eubie is another thing. When you're writing to his music, you never know who's going to sing it. You might know the *face* of the singer, but the style might not be as easily defined. The little lady who sang "Memories of You" in "Blackbirds" had a phenomenal range, and Eubie's melody is cleverly designed to show it off. An experienced lyricist has to watch out for certain things like, for instance, making sure that the high note is an open vowel sound. It's easier to sing a high 'you' than a high 'been.'

"When I write for Fats, I'm thinking of a stage with one piano, one great musician-entertainer who needs nothing but his talent and an audience. When I write for Eubie, I think of big sets, a chorus line, elaborate costumes. Of course Eubie's melodies lend themselves so perfectly to sophisticated lyrics, and they're sort of a challenge, too, because musically he's so far ahead of most contemporary popular composers. Some of those intervals in 'You're Lucky to Me' were really innovative at that time. Ethel [Waters] really enjoyed singing that song. She said, 'I've never sung changes like that before.' I told her, 'Neither has anyone else.' Eubie has been first with so many things.''

A Different World

Hard Times

  Alone and Going On

   Harlem

    Shooting Pool

Everybody knows about the great depression. Even people who don't remember it know about "Brother, Can You Spare a Dime?"—the theme song of the era. And if you're over fifty, you remember the world of entertainment between 1930 and 1935 mostly as cheap movie theaters and the radio, which was free. Kate Smith was successfully pushing the moon over the mountain every weekday evening. Bing Crosby was "The Cremo Minstrel"—"Spit is a horrid word, but it's worse on the end of your cigar." By far the most successful of the thirties radio shows, though, was the one performed by Charles Correll and Freeman Gosden, a pair of white midwesterners known to the nation as Amos 'n' Andy. Flournoy Miller wrote their early shows. In ads they were represented in blackface. Every American knew all about the Fresh Air Taxicab Company and such characters as the Kingfish and Sapphire. The act, clearly related to the Miller and Lyles formula, had a national audience.

Eubie and Broadway Jones appeared together once on a Newark, New Jersey station and were urged to buy shares in "The Blue Network," now NBC, at twenty-five cents a share.

"We could own New York now," Eubie groans. "I couldn't see how that business could make a livin' if nobody had to pay to listen to it."

Competing with radio were the talking-picture theaters where before 11 A.M. you could see two full-length features, a comedy, and a newsreel for a dime. Of a Tuesday night you might participate in a "bank night" with a chance to win a hundred dollars in a version of Bingo. In your neighborhood Thursday might be a "dish night," with every lady receiving a piece of crockery. Diligent and faithful attendance would eventually reward a lady with a full set. Today these same shoddy gimcracks are hot on the collectors' market. They're called "depression glass" and bring ridiculously high prices.

No matter what movie house you attended, the show would come to a sudden stop at seven o'clock and loudspeakers would bring to the audience the fifteen-minute Amos 'n' Andy show. Otherwise many or most of the customers would have forgotten their bank-night cards and cream pitchers and stayed home.

The most successful popular music of the first half of the decade was being performed by now almost forgotten commercial radio bands. Harry Reser and his Cliquot Club Eskimos, the Ipana Troubadours, the Fox Fur Trappers ("from the Land of Ice and Snow"), and Harry Horlick's A&P Gypsies dominated the music on the air.

There were late night "remote" broadcasts from major hotels and dining rooms. One might hear Harry Ford and His Orchestra direct from the Manger Hotel or Paul Tremaine's Lonely Acres Orchestra from the bandstand of Yeong's Chinese-American Restaurant.

It was going to be a while before the microphones would reach into Harlem's Cotton Club, Connie's Inn, and Small's Paradise, but if people stayed up late enough, they could become acquainted with Cab Calloway, Duke Ellington, Louis Armstrong, and Fletcher Henderson. Once a week some station was broadcasting an all-Negro program featuring the Mills Brothers and Don Redman's Orchestra. Starved for the sound of syncopation, lots of people were adjusting their living schedules to make sure they were near a radio at the critical hours.

Eubie Blake went about his business writing music that had nothing to do with the fashions of the moment. After the demise of "Blackbirds" in 1930 he wrote some pieces for a Will Morrissey production—white performers in a kind of American Folies-Bergère. He was in Morrissey's office when John Scholl, who had been one of the financial backers of "Shuffle Along," approached him for a favor.

"My son, Jack," he told Eubie, "thinks he can write lyrics. He's never written one, and I doubt that he has any talent. But I'd appreciate it if you'd take one of his lyrics and just scribble some music to go with it. I know it's an imposition, but I'm just asking as a friend."

"Loving You the Way I Do" by Jack Scholl and Eubie Blake became the big number of Morrissey's "Hot Rhythm" and the Broadway hit of the year. The film industry beckoned to young Scholl, and he became an extremely successful Hollywood songwriter.

"They sent for *him*," Eubie says. "They didn't send for *me*."

Translated, that means that Hollywood had room for white talent only. However, in justice to the industry it must be reported that many years earlier Eubie had been presented with an attractive proposition to go to Hollywood as half of a team with Henry Creamer, but couldn't go quickly enough because of other commitments.

In the face of the collapse of the show business they had known, Eubie and his former partners Flournoy Miller and Sissle quixotically attempted a revival of "Shuffle Along." Lyles died before rehearsals began in the late fall of 1932. It clearly was no time to try a musical show. People were psychologically down, but they weren't looking for escape, they were looking for answers. Even the dynamic gaiety of Sissle and Blake, with the celebrated talents of Miller and Edith Wilson thrown in, couldn't lure a depressed and disheartened public back to Broadway. It was a year in which even a high-budget Gershwin effort failed.

"Shuffle Along of 1933" was a first-class show that was too late. It held on on the Great White Way for just two weeks. "We saw it wasn't going anywhere," Eubie explains. "It wasn't the show, it was the times. When Miller suggested we cut it to a tab show and do the movie houses, it was already like we didn't have any choice. We already had costumes, scenery, and props, all that stuff. So we went on the road. We really worked. We gave it all we had. But it was no use. We got to L.A. and didn't even have enough money left to get home. By that time Sissle was already gone a couple of months. He went back to leading his band and did fairly well."

Among the unemployed created by the expiration of "Shuffle Along of 1933" was young Nat King Cole, who had just made his stage debut in this show. He was to go on to stardom that would be cut off by cigarette-induced lung cancer.

Suddenly Eubie could see there might be hard times ahead.

The new president, Franklin Delano Roosevelt, had done a lot of strange things during the first hundred days of his "New Deal." Show people had trouble understanding how this or that president could affect their business for better or worse. The more astute, however, suspected that the Broadway show as they had known it was gone for good, regardless of prosperity or depression. Eubie didn't know much about NRA, CCC, AAA, and the multitude of other government agencies being unveiled almost daily. Fortunately for him, though, a young and talented lyricist named Joshua Milton Reddie observed that one of the confusing sets of initials could be of some service. It was WPA.

President Roosevelt's Works Progress Administration had a disproportionate share of its job-creating funds allocated to provide mass employment for entertainers and other artists. The new first lady, Eleanor Roosevelt, never failed to show substantial affection for this segment of society. And so through the thirties there was a lot of federally subsidized entertainment in New York. Orson Welles and his Mercury Theater, fertilized by government sponsorship, did "The Death of Danton" and got ready to go on to bigger things. Message musicals like the government's "One Third of a Nation" and the International Ladies Garment Workers' "Pins and Needles," featuring amateur talent rounded up from the union's Local 22, dominated the scene. Proletarian dramas like Clifford Odets's "Waiting for Lefty" and "Awake and Sing" seemed to be something the public would pay to see—if the price was right. It didn't seem possible that Broadway shows would ever play to a two-dollar top.

Eubie doesn't remember how many shows he wrote with Reddie under WPA subsidy, but it was 1937 before one of them was produced. Entitled "Swing It," it was designed to exploit the musical style being popularized by Benny Goodman.

"Milton Reddie was the best lyricist I ever worked with," says Eubie. "He's from Baltimore too, you know. Now Sissle was good, but he always had trouble with the meters because he was always tryin' to fit those big words into them, and sometimes they lapped over. And of course Razaf and Henry Creamer were top men, but that Reddie—of course he's not famous like the rest of them, but he really had original ideas. Always carried a pad and a pencil with him, and if he hears somebody say something that hits him, he whips out his pad and writes down what the person said. Then later he twists it some way. You know, they're the same things that everybody always says, see, but he uses it some way to give it a different meaning. He twists it, you know, like Cole Porter. He idolized Cole Porter. Modeled himself after Cole. It's too bad he never got famous."

"I Can't Get You Out of My Mind" and "You Were Born to Be Loved" were modestly successful products of the efforts of Eubie and Reddie.

Around the turn of the decade Eubie also collaborated with Razaf on a beautiful production entitled "Tan Manhattan," which like "Shuffle Along" played Washington's Howard Theater before it was presented in New York, where it had a long run at the Ubangi Club. And even during the bleak years of the depression Eubie was able to keep more than one kind of professional activity going. He also had a ten-piece orchestra of his own touring the TOBA circuit—the Theater Owners Booking Association, known to performers as "Tough On Black Artists." These were mainly black theaters in New York, Philadelphia, Baltimore, Chicago, and Washington.

In 1938 Avis began to break down physically. Her illness was diagnosed as tuberculosis, and she had to be sent to a sanitarium. Eubie was distraught. He went to see her through all available visiting hours regardless of weather or other commitments. It was a long trip, including a ferry-boat ride. He brought her gifts, encouraged and cheered her, did what he could to keep her spirits up, but medical people didn't know enough yet to keep her alive. Of course when she died in 1939 at the age of fifty-eight, she was already approaching her normal life expectancy for that time, but Eubie never saw her as aging. For a time, Eubie was inconsolable. Here he was fifty-six years old and alone. He'd always wanted children, but they were not in his lot. Avis had always wanted them too.

"In my life I never knew what it was to be alone. At first when Avis got sick, I thought she just had a cold, but when time passed and she didn't get better, I made her go to a doctor and we found out she had TB. Now they know how to cure that, but forty years ago they really didn't know nothin' about it, see. So when it come time for me to take her to the sanitarium, I felt very bad. Doctors, they try to tell you she might get better—wait a while and see how she does. But no matter how much you hope, see, if they don't know how to fix it, it ain't gonna fix itself.

"I suppose I knew from when we found out she had the TB, I understood that it was just a matter of time. Of course, I couldn't let *her* see that. I guess she knew too, but she didn't want *me* to worry and be upset, you understand?"

No matter how well you know Eubie, you never really learn anything about his emotional patterns. His value structure is entirely personal. He's not a man who ever learned how to cry, and if he's in distress it's impossible to estimate the degree or even the nature of his pain. But now, even after almost forty years, when he talks about Avis's final days his voice and manner lose some of their customary control.

"If anybody asked me in 1935 or 1937 did I love Avis, I'd have told them, 'Sure I love my wife.' But I wouldn't be knowin' what I was talkin' about. When I *really* knew it is when I saw I was gonna lose her. God! People who got kids don't know how lucky they are. *We* never had any. I'd give *anything*—but anyway, all I could do then was to pay as much attention to her as I could. That became, for a year, the only thing I could think about. Then in 1939 she died. I didn't know what to do. I didn't have any *reason* to do anything. Who was I gonna do it for? No kids, see? Nobody."

I thought of the tragedy of that loneliness. Who *was* he going to do things for? What was really the point of the man's existence? Then suddenly I realized that he and I were talking forty years after the fact. He was right here across the table telling me all this. He was living and enjoying his life here in a different world, in another setting—it was as though it had happened to somebody else. He *had* found a reason to go on and had mustered whatever emotional resources it took. What was the reason? Where did the resources come from? Not from his contemporaries. He had never leaned emotionally on his friends and associates. And not from religion. "The only time anybody sees me in church is if it's a funeral or a benefit." I pressed him for *his* answer.

"Look," he told me, "I was fifty-six years old. I just decided right there I wasn't going to be an old man. God! If I could be fifty-six *again*, I'd feel like a kid. I had plenty goin' for me that other people don't. I had my health and a way of makin' a livin' doin' what was more important to me than anything else, and not only that, I knew *how* to live, and that's somethin' a lot of people older than me never learned."

As a star attraction on the B. F. Keith vaudeville circuit, the Sissle and Blake act had played that show-business mecca the Palace on Broadway, Keith's flagship theater. Variety is long gone from the old Palace, but for many Negro performers there has been another showplace that some feel has been of even greater importance—the venerable Apollo Theater on 125th Street in Harlem. The biggest names in black show business and many white stars have trod its boards since the late thirties. Originally Hurtig and Seamon's Burlesque Theater, it was taken over in 1939 by a remarkable entrepreneur named Frank Schiffman, who, picking up the pieces of the earlier Alhambra and Lafayette theaters and the failed Harlem Opera House, made an industry out of black show business. From time to time, Eubie served as conductor of the Apollo pit orchestra.

"Some shows are easy to cut. Anybody can do them," Schiffman told me, recalling his own practical experiences. "You don't need Toscanini for Pigmeat. But if you've got a real class act, say Pearl Primus or Bill Robinson, you need somebody like the old man"—Eubie. "You need him holding the stick. He's forgotten more about conducting than some of these new guys will ever learn."

Through the forties 125th Street was as exciting an artery as the nation had to offer. There was no visible racial conflict or antagonism in Harlem, and white people were still going uptown for class entertainment as they had been since early in the thirties when such *boîtes* as Connie's Inn, the Cotton Club, and Small's Paradise were offering shows featuring Don Redman, Louis Armstrong, Fletcher Henderson, Cab Calloway, and Duke Ellington and their orchestras, plus the most famous Negro acts.

Eubie had his chance to participate in all of this and did. He and Sissle had played the Harlem Opera House as early as 1919 and in 1925 they had been featured at the Lafayette, where young Fats Waller was in the pit playing the pipe organ. Now Schiffman was always glad to have Eubie conducting the Apollo orchestra when he was free to do so. Eubie appreciates Frank Schiffman and his role in providing a showcase for black talent.

"You know I never played too much for Negro audiences," Eubie laments. "I *love* to play for my own people. But in show business you play for anybody with a ticket and you don't ask who's out front—only how many. Now I'd go up there and conduct at the Apollo. You know it wasn't for the money, because they never paid the pit band very much. But just the feel of being part of a show with mostly my own people out there was a thrill. So I'd go up there if I could."

Harlem people were proud of their main street. They were proud of the Apollo and of Frank's Restaurant, a posh steak house that rivaled any in Manhattan. They enjoyed the knowledge that the Theresa Hotel, just around the corner on Lenox Avenue, was home to any number of the world-famous theater personalities. Billy Daniels, the Mills Brothers, Lucky Millinder, Peg Leg Bates, and Eddie Anderson ("Rochester") lived there. During the dinner hour the pages of *Variety* came alive in the dining room.

In those days Harlem was run by a powerful and respected political boss, Jimmy Pemberton, as a sort of enlightened monarchy. Pemberton died in 1949 at the age of thirty or so. His attitude toward his people, while paternalistic, was genuinely socially responsible and responsive. He owned and operated the Hollywood Cabaret, which served as his headquarters.

One day he and I were having lunch in a favorite restaurant of his, a Spanish place on the downtown side of 125th Street. I don't remember its name. It was near Frank's. Four-hundred-pound Pemberton knew how to appreciate the ambrosial food.

He asked me if I knew Eubie Blake, and I said I did.

He said, "I don't have any music in my place, and I've been thinking about getting a piano player, but I don't want some ham in there. I want the best, somebody with real class. Do you think he'd come and work for me?"

I told him I didn't think Eubie did solo club work any more, but I suggested that Jimmy ask him.

"It's not a matter of money," he assured me. "You *know* that. Whatever he'd want, we could get together on it. But to tell you the truth, I just haven't got the nerve to ask him. You know, he's a great man."

"Hell, Jimmy," I reminded him. "You've got a pretty good reputation yourself. I saw your picture hanging—the one with FDR. If you've got enough nerve to talk with *him*, you should be able to talk with Eubie on the phone. I'm sure his number is in the union book." I happened to have a Musicians Union Local 802 book in my pocket and I handed it to him.

Jimmy got up, always a laborious undertaking for him. He fished in his pin-stripe trousers, asked me if I had a nickel, and took it to the phone. I saw him try the number a couple of times and then hang up.

"It's busy," he said. "I've got the rest of the day taken up with appointments, and anyway I don't know what to say to him—how to approach him."

"How come you're scared of a musician?" I asked him. "I never knew you to be afraid of anything else. Anyway, Eubie's a friendly and mild-mannered gentleman. He can't shoot you over the phone."

Jimmy asked if I'd sound Eubie out about the job before he called. I owed Jimmy one very large favor, but I refused this one. I wasn't in a position to negotiate with Eubie, and I felt that Jimmy needed to overcome the groundless emotional block he had against making normal business overtures to Eubie.

"Hell!" Jimmy said. "You're right. I'll call him tomorrow."

Tomorrow was the day Jimmy died.

As the forties were beginning, Eubie, fifty-seven, his happy marriage of twenty-eight years having ended the year before with the death of Avis, had no responsibilities to anyone but himself and was spending his time visiting around with his old friends, writing a little music, and shooting more than a little pool. Admittedly this was an aimless activity, but Eubie was good at it, having had countless hours of leisure in which to hone the skill back at the Goldfield Hotel and in the Middle Section Club.

A great jazzman named Joe Sullivan, whose name is hallowed in the enclaves of authentic jazz fans, one observed to me, "Every hot piano player has a secret ambition to be either a pimp or a pool shark or both." Setting aside till some other time the pimping part of this, a proper census of the major keyboard wizards would tend to bear out the late Joe's contention on the pool-shark part. Certainly Jelly Roll Morton and Paul Wyer (the Pensacola Kid) not only held but realized these pool-shark aspirations. I had occasion myself to watch the late Fletcher Henderson run off thirty-five or so balls without coming up for air. James P. Johnson and Fats Waller spent lots of time with cue sticks and were more than reasonably proficient in their use. Claude Hopkins still is.

Very likely, though, it was Luckey Roberts who was the real king of the round ivories among piano players. He sometimes lived dangerously, hustling hard and notorious underworld characters. He'd make lots of money by losing in games in which the bets were low and then always managing to squeak out close victories when the big money was at stake.

"I used to beg him to cut that out" Eubie reports fervently. "I told him he was gonna get himself killed foolin' around like that. Some of the places he'd go in and pull that! But he always got away with it. Of course Luckey was strong and tough himself. Short as he was, he could grab a man in a bear hug and break every bone in his body. God, he was strong!"

I mentioned to Eubie that Luckey had once said to me that he could beat any musician alive playing pool except Eubie Blake.

"That's true," Eubie concurred with obvious satisfaction. "He never *could* beat me." Then he looked thoughtful for an instant and reminded himself, "Of course I never did play him for money."

Eubie points out that in the days when lots of piano players lived in the same neighborhood, as they frequently did in Harlem or around the market in Baltimore, they were the only people who weren't working in the daytime.

"A musician doesn't have anything to do all day, so he's got to have a place to hang around. Down at a pool room you meet everybody and talk about the latest fights and ball games and—well, you can't just hang around all the time. Every now and then you got to shoot a game.

"Well, you know how it is. You start doin' that every afternoon and pretty soon you begin to enjoy the competition, and then you get interested in who you can beat and who you can't beat, and before you know it that gets important and then you start in to *practice* it. Musicians know about practice. Then one day they find out they can beat a whole lot of people and then they're sharks! But it's very relaxin'. When I could stand up easier, I used to like to do all that."

Another Time Around

USO Days—and Marion
"Retirement" and Back to School
The Year of the Turkey
Elder Statesman of Ragtime
Onward and Upward

When music is your life, you don't really relate to events like Pearl Harbor. You express shock like everyone else, but what you don't do is relate it to yourself—to your own life and future. War is somebody else's business, you tell yourself. Maybe, *sotto voce*, only white men's business. And anyway, if you were too old to be drafted into World War I, you're certainly past the age of involvement in the sequel.

Nevertheless, the direction of Eubie's life was drastically altered by World War II.

Invited to lead an entertainment unit into army camps and hospitals under the auspices of the USO, he found some of his *joie de vivre* returning. With the aid of Grace Bouret and Bob Lee, two expert lyricists, he turned out lots of fresh material and was received at military installations throughout the country with great enthusiasm. He did the full tour this time, from Savannah to Seattle. The physical strain of all those one-night stands can be wearing on a sixty-year-old, but Eubie never seemed to notice. He felt

118

needed, he was a star again—and the show had plenty of girls. Eubie knew very well that sixty wasn't too old for *that!*

Working in military hospitals made him feel that his contributions were important. "Those kids are the greatest audience in the *world*. They really *appreciate* a show. That was a thrill. It made me feel so good I didn't even care if I got paid—but I took the money."

And toward the end of the war something happened to make life even more worth living. It had to be a lady.

Marion Gant Tyler, a native of the Eastern seaboard, was a Los Angeles business executive. She had been widowed for six years since the death of Willie Tyler, a distinguished musician who had worked with James Reese Europe and in orchestras directed by Will Vodery. Marion herself had performed in a few Negro musicals. It would have been difficult for her to qualify for these shows if she'd had to look Negro to get the parts. In short, Marion was seen as Negro because she said she was.

She didn't come from the kind of impoverished background Eubie did. Her grandfather, Hiram S. Thomas, a celebrated chef of the nineteenth century, had been, for a time, head waiter at the Grand Union Hotel in Saratoga Springs, the well-known race-track resort in New York State. He was the originator of record of the Saratoga chip—the old name for the potato chip. Later, he owned the posh hostelry Thomas' Rumson Inn, in Rumson, New Jersey. It was here that Marion's early childhood observations in a completely adult world endowed her with the keen sense of values and business acumen that has served her so well.

Marion enjoyed show-business life, both as a wife and as a performer. Later she found herself secretary to W. C. Handy, "father of the blues."

Eubie and Marion, having been widowed at about the same time and having found that this was long enough, married on December 27, 1945. At the time Eubie was on tour with the USO, and Marion traveled with him for some time. But at last the couple returned to New York and moved into Marion's four-story brownstone house in Brooklyn, which was being occupied by Marion's mother. As Eubie explains, "I got the coop with the chicken."

Turning her attention to the shambles of Eubie's fiscal affairs, she discovered that her husband, genius though he was, was completely unable to take care of himself—or even to think about it. And so, when Marion married Eubie she undertook a job for which a lifetime of training had equipped her. She understood the world of show business from the point of view of an administrator as well as a performer. Being married to a musical virtuoso was nothing new. She was used to the temperament, understood the specialized characteristics of the creative process. She knew how to get along with people, how to be a genuinely gracious hostess. And she was beautiful besides.

Eubie likes to be looked after. He doesn't know any other way of life. He wants someone else to make all nonmusical decisions. He wants complete freedom to play and compose and to enjoy his relationships with his friends and his audiences. Had it not been for this extraordinary woman there could have been no large-scale second career for Eubie Blake. He was nearly sixty-three when they were married—old enough, as society estimates careers, to call it quits.

Babies were born in 1945 who are stars today. That's the year Eubie got his second wind. The renown he won in "Shuffle Along" in 1921 is as nothing compared with his current fame. Good management, the expansion of communications media, and the growth of his own talent have all contributed to this.

One of Marion's first acts as Mrs. Blake was to note that Eubie's ASCAP rating had never been upgraded, mainly because her diffident groom had never bothered to apply to have it raised. ASCAP, shocked to learn of this situation, set it to rights at once, and his income instantly trebled. Then she set about screening the professional propositions that constantly were being made to her retired husband. She began to supervise the uses of his time, eventually bringing about a situation in which Eubie has nothing to do but perform if and when he pleases. He makes no appointments, reads no contracts, chooses no clothes, orders no meals, answers no phones, makes no deposits, cashes no checks.

But when artistic matters need to be resolved, Marion stays out of it. She has dedicated her life to making it possible for Eubie to spend whatever time he wants in bringing his gifts to the world. When he puts a program together for a personal appearance, he will consult with her, and at his direction she will make a list on a three-by-five card of what he's going to play. He usually stays with this list for the first three numbers. After that he goes out on his own.

There were going to be drastic changes in musical entertainment after World War II, and the promised postwar prosperity would keep entertainers working at their trade for a while—but maybe mostly white ones.

In 1946 Irving Berlin had "Annie Get Your Gun" on Broadway starring Ethel Merman. There also was "Call Me Mister," a long-awaited sequel to "This Is the Army." Buddy Ebsen was to be seen in a revival of "Showboat." Ray Bolger and Gordon MacRae were moderately successful in "Three to Make Ready." Black performers were scarce on the main stem. The protean Canada Lee, starring opposite Elisabeth Bergner in "The Duchess of Malfi," had to do his part in whiteface.

Brilliant Ellabelle Davis sang "Aida" in 1946, but she did it in Mexico City, where her duskiness was no obstacle to acceptance. Black actors of the stature of Fred O'Neill and Ossie Davis were bemused with "problem plays" that had to be heavily subsidized to last even a week.

There were some Negroes making it on the night-club circuit. Sammy Davis, Jr., Harry Belafonte, Eartha Kitt, and Lena Horne were prime Las Vegas attractions. But black musical theater as Eubie had known it had become history, though a few years earlier the black musicals "Cabin in the Sky," of 1940, and "Carmen Jones," a 1943 parody of the Bizet opera, had been on the boards. "Cabin" was heavy with talent. Rex Ingram, Todd Duncan, Dooley Wilson, Kathryn Dunham, and Ethel Waters were all available for this production, work on Broadway being so scarce for blacks. "Cabin's" real success was scored on the Hollywood screen, with only Miss Waters surviving from the original cast; in the film she was supported by Louis Armstrong, Eddie "Rochester" Anderson, and Lena Horne.

All these people, Eubie observed, were relative youngsters, and it was right and proper that show business should belong to them. He had had a full satisfying life and a prosperous career. He was happily married and living with his wonderful spouse in a comfortable home in Brooklyn, his ASCAP income was now pretty good, and his expenses were lower than most peoples'. Neither he nor Marion had any dependents. It was a magnificent opportunity to grow old gracefully and reap the benefits of retirement.

"So I knew I was sixty-three years old—*now* I know that ain't *nothin'*, but thirty-two years ago—you know how it is, the world gets you thinkin' that's old enough to quit.

"Still, it didn't take long for me to get enough of sittin' in my easy chair readin' my newspapers. Then I got to rememberin' not only the great things that happened to me in my life, but I got to thinkin' of all the things I *missed*, too. I says to myself, 'Man, you not *doin'* nothin', this is a great chance to fill in some of those things, and who knows what might come of it.' So right then and there I decided. Made me feel like a kid again! I just went to school."

So here we find him at sixty-three enrolled in New York University studying the Joseph Schillinger system of composition under one of Schillinger's own pupils, Professor Rudolph Schramm.

"He really got upset one time when he asked the class for opinions about the greatest composers in history. The professor admired the modern symphony composers, and I don't. He really pressed me for my opinion of Stravinsky's music, and I said I thought it was lousy. It bothered him because I was so much older than the rest of the people in the class and because I was a well-known composer. He thought I might prejudice them against modern music. I hope I did. I told him, 'You asked for my opinion and that's my opinion.'"

Eubie contends that the NYU experience was a great help, if only for its time-saving advantages in composition, and he liked Professor Schramm. In June 1950, at the age of sixty-seven, he graduated from the university with his degree in music. In 1955 his "Dictys on Seventh Avenue" was published. It had been his thesis equivalent for Dr. Schramm's course, an application of the Schillinger system to Eubie's own compositional style.

During the period of his studies, Eubie's association with Sissle was reactivated in a relationship more social now than professional.

Much of the impetus for the reunion came about as a result of the sudden boom in the popularity of "I'm Just Wild about Harry" in 1948. The Truman for President campaign committee used it for a campaign song. The impact of this on the ASCAP ratings of Sissle and Blake was substantial.

That year they wrote "Swingtime at the Savoy." In 1950 they came on with "Alone with Love" and then admitted to each other that individually they'd been thinking about yet another revival of "Shuffle Along." They put together a dozen or so songs to "put in the safe" against such a revival.

"Nothin' much was happenin' on Broadway for the Joneses," Eubie recalls. "Sammy Davis had a good hit ["Mr. Wonderful"], but Ellington tried for a show of his own that didn't do good at all" ["Pousse Cafe"]. Our people got *some* parts in legit plays. Ethel [Waters] *always* worked.

"For me and Sissle, 1952 was the year of the turkey. You know how the Chinese people got the Year of the Dog and the Year of the Snake? Well, we had the Year of the Turkey"—the disastrous, ill-received revival of "Shuffle Along." "I could tell from that it wasn't only the *talent* that changed. It was the business itself. The kind of people that came into it."

Eubie turned back to the situation blacks faced in the entertainment world in those years. "And TV! In those times if you looked at the TV, you'd think there was no Negroes in the whole world. Well, Amos 'n' Andy. They *had* to go for Negroes for that show *on* TV. On radio those parts were played by white actors. Sometimes a Jones could get a part as a maid or a porter. In fact one lady got her own *series* playin' a maid"—Louise Beavers in "Beulah." "But they shoulda been more advanced by that time. But they weren't. People don't realize, but Martin Luther King done all that. He *started* everything for Negroes."

Eubie's appraisal of the objective situation in the industry was all too true. It was many years later that militants and activists altered that state of affairs. But I wondered if that was the whole story behind "the turkey," and I imposed on Eubie to tell me how he really felt about that flop—what it had done to him emotionally. I knew he didn't like to talk about it but also that he felt a certain responsibility to posterity to address such matters. Because he *hadn't* discussed it very much, I had the feeling that much of what he said about it was formulated on the spot. Before, he had merely put it out of his mind as a generally distasteful subject.

"I gotta keep remindin' you of my age," Eubie insisted. "You know when you ask me how I felt about the turkey—sure I was disappointed. I knew it wasn't my fault or Sissle's fault that it was no good. My God, we had some of the most talented people in the *world*. But I wasn't broken up like some kid seeing his first show go down the drain. Now I was almost seventy years old.

"Most men seventy years old—I felt it myself—they think there's not much future left. But I got to tell you that the year of the turkey there was babies born in the United States, white ones and Negro ones, they grew up and went to school, got in show business. They became stars, did shows, made records, and got married and had kids of their own—and I'm still here with Marion keepin' my bookin's straight and Carl [Seltzer] takin' care of the record business, and I'm gettin' ready to go to Europe again to do more concerts. But after seventy I never *planned* on any of that stuff. I'm long past the time when a flop can be a disaster, and I already was *then*.

"Of course, while it's happenin' it's no fun at all. You look at what they done to your show and you know they don't know what the—what they're doin'. And if you been in show business all your life, it hurts more than anything to see an audience that's not gettin' what it paid to see."

What the audience paid to see was, according to some who were there, a "damn good show." *But*, it wasn't "Shuffle Along."

The failure of the show was certainly not due to lack of a talented cast. Sissle and Blake had rounded up some big names. Thelma Carpenter, who had established her credentials as a singer on some excellent Majestic records, was in the cast, as was Hamtree Harrington, by now an old name in show business, famed for his Bert Williams impressions. Talented younger people like Avon Long and Mable Lee also involved themselves.

The show flopped because drastic, last-minute changes destroyed the original concept. The producer, Irving Gaumont, had asked Flournoy Miller to modernize the script, to bring it up to date. Sissle and Blake meanwhile auditioned for prospective backers, eventually raising 250 thousand dollars. When Miller presented his updated script, Gaumont was not satisfied. (Neither was Pearl Bailey, who, finding the material unacceptable, dropped out of the cast.) By this time, rehearsals had already been called and out-of-town opening dates were set. A ghostwriter was hastily called in to doctor the book. But time was running out. Gaumont, in a state of panic, accepted and produced an entirely new book, a story that had nothing to do with "Shuffle Along" except for a few of the original songs.

Audiences, who remembered the 1921 hit, were disappointed. The critics made no charitable sounds at all. After four performances, the show closed.

Eubie, though not totally broken up, was still depressed by the high-budget catastrophe that had just occurred before his very eyes. He had been perfectly confident that the show could have made it—if they'd just left him and Sissle alone with it for a couple of months. The turkey made him feel like retiring again. Sometimes, he says, "a man gets to feelin' that enough is enough."

Among nonmusicians there was at mid-century still no concept of the classic rag, but almost everyone thought he knew what ragtime was. The word conjured up images of derbies and checked vests, silk shirts with arm garters, and a piano, an upright, with thumb tacks in the hammers to produce a ricky-tick sound. Those were days when almost nobody listening to Eubie Blake playing "Charleston Rag" could have identified it as a rag.

But all this was starting to change. A main factor in this was the publication in 1950 of the book *They All Played Ragtime* by Rudi Blesh and Harriet Janis. It had a profound effect as a rallying point for people who identified with the idiom. The book rediscovered Scott Joplin and directed substantial attention to artists like Joseph Lamb, Arthur Marshall, Charlie Thompson, Artie Matthews, and Joe Jordan while they were still alive, and it took due note of the life and work of Eubie Blake.

Other things began to happen. An exceptional musician and superb showman, Max Morath, found his way to Public Broadcasting television with a series on the ragtime years that helped organize a consciousness and appreciation of the music. Recordings by Turk Murphy and Wally Rose harked back to the real sound. The amazing Knocky Parker did some beautifully recorded piano solos for Audiophile on an LP called "Old Rags." It began to be apparent that there was a revival of interest in this great music.

Eubie appeared in a beautifully mounted TV production in which he and three other piano players—Hoagy Carmichael, Dick Wellstood, and Ralph Sutton—presented the ragtime years. Those who knew something about the idiom began to realize that there were more excellent ragtime players than they had suspected. The Parisian Claude Bolling, already established in the European jazz world, suddenly demonstrated superb ragtime skills. Youngsters like Trebor Tichenor and Mike Montgomery were not only playing the music but also amassing huge collections of it, written and recorded, which a few years later were to contribute heavily to the growth and understanding of genuine ragtime.

Nearing the ends of their careers, some of Eubie's old sidekicks belatedly had their chance to take bows to large and enthusiastic audiences. Willie the Lion, James P. Johnson, and Don Lambert all discovered at the ends of their lives that all that music they'd put out had not been for naught as far as wide recognition was concerned.

Eubie himself was rarely seen in live performance except at benefits, but he did not go unrecorded in this period. Blesh made a session in his Greenwich Village apartment on January 7, 1951, in which Eubie recorded "Maryland, My Maryland" and "Maple Leaf Rag." They also made a tape of other tunes, mainly original rags of Eubie's. This tape was assimilated by George H. Buck, Jr., when he bought Circle Records to add to his Jazzology Record catalog. They remain unissued as of this writing. Although the attempted revival of "Shuffle Along" failed, it did produce a good recording session for RCA Victor. "Love Will Find a Way," "I'm Just Wild about Harry," "Bandana Days," and "Gypsy Blues" came out on Victor's "Showtime" series with vocals by the principals in the 1952 show, orchestra led by Eubie. In 1958 and 1959, Twentieth Century–Fox Records felicitously combined the skills of Buster Bailey with Eubie's for two great LPs. The first, with vocals by Sissle, was entitled "The Wizard of the Ragtime Piano." The second, without Sissle, was called "The Marches I Played on the Old Ragtime Piano."

Eubie remembers very little specifically about what live performing he did do during the fifties. It's doubtful that many of those
who heard him have been so forgetful. In 1955 I was having lunch
in New Orleans with my old friend the late Johnny Wiggs, the real
king of New Orleans jazz cornets. He had just returned from a
summer musical get-together at Music Inn at Tanglewood, in
Lenox, Massachusetts, and there was only one thing he wanted to
talk about: a piano player he'd heard there. "You think you've
heard piano players? There's only *one* piano player. Greatest thing
I ever heard!"

Wiggs couldn't recall his name. An old guy, yes, and a Negro.
That's as far as we got. Yes, he played in a session with him—like
floating on a cloud. Further grilling of Wiggs was fruitless. Dr. Edmond Souchon, who'd been there with Wiggs, told me later it was
Eubie Blake.

But there were getting to be fewer and fewer such occasions, and
in general Eubie began in the fifties to act like a man who was in
fact retired. When you're seventy years old, as he was in 1953, it's
not abnormal to think your career is over. If you're a realistic sep-
tuagenarian, you don't make a lot of career plans, and if you don't
retire yourself, society tends to do it for you by asking less and less
of you. Eubie didn't *feel* old, but being seventy was like this for
him, and he wasn't working much.

But he had the chance to renew old friendships and associations.
Now there was time. He had occasion sometimes to hear other
piano players perform, and he enjoyed this—Willie the Lion,
James P., Don Lambert, all his juniors, and Luckey Roberts too,
who he always says was like a son to him. Among them all, Eubie
was dazzled by the performance of a young man named Don
Ewell. "He's white," he says, "but he doesn't *play* white."

So, Eubie was satisfied with his role as the elder statesman of
ragtime. Fewer and fewer of the younger folks remembered him,
but that, he was ready to acknowledge, was the way of the world.
Not that he couldn't have gone on delighting in the give and take
with audiences, but that sort of thing just seemed to be slipping
into the past.

And then the 1960s came on and soon Eubie's eighties came on,
and when a man gets to be eighty years old people don't expect too
much from him anymore. Eubie had always turned out for almost

every benefit he was invited to, and he still did. He and Marion lived mainly on his now substantial participation in ASCAP funds. They took to spending winters in California and were frequent guests of friends in various parts of the country. They continued to spend some of their time in New York. All travel by the Blakes was by train or ship. Eubie was frankly fearful of air transportation.

It soon became apparent that all the moving about wasn't going to wear Eubie down. Having lived so much of his life on the road, he'd learned to thrive on it.

The role of elder statesman of ragtime now began to make demands. There were frequent newspaper interviews and occasional radio appearances. Eubie made an extended biographical tape for Rutgers University. By now he was in the process of being "rediscovered" by the academic world. He found out he was a Black Study.

And there were honors and recognition. In 1965 ASCAP honored Eubie and his old partner Noble Sissle in a major event at Town Hall in New York. In the same year the pair were honored as guests of the *Chicago Tribune* at the thirty-sixth annual Chicagoland Music Festival. A bust of Eubie by sculptress Estelle V. Wright was unveiled in the Museum of the City of New York in May 1967. Distinguished notables present included Judge Jonah Goldstein, president of the Grand Street Boys; Fred O'Neill, president of Actors Equity; George A. Hoffman, treasurer of ASCAP; Rudi Blesh; and Honi Coles, president of the Negro Actors Guild.

Eubie continued to see Sissle frequently, and they'd write a few more songs just to keep their hands in. Mainly they were showing each other they could still do it, after the manner of true professionals in all pursuits.

All this was as nothing compared with what was in store for Eubie. Musical forces bubbling under the surface of American culture were about to erupt.

In St. Louis, Trebor Jay Tichenor, a ragtime piano player of top-grade stature, had been carefully collecting ragtime memorabilia, piano rolls, records, cylinders, catalogs, and sheet music. Included in his vast knowledge of the subject was the fact that many of the idiom's pioneers still lived. There were also many younger people playing great ragtime. Tichenor had them all located and classified. Most excitingly, he and some associates organized the first St. Louis Ragfest in 1966.

The Ragfest brought together artists like Max Morath, Knocky Parker, Mike Montgomery, Charlie Rasch, and Dr. Edmond Souchon and some *very*-old-timers like Homer Denny and Curtis Hitch (of Hitch's Happy Harmonists on early-twenties Gennett records). The festival was held on the ancient showboat *Goldenrod*, docked in the mighty Mississippi sans engine. It was being used for the presentation of old-time melodramas. The festival also happened in the Levee House, a club on the river, and around every hotel piano in St. Louis. Hordes of ragtimers showed up from across the nation. It was a delightful, warm experience (literally, too: the thermometer hit 100 degrees!) for the hundreds of participants and it became a foregone conclusion that it would be repeated the following year.

By 1967 the Ragfest felt like a big-time operation and Tichenor decided to go after the biggest-time ragtimer of them all. The principals didn't expect much in the way of performance from an eighty-four-year-old but considered that his presence alone would be a major asset. It would bring prestige to the festival and a thrill for the surprisingly large hard core of ragtime fanciers.

So along came Marion and Eubie to St. Louis in that hot June of 1967.

St. Louis they found to be a beautiful and exciting metropolis offering all modern conveniences—but not all through the night. The Blakes arrived very late. Bob Greene and I were in the lobby of the Belair Hotel when they arrived. Bob Greene, the living shade of Jelly Roll Morton, does concert tours with his new Red Hot Peppers, recreating the music of the immortal Ferdinand. Eubie hadn't eaten in a long time, and the only place for a sandwich at 1:00 A.M. was the lunchroom of the Greyhound bus terminal. That was a taxi ride away. I hadn't seen Eubie in a couple of years. He looked strong and alert, but I was beyond being amazed to see him looking well at any age. He wanted to wash up before going out. He slapped his palm on the reservation desk of the hotel and said, "Twenty minutes! I'll meet you right here at the box office."

For most of the remainder of the night, Bob, Eubie, and I sat eating poor cheese sandwiches on store bread, the only item left on the all-night menu, and talking about the state of the underground art of ragtime. I pointed out that on the next day Eubie, at eighty-four, would be doing the very first concert of his life. He didn't grasp the point easily. I explained that he was about to perform in a situation in which people bought tickets to come and sit in theater seats in an auditorium for the sole purpose of seeing and hearing his performance. No drinks, no floor show, just Eubie. His reply was sleepy-eyed and laconic: "Just like Horowitz, huh?" It didn't seem to Bob or me that he was impressed.

I asked him, "Have you ever had stage fright? Do you know how it feels to walk out on the stage and want to run off again when you see the audience?"

Eubie put on his amazed look. "That's a funny thing. So *many* show people I know get that stage fright. I mean *good* people. Sophie Tucker. They start to sweat like hell even before the leader strikes up their introduction. I never could understand that." He gave the matter a second thought. "You know, I don't think that *ever* happens to the Joneses. White people got so much to lose, it seems that *they* can get scared, but a Jones ain't got nothin' to lose. Nothin' can scare him."

Tichenor and the other people who had organized the festival had no idea what to expect from Eubie's appearance the next day. There was no way to predict what his performance would be like or how the audience would respond.

There was no piano on the stage of the exquisite theater of the *Goldenrod*. The instrument was in its usual place in the orchestra pit. When Eubie was introduced, he went to the piano, sat down, made as if to play, then suddenly interrupted himself and turned to face the audience. Then he got up and spoke.

"Ladies and gentleman! I've been playing the piano for seventy years." Applause. Only natural to think he's making a bid for rapport on the basis of his advanced years. Wrong! "But this is a first." I expect him to say it's his first real concert, as I'd reminded him the night before. Wrong! "This is the *first* time—the first time I ever played with my back to the audience."

Ovation.

He turns and sits on the stool, spins around and faces the crowd again. "With your permission," he says, "after each number I'll turn around and we'll talk awhile."

Standing and cheering.

He hasn't touched the piano yet, and the crowd is wild with delight. Blesh, sitting next to me, says, *"That's* show biz."

Then Eubie plays.

I never made notes of what he played. I remember a deliriously joyful audience couldn't contain itself through "The Stars and Stripes Forever." The program, as Eubie's usually does, ran way overtime. At the end the audience response was more excited than any I had ever seen.

Eubie, after a concert, is never exhausted. He's never rumpled. I don't think there's a change in his pulse rate. He doesn't perspire. His breathing is steady and composed. There's no excitement in his voice. Backstage were most of the key figures in the ragtime revival. Bill Russell, Rudi Blesh, Knocky Parker, Edmond Souchon, Terry Waldo, Mike Montgomery—they all paid their respects. Eubie had stopped being a quaint relic of a romantic past.

One young woman, a good pianist, said, "I never expected anything like *that.* All I wanted was to hear this man in person, just to get an idea of what he might have sounded like fifty years ago. I can't even imagine *anybody* right now who could give that quality performance." She spoke for the crowd.

Any more talk of retirement was frivolous and unrealistic. Eighty-four was just a number, not an age. Here, clearly, was the brightest star of a reborn art.

How did Eubie feel about it?

"I'm jus' doin' what I *always* do. *This* year, everybody's watchin'."

In 1969 record producer John Hammond waved his magic wand and made Eubie's life and work available on Columbia records. The result was a showcase set, a double LP album. The front and back covers show Eubie in "Shuffle Along" days and, identically posed, at eighty-six. The set is a highlight reprise of his musical career with a guest appearance by Noble Sissle. It is beautifully recorded, and Hammond's superior ear caught every musical mishap to be rerecorded. A complete artistic and commercial success.

Suddenly Eubie was a celebrity all over again. His face began to appear on the covers of musical publications. His fans could follow his action in the *Mississippi Rag*, the *Rag Times* of California's Maple Leaf Club, and the *Ragtimer*, published in Canada. He turned up in *Time* and in *Newsweek*. Eventually Marion, who among her other self-imposed duties keeps the archives and the scrapbooks, could no longer keep track of Eubie in print. Sacks of fan mail had to be dealt with. He loved it.

Ragtime was suddenly "in." The Scott Joplin boom added to Eubie's celebrity because Eubie was the only living contemporary from the early ragtime days. There was increasing demand for his performances. The world went ragtime mad.

Joshua Rivkin made number one on the best-seller list with his Joplin LP. Orchestral ragtime began to flourish. Gunther Schuller unveiled his New England Conservatory Ragtime Ensemble on records. The New Leviathan Oriental Fox-Trot Orchestra played twenty-two–piece arrangements of Blake items like "Fizz Water."

Eubie's life went into a still higher gear in 1972. With his close friend Carl Seltzer he formed a partnership to start Eubie Blake Music, a record company, which has been successful and has an expanding catalog. Eubie himself not only performs but acts as artists and repertoire ("A&R") executive.

Early in 1972 Marion and Eubie went to Atlanta for the premiere of Joplin's opera "Treemonisha." Eubie was the star of the weekend. A "tribute" luncheon at a Holiday Inn found Max Morath, Knocky Parker, and Terry Waldo in turn playing "Charleston Rag." Also present were T. J. Anderson, who wrote the first and best score for the opera, Dr. Eileen Southern of Yale University, dance director Kathryn Dunham, and the nation's most effective researcher in black music of the eighteenth and nineteenth centuries, Arthur La Brew. With all of these people, Eubie participated in a panel discussion that also included Rudi Blesh, Bill Russell, and choral and orchestral conductor Robert Shaw.

During the rest of the year, Eubie made more than forty public appearances. On July 4 he starred at the Newport–New York Jazz Festival. On November 4 and 5 he played the Berlin Jazz Festival in Germany and made it back to New York for a December 3 concert at Alice Tully Hall. A Philharmonic appearance on the 27th closed out the year for him.

The pace quickened further as 1973 began. He did his first

Tonight show with Johnny Carson on January 27 and during the month was on Black Omnibus and the Ralph Story show. On the way back home he stopped in Chicago to join pianist Bill Bolcom in concert at the Goodman Theater and appeared on Bookbeat, where he promoted the beautiful pictorial history *Reminiscing with Sissle and Blake* by Bolcom and Bob Kimball. Marion and Eubie had to hurry back to New York to celebrate his ninetieth birthday on February 7.

The big day began with birthday greetings from the president of the United States. ASCAP honored Eubie with a luncheon at the Hampshire House. There were get-togethers with old friends. The celebration continued into the next day on the John Bartholomew Tucker TV show.

With all this going on, Eubie couldn't make it to Baltimore for his ninetieth birthday, so it was observed there a week later when he could attend. February 14 in that city was officially declared "Salute Eubie Blake Day," with special events and concerts at Peabody Institute and Morgan State University honoring Eubie. The highlight of the day, sponsored by the Commission of the Governor of Maryland on the Study of Negro History and Culture, was a luncheon with Mayor William Donald Schaefer.

On February 16 Eubie made an appearance at New York's La Guardia College, and on the 28th he played a solo concert at Town Hall.

As I run down my lengthening list of events in 1973, Eubie grins and says, "How'm I doin', kid?"

The list goes on. Eubie turned up on the Mike Douglas show in Philadelphia on March 8, did his act at NYU on the 15th, and then hurried out to L.A. for the Billy Rose show on the 26th. Encore with Johnny Carson two nights later. April Fool's Day he spent doing the Leonard Feather show. Next day there was a concert at the Wilshire-Ebell Theater.

Back in New York, he was interviewed by *Ebony* and *Women's Wear Daily* on April 18 and 19, and on the 24th he appeared once more on TV with John Bartholomew Tucker.

He accepted honors from the Brooklyn Business and Professional Women's Club on May 6. The Tonight show came to New York on the 11th, and Eubie was on it again. On the 16th he composed some impromptu music for a film called "Harlem Renaissance."

Three days later Eubie made a big change in the way he gets himself around—a change appropriate to the accelerating tempo of his life in general. After ninety years on the ground, he at last took to the air.

When Eubie was twenty years old, he was informed by the *Baltimore Sun* that Dr. Sam Langley, a director of the Smithsonian Institution not far away in Washington, had plunged his flying machine directly off a barge into the waters of the Potomac. The press made much of this debacle, complaining that the government had squandered 50,000 dollars on a ridiculous experiment and then explaining in careful and authoritative scientific terms why man could never possibly be airborne. The incident happened on December 8, 1903. Nine days later, at Kitty Hawk, North Carolina, the Wright brothers got *their* version of an airplane off the ground and safely back again, and in the following decades humanity took to the air. But Eubie, remembering the story of Langley, was afraid to go along, and he resolved never to find himself aloft. He stood by this resolution for seven decades. Then, on May 19, 1973, at the age of ninety, he overcame his fear and made his initial airplane flight—to Buffalo, New York, to cut some piano rolls, of which more later.

He's been on wings ever since.

On May 22 Eubie performed for the Yesteryear Museum in New Brunswick, New Jersey; the next day he was honored by the Senior Musicians of Local 802 in New York; and on May 27 he appeared with Arthur Fiedler and the Boston Pops.

That day—May 27, a little over ninety years after James Hubert Blake first saw the light in Baltimore, in another world, another century—was a red-letter day in Eubie's life. This was no revival of the "Shuffle Along" Orchestra, even though Eubie would have been the first to insist that that band did, in fact, play high-class music. But this was even higher class. This was about as high class as you could get.

Up there on the podium was Fiedler, the chubby white-haired maestro known and loved around the world, about to tap for the orchestra's attention with his baton. One hundred and five musicians were poised and ready. Count em, a hundred and *five!* Today, as the papers had said, the Boston Pops concert was "to honor Eubie Blake." They were going to play his music. And here he was at the piano—Eubie Blake, the little colored kid who had started his piano playing career in the hookshops of East Street. Could he really be sitting there? In a minute they were going to shine the spotlight on him and he'd be playing. Well, *he'd* played his songs often enough before, but now a great orchestra—*a hundred and five* musicians, all at the same time—would be playing his music: violins, brass, cellos, woodwinds, percussion! Even Emily would have found it hard to disapprove *this* performance—in spite of the ragtime.

Now they were playing "Memories of You" and he was getting ready to play his solo and he couldn't even see his fingers because of the tears in his eyes. Lucky it wasn't something he didn't know too well. He could do this one with no trouble.

Right on cue, there was the spotlight, and now he was into it. Memories, memories! Here was the chorus now. Relax, kid, the crowd is eating it up! Then pretty soon came the part where he did the ragtime thing. He hit it. He heard, he felt, the crowd come to life. They loved it! And underneath there was that great orchestra ready to pick him up at the end and lift his piano and his music into the sky!

He finished the chorus for the spellbound audience, and Fiedler, who understands audiences as well as anyone alive, moved with all possible drama to the kind of crescendo they expect from the Boston Pops. Eubie sat with tears of joy rolling down his cheeks. His life had had many crescendos, some of them exciting or satisfying enough to be called magnificent. But this one, he felt as it drew to its inevitable close, was the ultimate accolade.

He bowed and smiled through the thunderous applause, seeing nothing through the bright lights and the tears. He did his familiar overhead handclasp. He was aware of people around him in motion. There were the inevitable autographs, the crowds waiting to say a word to him, the familiar low surge that would get him outdoors and into his waiting vehicle. It always takes so long for Eubie to get through his army of admirers. At last he settled himself into the front seat. Then he turned to Marion and asked, "Where do we go from here?"

Among other places, they went to Brooklyn College to attend

the commencement ceremonies. On June 5, 1973, a warm summer's day, the college president handed Eubie a sheepskin that made him a Doctor of Humane Letters. On the 10th Eubie attended another ceremony, at which the theater in New York's Tompkins Park was named the Eubie Blake Theater. And on the 24th—Emily would have been *so* proud!—he was honored by the Abyssinian Baptist Church. Then, on the 28th, three solos for the annual Princeton Harpsichord Festival.

On the Fourth of July Eubie was featured at a Louis Armstrong Memorial at Singer Bowl in New York. "He was a great artist and a great man," Eubie said, "I'm glad we had a chance to help with the statue of Louis for Armstrong Park" in New Orleans. Eubie returned to the Newport–New York Jazz Festival and played at Carnegie Hall on July 7. Then, off to Europe, airborne now. July 19 to August 5: Baden, Copenhagen, the Mölde (Norway) Jazz Festival. Packed auditoriums and standing ovations!

"So I'm ninety years old," Eubie comments. "There's no law says I got to get tired. It's a tough schedule, but other people take care of it. All *I* do is play. If I was *home*, I'd be doin' that."

Back to New York on August 6 for the Jack Paar show. A little time at home, then a big concert at Bryant Park on the 27th.

"We just saw you in Germany," a fan says to Eubie as he comes off stage.

"Did I make you happy?" he wants to know.

"You certainly did, Mr. Blake. You made us all happy!"

"Then," he assures her, "then I'm happy."

A standard piece of dialogue. No time for too much small talk these days—got to help Jerry Lewis's muscular dystrophy telethon on September 3, do the Seagram Noontime show on the 5th. The *Wall Street Journal* wants an interview on the 12th—"I guess ragtime's going up!"—and next day there's a tape to be made for Brooklyn College.

October is concert season. New York University on the 10th, the Toronto Rag Bash on the 13th. Chicago on the 22nd for another go-round at the Goodman Theater, sharing the stage with old friend Bill Bolcom. Back to New York for the Town Hall Interlude Program on the 31st.

It never lets up. Here's November 5 and a benefit for the Bronx

Veterans Hospital. On the 9th a concert at Yale. The concert year ends with Bolcom on stage at Carnegie Hall on the 27th of December.

On January 27, 1974, Eubie went to Nashville for the presentation of the original Sissle and Blake sound film to Fisk University. Two days later Eubie and Marion went to Florida to visit Noble Sissle in Tampa.

"Oh, that was terrible. I should never have gone. Poor Sissle. He kept asking me if I had any trouble finding his place on the subway. There's no subway in Tampa. He don't even know he ain't in New York. I felt so bad seeing him like that."

Eubie and Marion had planned to stay with Sissle, but he didn't seem well enough to have guests, so Marion called their pianist friend Jim Hession in Disney World and they went and stayed with him.

Despite Noble's poor health, he and Eubie did tape an autobiographical film, "Reminiscin' with Sissle and Blake," on this visit. "I never thought he could make it," Eubie reports. "His son works around TV. He said Sissle would be all right, but I didn't believe it. Anyway, they started to tape the act, and I went into 'Gee! I'm Glad That I'm from Dixie.' But Sissle don't come in. I tried again, but poor Sissle looks like he don't know where he is or what we're doin.' Then I played a Shubert—that's a standard opening for all vaudeville shows in Shubert theaters—and he come *right* in and did the whole act with me perfectly. Right after we got done, he started talkin' nonsense like his mind is gone. I couldn't *stand* that."

Sissle, Eubie's partner since 1915, died in Tampa on December 17, 1975.

Back at home, Eubie passed a quiet ninety-first birthday on February 7, 1974. On the 24th, the *Washington Post* sponsored a one-hour TV special starring Eubie, with the old-time singer Edith Wilson. "Ragtime with Gunther Schuller and Max Morath" on WGBH-TV in Boston had Eubie as a guest on March 1. He did concerts on the 4th and 5th at the University of Massachusetts and Smith College. Then, on the 18th, three of Eubie's young colleagues—Jim Hession, Terry Waldo, and Mike Lipskin—joined him for a musical presentation at the Theater De Lys in New York.

There was another time in Carnegie Hall on April 3, guesting with Benny Goodman, then on the 5th Eubie traveled to Philadelphia for a repeat with Mike Douglas.

As must appear increasingly obvious, Eubie's health has always been excellent, but, on April 11 internal disorders put him out of commission temporarily. He went into the hospital and was persuaded to stay there until the 24th, when his convalescence was declared at an end and he was again eager to go.

On Memorial Day he showed up to accept his Doctor of Fine Arts degree from Rutgers, and three days later he got his doctorate in music from the New England Conservatory, with Gunther Schuller making the presentation. Exactly a week later, June 9, Dartmouth bestowed on him his second doctorate in humane letters. "Hughie Wolford," he muses, "was better in *math* than me."

On the 19th of June he did Princeton's Harpsichord Festival again. He appeared on the Today show on the 25th, then failed to stump any experts on "What's My Line?" on the 27th. He did the TV show Sunday on June 30. Eubie loves France and was delighted to go to Nice for its jazz festival on July 13.

All this demonstrates that to the general public Eubie is a star. Millions have seen him time and again on the tube. His recognition factor is very high. But at these concerts and other public functions he's not facing audiences that really know his music or grasp his significance in the history of American culture. They relate to this kindly and pleasant nonagenarian who happens to be—and this they *can* tell—a hell of a piano player. For Eubie these are not the critical audiences. But on July 26 and 27 he went to sit among the modern "sharks," *the* critical audience. Followers and expert performers of authentic ragtime converged from everywhere for a festival in the little town of Sedalia, Missouri, ninety miles southeast of Kansas City.

This was Joplin's old stamping ground. Eubie visited the site of the original Maple Leaf Club after which Joplin named the immortal rag. The grade school is where Scott Hayden and Arthur Marshall labored over the three R's. The musical explosion was ignited here.

Many residents of Sedalia could still remember the times and even Joplin himself. Arthur Marshall's daughter showed up. The parade of participating ragtime stars seemed endless. Max Morath came to play. "Ragtime Bob" Darch showed up direct from an engagement in Alaska. There were Dick Zimmerman and Wally Rose from the West Coast, Steve Pistorius from New Orleans, Terry Waldo from Columbus, Ohio, Knocky Parker from the University of South Florida, Bill Bolcom and William Albright from the University of Michigan. This was the major league of ragtime. It was a distinguished company and Eubie was well aware of it. In the audience were scholars who could date the events of his life, name the master numbers of his records, who knew, note by note, every piece of the hundreds that were published in his name. This fact astonished Eubie. He had no idea that attention was focused on his work as intensely as it was focused on the work of Beethoven or Mozart.

"Man!" he told me. "If ever I was gonna get stage fright, this should be the place."

No need. By the time he left Sedalia, the town, its people, and its weekend guests were his.

And on and on it went, with the range of things Eubie was doing ever widening. The following paragraphs give a few highlights of his busy life from mid-1974 on.

Woodstock, Vermont, on the 15th and 16th of August offered a tribute to Sissle and Blake in the town's art festival, including an appropriate citation from Governor Salmon.

Eubie was off to Paris again in the fall of '74. If the quality of nobility occurs on TV, it would have to be represented by Jean-Cristophe Averty. From the 18th to the 21st of November this colossus of the tube put Eubie through his paces and produced four hours of bio-documentary. Knowledgeable and sensitive, Averty, who is himself a former professional ragtime pianist with a vast repertoire, wrought a definitive portrait of the man and his music. It is to be hoped that someday American audiences will have a chance to see this masterpiece.

On the eve of Eubie's next birthday, WCVB in Boston saluted Eubie on its Good Morning show. His 1975 birthday concert was at Harvard. At ninety-two he showed no sign of fatigue after a full production. On February 10 there was a tribute to Eubie from the American Guild of Authors and Composers at New York's

Princeton Club. Good friend Bill Cosby invited him for a live telecast from Cleveland on the 22nd and 23rd.

On March 17 Eubie recorded "Joplin's School of Ragtime" for RCA. This is no less than an instruction book for ragtime piano by the master composer.

May 16 and 17 Eubie was on stage at the Morris Mechanic Theater in Baltimore. Also on the 16th he watched the running of the Eubie Blake Purse at Pimlico. Carnegie Hall welcomed Eubie again on the 22nd as he and other piano prodigies offered "An Evening of Harlem Stride." Two days later he completed an original musical score for the film "Roots."

Pratt Institution made him a Doctor of Music on June 6th. Then back to France for the Nice Festival from July 16 to 29.

On September 11 Eubie testified on copyrights before a congressional committee in Washington. On the 17th he accepted the Senior Citizen Award from the City of New York. On the 28th he was back in the nation's capital to play for the National Council for the Aging.

In mid-October he was off for Toronto for the Rag Bash and collapsed of exhaustion following his performance. Who wouldn't? He was doing too much work for anyone. Eubie paid the price by being stuck in the hospital from October 19 through November 2 and had to hang it up for the rest of the year to recuperate.

He was back in his old form by mid-January 1976, and his ninety-third birthday was celebrated at the Waldorf-Astoria Hotel. Next day he flew to Oakland, California, to be honored by the Black Filmmakers Hall of Fame. On March 20 he was a guest of the Brooklyn Philharmonic, and on the 27th he joined Bill Bolcom and singer Joan Morris for a concert at Alice Tully Hall.

Many of Marion and Eubie's close personal friends live in New Orleans—for instance, old show-business folks Danny and Blue Lu Barker; Bill Russell, Lars Edegran, and Orange Kellin, musicians of the New Orleans Ragtime Orchestra; nurses Mary Tunis and Pat Quina; photographer Jules Cahn and his wife June, an attorney; Allen and Sandra Jaffe, the proprietors of Preservation Hall; Dick Allen, curator of the Archive of New Orleans Jazz at Tulane; Vaughn Glasgow, curator of the Louisiana State Museum; man-about-town Jamie Charbonnet. Accordingly, there was almost as

Eubie Blake as a young man. Elegant dress was a trademark of Sissle and Blake.

Noble Sissle, lyricist for some of Eubie's greatest songs.

"It's All Your Fault," Eubie Blake's first song and first collaboration with Noble Sissle, written in 1915.

Sophie Tucker accepted and sang their first song, introduced to her by Al Herman, who shared the bill with her at the Maryland Theater, Baltimore. Later, when they were writing shows, Sissle and Blake often shared Sunday-night bills with her in New York.

James Reese Europe and his Clef Club Orchestra, 1914. Europe was a principal organizer of black musicians and a leader of society orchestras. Eubie said of him, "He was our benefactor and inspiration. Even more, he was the Martin Luther King of music."

Noble Sissle and Lieut. James Reese Europe with the 369th U.S. Infantry in France during World War I. Europe organized a regimental band with Sissle as drum major.

Left: Thomas (Fats) Waller, great jazz piano player and songwriter, who was later to do his own black Broadway show.

Above: James P. Johnson, great Harlem pianist and songwriter, father of "stride" piano and teacher of Fats Waller.

Joe Jordan, composer of "Lovie Joe," the first Fanny Brice hit.

Out-of-town flyer for "In Bamville," renamed "The Chocolate Dandies" for its New York opening in 1924. With an enormous production cost, a cast of more than a hundred, and a fantasy, "non-Negro" plot, the show was not a financial success, but its score remains the one of which Eubie is most proud: "I have never written a score to compare with 'The Chocolate Dandies.' I know there is nothing in 'Shuffle Along' anywhere near the melodies of 'Dixie Moon' and 'Jassamine Lane.'"

SISSLE & BLAKE
STARS & COMPOSERS
"IN BAMVILLE"
ILLINOIS THEATRE
SUNDAY MARCH 30TH.

yours Musically,
Noble Sissle Eubie Bla

"Brown Sugar," showgirl in "The Chocolate Dandies."

Valada Snow, one of the singing stars in "The Chocolate Dandies." She had absolute pitch (she once corrected Eubie's tuning fork, which had gotten slightly bent) and was able to play every instrument in the orchestra.

Lyricist Joshua Milton Reddie and Eubie in 1947. Eubie began writing with Reddie in the mid-thirties under WPA's subsidy. Their "Swing It" was produced in 1937.

Eubie Blake's hands. Playing every day wards off arthritis.

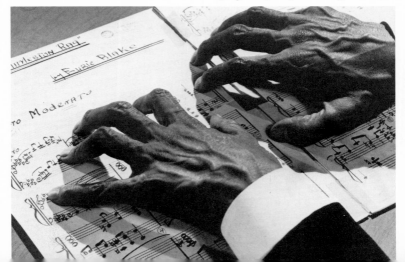

much socializing as performing on April 17 and 18 at the New Orleans Jazz and Heritage Festival, where Eubie played "Chevy Chase" and "Poor Katie Redd" with the New Orleans Ragtime Orchestra. Watching him rehearse with this group the night before was a revelation. In recent years few people have had the opportunity to see Eubie conduct. At 93 he clearly knew what to do to whip an orchestra into shape and demonstrated an infallible ear. Band members learned things they never realized before about the performance of rags. The actual performances in the huge tent were just another pair of triumphs. My two sons, Rex and Forrest, ran a certain amount of interference for him as he left, but Eubie turned and bucked into the crowd like a candidate for city council and let himself be mobbed by autograph hounds.

"How do you spell 'from'?" he often asked.

Eubie was back in L.A. to help Merv Griffin salute Irving Berlin on April 27. On the 29th there was a Columbia recording session back in New York with Bill Bolcom and Joanie Morris. The music on the album is all Eubie Blake composition. On the 6th of May he was a dais guest at the Frederick Douglass Award dinner sponsored by the Urban League.

He made his third trip of the year to California on July 22 and spent a week working on a movie of Scott Joplin's life for TV. He played the part of Will Williams, proprietor of the Maple Leaf Club in Sedalia, Missouri. September 3 to 6 Eubie was in Colorado Springs for Dick Gibson's "Rocky Mountain Jazz Party" at the Broadmoor Hotel. A documentary film of this event was produced.

Eubie participated in a Jimmy Carter rally in Asbury Park, New Jersey, on October 28 and attended his candidate's victory celebration at the Mayflower Hotel in Washington on November 2. On the 3rd there was a press-party tribute to Josephine Baker at Gallagher's in New York, where Eubie had his picture taken with cochairman Jackie Onassis at her gracious request. On the 7th he appeared for the Josephine Baker tribute at the Metropolitan Opera House. On the 14th he did a gala benefit for Town Hall in New York. On the 30th he taped a Voice of America show.

Then, on December 14 Kazuko Hillyer interviewed Eubie for a documentary to be shown in Japan, and in early January Eubie and

Marion came to New Orleans for three days for its filming. The show was done at the Royal Orleans Hotel, and Eubie played his duet of "I'm Just Wild about Harry" with then eight-year-old Harry Connick, Jr., the son of good New Orleans friends.

On the last day of his visit Eubie and Marion, Jamie Charbonnet, my wife Diana and I had breakfast together at the hotel. Between the Creole cream cheese and the eggs Florentine Eubie paid me one of the big compliments of my life when he asked, "Al, would you consider writing my biography?" We were all stunned for a moment, but I quickly caught my breath, accepted, and we shook hands on it. Then principals and witnesses signed a Royal Orleans Hotel menu, and that's our contract.

On January 9 Ms. Lorraine Brown of George Mason University, Fairfax, Virginia, interviewed Eubie about old WPA material he had composed, including the 1937 show "Swing It." On the 15th he was on stage playing ragtime again in Carnegie Hall as a special guest in Bob Greene's "The World of Jelly Roll Morton." Later in the winter there were trips, both to California and to Europe, and then it was back to New Orleans again. The New Orleans Jazz and Heritage Festival, or Newport South, showcased Eubie in a concert performance on the steamer *President* April 12, 1977.

The Blakes' visit to New Orleans for this was a mellow occasion. Eubie's appearance became a fleeting incident in four or five days of New Orleans merrymaking and, for Eubie, a journey back to his roots.

Eubie and Marion arrived at the airport and were limousined to their quarters at our house, and soon we were all on our way to a dinner at Antoine's hosted by Mary Tunis. This is one of the world's famous restaurants, but Eubie didn't notice what he was eating; he was busy regaling his friends with reports of his recent activities, telling tales of long ago, and engaging in the quick repartee that is so much a part of his style.

Later, at the house, he practiced a while on the piano upstairs and then, before going to bed around three in the morning, worked out on the downstairs piano, but not before a foray to the doughnuts and 7-Up lardered especially for his visit. The next day, he was up early (more doughnuts); there was a quick auto tour of the downtown area; and he was ready for a press conference in the music room. Photographers shot several hundred views. Eubie became, again, the cover story for the *Mississippi Rag.* Terry Dash, publisher of England's *Footnote* magazine, got an interview, as did Angie King of the Tulane University *Hullabaloo.* The conference was planned for thirty minutes. It ran two hours.

That night there was the matter of getting him aboard the huge steamer, where everybody recognized him, and seated at the best table on the huge floor, with friends deployed so that the many well-wishers and autograph seekers he was attracting would not have too ready access to the star before he performed. This accomplished, Eubie had a chance to take in all that went on. Eubie pays close attention to other entertainers, and that night he was taken with a swinging gospel group and with the expert playing of Louis Cottrell's Orchestra. Joy in New Orleans is traditionally unconfined, and when they played "The Saints," some fifty or sixty members of the audience got up and performed the time-honored "second line," which is the Creole version of the snake dance, except that in New Orleans participants are equipped with spectacularly decorated umbrellas and they strut and shuffle in a unique movement that's indigenous to the city.

I had all I could do to keep Eubie from joining the line.

"Anybody needs to learn about having a good time," he observed, "this is the place."

His performance over, the Blakes and the Roses went home and stayed up very late talking. Finally everyone had drifted off to bed except Eubie and me. He said, "They all went off and left us. It must be time to go to bed." I agreed and reminded him he'd find doughnuts and milk in his apartment. I asked if he was tired, but he misunderstood. "People keep tellin' me I'm tired. They don't mean *I'm* tired. They mean *they're* tired. I'll see you in the morning."

Eubie's journey into the past came the next day. Vaughn Glasgow had arranged a plantation tour for the Blakes which would culminate at historic Tezcuco, where they would be greeted and guided by the proprietress herself, Mrs. Roberta Potts, who had lived there all of her married life. She welcomed Eubie and Marion and a small company of friends and led the way through the grand old establishment.

Eubie was interested, and clearly became *very* interested when the group came to an ancient slave cabin on the river road. This he examined at considerable length, even feeling the texture of its walls. Lester Dilmore, overseer of the plantation, himself a show-business veteran, solicitously supplied details about the place.

In Eubie's mind stirred images of John Sumner Blake and Emily Johnston Blake—early images, images that went back before Eubie knew them. They had known plantations, cotton acres, and cabins like this—very much like this, that must have felt and maybe smelled like this. He was suddenly very close to the past—not his, but *theirs*—and closer to *them*, standing in the doorway of what could well have been their home.

Eubie stopped the progress of the tour and asked that his picture be taken right there, in that entrance. He seemed to be telling himself, "This is where I really began. I know about Europe and jet planes. I know what the world's applause sounds like. I've had things named after me. I've been honored by great institutions of learning, by the White House itself. But this is where I began, and my father made sure I wouldn't forget where I started and I haven't. I'm ninety-four years old and I remember. And it's what he and my mother gave me that made it possible for me to go so far!"

Pictures were taken until he was satisfied.

This would have been a fit and satisfying climax to a New Orleans visit, but there was more to come, for the next night Eubie was to belong to the fabulous Rosalie Wilson. Rosalie operated the posh bistro Rosy's, where the nation's main musical-entertainment attractions rotated. At seventeen she was orphaned but not left penniless. Now only in her early twenties she already is in the direct line of the great bonifaces of the country. With the aid of the ebullient and imaginative Jamie Charbonnet, she was hostess to a party for Eubie and Marion—not at her beautiful club, but at her spectacular St. Charles Avenue mansion.

Rosy and Jamie, who are young and atypical members of New Orleans Garden District high society, threw a function in Eubie's honor for a group of five hundred or so, directly in the Gatsby tradition. And they jolted their friends and families by rending the uptown New Orleans color line once and for all, though this purpose was unstated. The affair was duly announced in the society pages of the *Times-Picayune*. The New Leviathan Oriental Fox-Trot Orchestra, which at full strength has about twenty-three pieces, played for the occasion. Eubie performed his own "Chevy Chase" with them.

This significant event in the history of New Orleans society went beautifully, under Jamie's unobtrusive, Machiavellian direction, and the "ancien régime" of New Orleans was never to be the same.

Clearly, Eubie had a wonderful time, as did Marion. They no longer go anywhere without encountering old friends from all over the world, and many were invited to, and attended, this soiree. Eubie's only regret was that he had missed seeing the naked girls in Rosy's swimming pool. Nobody had called them to his attention.

Musical Matters

Piano Players
Piano Rolls
Eubie on How to Play Rags
His Own Music and Playing

"In small bands back in the early days," Eubie comments, "musicians who played the same instrument rarely got to know each other. If a band had one cornet player and somebody had to sit in for him for a night, the new guy met the other horn players and the rhythm men, but he didn't meet the guy he was replacing. It was different with piano players. If you had a half-hour break, you go around the corner and listen to the other guy a while. Piano players *had* to do that to try to steal each other's stuff. That's how you stayed up to date, and that's how you could hold your own when the other guys tried to cut you.

"A lot of piano players got to be good friends—shoot pool together in the daytime, stuff like that. When you're real young, you hear another guy play and you say to yourself, 'Man, listen to that! I wish I could play that good.' Then you hear somebody else and you say the same thing. Then comes a time when you realize that the first guy can't do what the second guy can and the second guy can't do what the first guy can. That makes you feel a little better when you know that. Well, then, when you come to find out *you* can do things *both* them other guys can't do, you discover that ain't got anything to do with who's good and who isn't. It's just that everybody puts his own personal *style* to the music. Of course, if he *doesn't*, then he just ain't a musician."

Eubie's been asked frequently who was the greatest piano player he's ever heard and he usually names One Leg Willie Joseph. But at times, overcome with enthusiasm for a recently heard performance or even suddenly recalling a spectacular pianistic achievement from earlier times, he'll unpredictably bestow the palm on someone else. I asked specific questions about the keyboard stars of past and present, and got the following answers.

"Sam Wooding was a youngster around Atlantic City before 1915. He was always playing a show with three or five singers. That hurt him because he always played in *their* keys. He didn't have any rags of his own. He was a dark, chunky fellow. Never got tired, and you know cabaret pianos never stopped in those days. Some people say I taught him, but *I* never taught him. He could *read* good. He was also a *showman.* He had a regular organized act, and I think he took it to Europe.

"Me and Willie the Lion played a concert with Don Lambert once. We didn't know him at that time, and Willie made fun of him before he started to play. Lambert wiped us *both* out. He didn't *look* like nothin'. His mouth hung open like this"—Eubie demonstrates—"and his clothes—baggy, they didn't fit—and he's got no personality at all. Then he starts in to play and I look at the Lion and Willie says, 'He'll do.' He'll *do?* You can't believe what that fellow *could* do with a piano. Of course the Lion never had *nothin'* good to say about *anybody*, you know. Big mouth. But the Lion could play! He *could* play. But Willie always wanted to be the whole show. I guess he thought if you always put the other guy down, it made *you* look good. But things don't work that way. Willie was good enough that he didn't need to act that way.

"Now Hughie Wolford, we grew up together from *babies* in Baltimore. I mean we were *really* shirt-tail babies in the same block. He was my competitor, and when I say competitor, I *mean* competitor. He was known in show business in his time because he was such a fine musician, but now hardly anybody remembers him. I don't think he ever made any records. He had a marvelous, complicated way with chords, and he could keep so *many* things goin' in his head at once. He worked with Broadway Jones too, after me and Broadway stopped doin' our act.

"What I *don't* understand is these bebop guys. You know this fellow, blind guy, works down in the Village. It seems like he just bangs his hands down on the piano just anywhere." Eubie was talking about Thelonius Monk. "You know, if you got no melody, you got no music. There's a big difference between playin' the piano and playin' *with* the piano. I think the world will get over that stuff.

"I'll tell you about Jack the Bear. His real name was Wilson. *He* had a lot of tricks. You could learn a lot from *watchin'* him. He didn't have to work because he always had women keepin' him. He was always dressed to kill. Diamonds, everything. In Baltimore when I was workin' at the Middle Section Club or at the Goldfield Hotel, he used to lecture to me to never use no dope. I *saw* what it did to *him*. He would always say he needed to go someplace and lie down. What he meant was to smoke some opium. But still he used to tell me not to use no dope. He had so *much* talent and he wasted it.

"And James P. Johnson! Black James we called him. I wrote 'Troublesome Ivories' to have a number to cut everybody with. It was even hard for *me* to play. Black James, he was only sixteen years old, he came by where I was workin' in Atlantic City and he heard me play the piece twice and he *had* it. Only *sixteen!* He was still drinkin' sarsaparilla then. Greatest piano player I ever heard. I let him sit in for me for twenty minutes while I took a break. I come back and he's playin' 'Troublesome Ivories' without no mistakes. *I* make mistakes, but not him.

"There was a guy in Baltimore, you never heard of him, his name was Sammy Ewell. He had more suits than Broadway Jones. He couldn't read music, but he had a great memory and a great ear. He could hear a new number once as soon as it came out and he'd *have* it. All the piano players in Baltimore hung around him to learn the new numbers. Of course by that time we were all *sharks*, and that was some of the best piano music the world ever heard, right there in Baltimore.

"Fats Waller knew how to hold an audience, and he could really play too. Between you and me, though, he wasn't no James P. But he learned a lot from Black James. Poor Fats! I pleaded with him not to be flashin' those whisky bottles around and makin' the white folks think that colored people ain't civilized yet. I remember one night, he's goin' to Europe the next day and he can't get his passport because his agent or his manager forgot to pay his income taxes. I got Bill Robinson and we got *him* to call Mayor La Guardia, who was in California at the time—he loved Bill Robinson—and Bill got La Guardia to call somebody in the government to fix it so Fats could get his passport. The things that used to happen in New York!

"Art Tatum was a master of those runs. He had two right hands, that guy. You listen to him you think what he's doin' ain't possible. He had a big success. I wonder if the people who heard him enjoyed the music or if they got excited hearin' all those notes comin' so fast. But he could get so much out of a simple tune, sometimes a lot more than it had in it.

"'Luckey Roberts wasn't much younger than me, but he was like a son. He came from Philadelphia, but he used to hang around wherever I played in Baltimore. There wasn't anything *he* couldn't play! Greatest piano player I ever heard. Nothin' was too hard for him." The subject of Roberts's pool hustling comes back into Eubie's thoughts. "I used to try to stop him from gettin' in those lemon pool games with those big-time Harlem hustlers. He could have gotten himself killed. But you wouldn't believe how strong he was. He was this wide"—arms fully extended.

"He had a real flowery style and they used to love him at those millionaire parties in Long Island. He had a *big* hit, 'Moonlight Cocktail.' It was really part of something else he wrote, but it made more money then everything else he wrote put together.

"Now I *knew* Jelly Roll Morton, and I talked with him once in a while. He was *always* talkin' like Mule Bradford or the Lion. I never paid much attention to him. To tell you the truth, I never *did* hear him play except on records, and you can't always tell off of records—but you know Bob Greene? He says he's imitatin' Jelly Roll. Well if Jelly really played *that* good, he was a hell of musician. But Jelly Roll had good tunes he wrote, and a lot of bands play them. *Still* play them.

"I only met Scott Joplin one time, in Washington. Some kind of a big dinner in a big hotel. I guess I have to *say* I heard him play, but the poor fellow, they *made* him play 'Maple Leaf.' It was about 1915. So pitiful. He was so far gone with the dog [syphilis] and he sounded like a little child tryin' to pick out a tune. They shouldn't have made him do it. I hate to see things like that. I hated to see him tryin' so hard. He was so weak. And he did such great things in his life. And nobody appreciated him until so much later after he died. You remember in Atlanta, when was that? They had the premiere performance of his opera. You were there. He's already dead fifty-five years then and that was the first time they showed it! And our people owe a lot to him." The year was 1972, the opera Joplin's "Treemonisha."

"Slew Foot Nelson was the greatest piano player I ever heard. There was a big hall in Atlantic City where piano players used to sit around and wait for jobs. It was like a hirin' hall. When Slew Foot was there, nobody but him touched that piano. He was really feared—musically, I mean. Real black guy. He had a very heavy rhythm style, but he played a *lot* of notes. Even more than Big Head Wilbur, who was the greatest piano player I ever heard.

"Poor Jimmy Green! That's *little* Jimmy Green. There was a *big* Jimmy Green too. But little Jimmy was a great musician. I wrote a rag about him called 'Poor Jimmy Green.' He could have been the *most* famous of all if not for whisky and dope. Back in Baltimore after I saw Jack the Bear and Jimmy Green kill theirselves with that stuff, I decided right there to stay away from things like that. I never smoked no dope, and I was never a real drinker. Of course *now* I never take a drink at all.

"Another one, Paul Seminole—he was a real Indian. He played things I didn't believe. I think he came from Pensacola, same as the Pensacola Kid [Paul Wyer], in Florida. but Seminole wasn't a big pool shark like the Kid.

"Old Jesse Pickett, I learned 'The Dream' off of him. He was an old pimp. He was pretty old already back in 1898. But if you heard him *then*, you knew he was playin' that music a long time before that. These guys that say they invented this music, they never heard Jesse Pickett, and even he wasn't the only one or even the oldest. Old Man "Metronome" French, I heard he played piano some, but when I was a *little* kid in Baltimore he played ragtime on a banjo. He was really old *then*, it must have been before 1890. He went *way* back, before the Civil War."

As Eubie reminisces about his colleagues, there passes a parade of exotic names—Abba Labba (Richard McLean), the Shadow (Walter Gould), the Beetle (Stephen Henderson), Fats Harris, William Turk, No Legs Cagey, Cat Eye Harry, Sparrow, Sheet Iron Brown, Wildcat Joe, Black Diamond, Squirrel, John the Baptist, Sam Gordon. Each had poured his unique seasoning into the giant ragtime pot. Most are all but forgotten.

But Eubie never stopped listening. After his generation of ragtimers vanished from the scene, younger musicians captured his attention—and his admiration. He bemoans the fact that authentic ragtime has become a white monopoly because black artists have turned their backs on it. He is aware, however, that he has influenced the music profoundly, and he speaks with affection of those who have carried forward the tradition.

"Never play a piano after *he* gets done with it," warns Eubie about Dr. John W. (Knocky) Parker. "First you call a carpenter and then a tuner. I never saw a man beat a piano to death like him. I always thought of him as a kid, but he's been around for a good, long time, hasn't he?" Knocky is sixty-five.

Of John Arpin Eubie says, "I call him the Chopin of ragtime. I sat around all night waiting to hear him make a mistake. He never made one. He plays so beautiful it makes me cry. And he really did a lot for ragtime in Canada.

"You talk about *great* piano players! You know Don Ewell? He's from Baltimore too. Plays just like the old-time stars, but *better*. He's the greatest piano player I ever heard.

"Max Morath? You're gettin' close to home when you talk about Max. He's our great friend, and Marion and I love him. *Everybody* loves him, not only because he's a show-business genius and a wonderful piano player—I love to hear him play—but he's such a wonderful *person* too. We're lucky to have friends like Max and Bill Bolcom.

"*There's* a real musician," Eubie says of Bolcom. "We watched him and Joanie [singer Joan Morris] get married. We were so happy! He's a true classical pianist. I wish I could play my own classical pieces as good as Bolcom. You hear him at the concert playin' 'Capricious Harlem'? Better than me, ain't he?

"Then when you listen to Johnny Guarnieri, you feel like you never want to touch a piano yourself again. How can he *do* those things?"

Eubie calls Terry Waldo "my ofay son"—white son. "Only one I could ever show anything to. He learns easy. Every time I see him he sounds better. And he *knows* what to do on the stage. A real comedian. He could have a great future.

"Bob Darch is *real* ragtime. He's what people expect to see when they think of a ragtime piano player. He's done a lot for the music. The funny places he plays! The Malemute Saloon in Alaska!

"And the fellow in Chicago?" This is Bob Wright. "My God, he knows every rag ever written. You tell him any rag, he plays it. I mean *any* rag. Plays it right off!

"Now there are guys who not only *play* the music, but they *know* all about it, just like college professors. In fact, some of them *are* college professors. David Jasen right here in New York and Trebor Tichenor in St. Louis. These guys are great musicians and they're real historians. You know [Dick] Zimmerman, the magician from California, and the guy in Detroit, Mike Montgomery. They know the old records, piano rolls, films, things I forgot myself that I ever made.

"There are so many great young piano players now. I can't keep track of them all. Some of them are so perfect they scare you. I'm glad I didn't have to go up against a Morten Gunnar Larsen when I was twenty like him. He's from Oslo. And Jim Hession in Orlando, Florida? He's amazing. Girls too. I don't even know their names. Too many to remember.

"There's enough of them around so you know our music will be around for a very long time. I never get tired of hearing it, and I'm so proud of them all!"

The 1970s have seen a nostalgia boom in which people are eager to recreate the attractive accoutrements of living from an earlier part of the century. Among the most prized items are automatic music machines, player pianos, and piano rolls. Also, player pianos are still in production, and on May 19, 1973, Eubie Blake made his very first airplane flight—ninety years after his birth—to Buffalo, New York, to cut five piano rolls for QRS, the same company that dominated the field in the first decade of the century.

"In Buffalo," Eubie confesses, "I made mistakes, and they said, 'Don't worry about it, we'll fix it,' and they did."

The thought carries him back. "I recorded so *many* piano rolls in the old days. I remember one company, Mel-O-Dee, on Forty-second Street, between Fifth and Sixth Avenue. You played on a regular piano, but it has a whole lot of mechanical stuff underneath. It doesn't get in your way when you play or anything. You can't even see it.

"This man was from Georgia and he *idolized* me. Not one of them things where a Georgia redneck says, 'He's my nigger, don't bother him,' nothin' like that. He just loved *me*, and if he sees me on Broadway he calls me and tries to take me in for a drink or a sandwich. I didn't go because I didn't want to get him in trouble—that could happen in those days. But I *did* cut these rolls for him.

"Another time—this is in the twenties—I'm comin' down from Boston on the train and I get to Meriden, Connecticut. A guy says, 'Do I know you?' I tell him I don't know. He says, 'Don't you play the piano?' I say, 'Yeah.' He says, 'You want to cut some piano rolls right now, right here in Meriden?' I say, 'Sure.'

"This is Sunday, now, but we get off the train and go someplace to cut the rolls.

"He says, 'You can play anything you want to and just tell me the name of it, and who wrote it, if *you* didn't write it.' Five hundred dollars! They gave me five hundred dollars. No, not the twenties—that's gotta be 1919. I can't remember what I played.

"I did about seven or eight numbers. There were just three guys there. No crow's nest [engineer's booth] like in a record place. I'd just say, 'This number is so-and-so, written by so-and-so, and published by so-and-so, or I'd say, 'Unpublished'—and I'd play it. They gave me five hundred dollars for that. It took about an hour and a half. I didn't make any mistakes. I was young then."

Eubie is known to have made thirty-nine rolls. These all are listed in the rollography. It is likely he made—and forgot—quite a few others. Thus a complete rollography may never be possible. It is encouraging that there are a number of avid collectors constantly turning up unknown items, and it's reasonable to hope that some of the finds will be Eubie's.

Terry Waldo, a young man of extraordinary performing skill at the piano, has said that any piano player lucky enough to have Eubie Blake tell him about how to play can learn something about both technique and presentation—that there's nothing old-fashioned about Eubie and his style, but that everything he has to say "applies right now, this minute, to every musician."

What is it, actually, that Eubie does say? He was interviewed for the November 1973 issue of the *Rag Times*, which then passed on these highlights: The most important element of ragtime is the bass. Since the left hand provides the rhythmic pulse of the rag as well as the notes against which the melody is syncopated, it has to be strong, even, and clear. A second extremely important element is proper use of the sustaining pedal so that it doesn't sound too long or at the wrong times, causing the notes to sound muddy. The pedal is essential for achieving desired tones and coloring, Eubie says, but must never be used indiscriminately. He names incorrect pedaling as probably the most heard error among ragtime pianists and says that one common fault is beating time with the pedal.

To learn a rag, Eubie suggests mastering and memorizing four bars at a time. After the entire rag is learned, he advises, it can be played however one chooses. He sees no reason why a rag should be played exactly as written and believes that the player should inject his own ideas and personality. He is against the idea that ragtime sounds best played at a snail's pace. The more classic rags should not be rushed, he says, but rags containing many single notes and runs, such as Scott Joplin's "The Cascades," benefit from slightly increased tempos.

Eubie points out that the piano has basically one "color" and that variety in coloring leads to more interesting performance. The sudden use of treble notes or a bass melody line, for instance, changes the color in a dramatic manner.

"These modern piano players," Eubie adds, "all sound alike because they don't know how to use this [the left] hand." Eubie's

left hand has a span that has made it easy for him to stretch over a
twelfth on the piano, so that, as Terry Waldo wrote in his liner
notes for "Sincerely, Eubie Blake," playing tenths is nothing for
him—and the use of tenths in the left hand is central to his music.
"But this [left hand] is the chords! And it's the rhythm! You've got
to use your left hand to go 'boom cha, boom cha.' We *had* to do it
that way in cabarets and dance halls. Lots of times you're the only
musician. No drums, no bass. *You're* the rhythm. You don't play
rhythm, they can't dance, and then you ain't workin'. My wife tells
me not to say 'ain't.' So that's why the *old*-timers—Willie the Lion,
Luckey Roberts, Black James—that's why they learned to play
with *both* hands."

Most everyone with a TV set has by now had a look at Eubie
Blake. What they've seen is a delightful gentleman, very quick
with his repartee, matching the skills of the most experienced wits
and program hosts in the nation. In these situations, when he's
asked to play the piano, he tends to perform his best-known
popular hits. That's what his hosts generally ask for. The most re-
quested of them are "I'm Just Wild about Harry" and "Memories of
You." If there's time—which there usually isn't—he tries to get in a
little Gershwin to show he's not limited to his own material and
because "Rhapsody in Blue" and "The Man I Love" are readily
recognizable to his audiences.

But after you get by the ready wit and mastery of show business
and audience manipulation that these situations bring out and get
further into Eubie's intrinsic musical merit, you begin to see the artist emerging from the cocoon of the entertainer. His performance,
as heard on records, is masterful and personal, and the quality and
variety of his compositions are amazing.

Any attempt to analyze the origins of Eubie Blake's music must
steer clear of the clichés and assumptions of most authors on the
subject of American popular music in general and so-called black
music in particular. Jesse Pickett and Jack the Bear, whose musical
products reflect slave and plantation days, were important but not
primary influences on Eubie's output. Stylistically, Eubie's compositions hark back to Francis Johnson of Philadelphia, a Negro
cornetist, composer, and bandleader who died in 1844. Johnson's

marches and waltzes influenced the music of Patrick Sarsfield Gilmore and, later, John Philip Sousa. A direct model was the Englishman Leslie Stuart, composer of "Florodora," whose music for the Florodora Sextette took turn-of-the-century America by storm. And Eubie has been deeply affected by the music of Mozart, Chopin, Tchaikovsky, and George Gershwin.

A white artist could as easily have felt just such a mix of influences. Eubie's color has little if anything to do with his style or his musical thinking. Genuine American popular music—and that includes jazz, ragtime, and Tin Pan Alley tunes—springs from a racial amalgam that includes Eubie as it includes Hoagy Carmichael and Jerome Kern. Listening to Eubie performing a truly representative selection of his own compositions without knowing of him or seeing him, one would hear nothing to make one assume that he was black or he was white.

While he was fortunate enough to have lyricists of the stature of Andy Razaf, Jack Scholl, and Milton Reddie to work with—and Sissle, despite his technical flaws—it's mainly Eubie's melodies that have endured from such collaborations. "Memories of You" is rarely sung, the great Razaf words little known, but the melody is universally recognized and loved. Its long melodic line developing into a classic call-and-response pattern is a brilliant conception. Its almost half century of popularity, supported by recordings by Benny Goodman, Louis Armstrong, the Casa Loma Orchestra, and others, is clear evidence of that assessment. "I'm Just Wild about Harry," originally written as a waltz, became popular as a fox trot. Nobody sings it anymore, but it remains standard production music for TV variety shows, and it too is a worldwide standard.

"You're Lucky to Me" was a technical wonder when it came out in 1930 in "Blackbirds." It introduced new and modern concepts about intervals that challenged other musicians and won enough adherents to become permanently incorporated into common musical idiom. "Loving You the Way I Do," a gem of simplicity, is a lush and exciting vehicle for instrumental solos. Nobody ever sings it anymore, but lots of people play it.

The great Blake rags "Charleston Rag," "Chevy Chase," "Brittwood Rag," "Troublesome Ivories," and "Tricky Fingers" have found their way into the repertoires of the incredibly skilled younger generation of ragtimers of "the revival." The one-step "Fizz Water" was recorded by a full orchestra as late as 1975—the New Leviathan Oriental Fox-Trot Orchestra—though copyrighted sixty years earlier. In the early days, as William J. Schafer pointed out in discussing Eubie's compositions in the *Mississippi Rag* of December 1975 (page 2), Blake's and many of his peers' rags were rejected by publishers as too difficult for the parlor pianist. Blake simplified them, staff arrangers worked them over, and versions considerably less complex than his performance style were finally printed. But even in this form, Schafer says, Blake's ragtime is "dense, intricate music, at once highly melodic, ingeniously 'or-namented' in a kind of neobaroque fashion and compellingly rhythmic."

"Love Will Find a Way" and "In Honeysuckle Time," those fabulous ballads that Eubie wrote for "Shuffle Along," were featured in "Bubbling Brown Sugar" on Broadway in 1976. Those songs and Florence Mills's great hit "I'm Craving for That Kind of Love" are available on records and are still in the repertoires of many contemporary night-club singers. It's a safe bet that these melodies will be around again and again in revivals—and not for their nostalgic appeal, but for their musical merit.

It is as a composer of classics and semiclassics that Eubie has done some of his most exciting, though least known, work. "Dictys on Seventh Avenue," his "graduation piece" for his New York University degree, is in the Reginald Forsythe–David Rose mold but is nevertheless pure Eubie, as is his Gershwinesque "Ca-pricious Harlem." Most surprising and most difficult to identify with Eubie are the two exotic etudes "Rain Drops" and "Butterfly." These delicate little tone poems are clearly in the genre of Debussy, with a hint of Richard Strauss. They are in no way imitative, though. It's just that these earlier composers established forms in which Eubie is supremely at ease. "Rain Drops" is built on a single note set ingeniously, like a diamond, in a ring of complex chords. It is slow in tempo, a "mood" piece, yet it is exciting. Excruciatingly restrained and suspenseful, it may ultimately go farthest in establishing Eubie's credentials in the ranks of formal classical composers. "Butterfly" has a more programmatic character. Eubie captures flutters and silences in a gossamer of taste and sensitivity. It's almost impossible to believe that the man who composed "Butterfly" and "Rain Drops" could also have written "If You've Never Been Vamped by a Brownskin" and "My Handy Man Ain't Handy No More."

Some of Eubie's waltzes, composed in the Viennese style, without modern innovation, are named for lovely ladies he has known. One is "Valse Marion," dedicated to his wife. Another is "Valse Erda." This waltz intrigued me because Erda is such an unusual name and because I happen to know a lady who bears it. I questioned Eubie, but he wasn't much help. He's not good at remembering names anyway, and he convinced me that he had no idea who "Valse Erda" was named for. After all, he'd written it ten years earlier.

"What'd you say the name is? Erda? And one of my waltzes is named after her? Beautiful name, ain't it? That's what old age'll do to you. Imagine naming a piece after somebody and not to remember *nothin'* about it. Erda? Marion, do we know an Erda?"

Marion shrugs. "Maybe *you* know an Erda," she says, ever so slightly annoyed. "*I* don't know anybody by that name."

So I was prepared to accept it as an unsolved mystery until I got a letter from an old friend in York, Pennsylvania, who said he had a story to tell that I might want to use in Eubie's biography. I quote it from his letter: "[On the train] on the way home from the St. Louis Ragtime Festival in the summer of 1968 . . . I heard a recognizable voice in the next compartment. . . . Those were the days when Eubie was afraid to fly, too. . . . I confirmed the evidence of my ears by looking in and . . . inviting Eubie to have dinner with my wife and me. . . . Dinner was a delight, with Eubie sharing so many of his experiences and ideas with us, virtual strangers.

"As dinner ended, Eubie indicated that in appreciation of our taking him to dinner he would compose a piece dedicated to my wife, Erda. . . .

"Several weeks later we received a letter from Eubie. . . . He was working on a waltz, and shortly afterwards, there was delivered, by registered mail, a beautiful six-page document entitled "Valse Erda," with the inscription 'Respectfully dedicated to Mrs. Robert W. Erdos by Eubie Blake.'"

On yet another plane is the music Eubie tailored specially for Broadway production numbers. The rousing "Bandana Days" and "Baltimore Buzz" hold up for modern listeners even without the capering chorines for whom they were written. He's done it all, from etudes to boogie-woogie.

Eubie's audiences never fail to be transfixed. Even if they've heard him before, they're brought up short anew by the quality of his music and the brilliance of his execution. He never loses sight of his objective—to please and satisfy. He plays his audiences like his scores. A sixth sense seems to tell him what they'll enjoy. At the end his listeners realize that they've had a profound musical experience. If they're the right audience and particularly lucky, they may have heard one of the etudes. His classical compositions will find an enduring place as standard American works in the field of conventional composition just as his rags and ballads have made their way into the mainstream of American culture.

Aside from his blues, ballads, and "hot" songs, most of Eubie's musical product is very difficult to play, though many works are published in simplified form to put them within the scope of lesser artists. His own technique—even at ninety-six—continues to sparkle enough to dazzle today's skilled musicians. His approach to accenting remains a marvel to other performers.

He *does* make a few mistakes now, but not enough to detract from the joy and vitality of his presentation. In his concerts one feels a certain turn when the audience's response clearly changes from mere delight in his presence to awe and respect for his extraordinary musical talent.

Fortunately, there's now so much of Eubie available on LP (see the discography) that some of us feel a stronger sense of security about it than we once did. It's good to know that Eubie's great music and skill will forever remain with us.

Curtain Going Up

"People keep askin' me how it feels to be ninety-six years old. Last year they asked me how it feels to be ninety-five. That's been goin' on quite a few years.

"I sleep a little more than I did when I was thirty," Eubie explains patiently, "and I started havin' trouble with my legs maybe forty years ago, so I don't walk too good, but that ain't from bein' ninety-six. I don't hear too good without my hearin' aid, but I don't like that thing. It keeps makin' static.

"I know I got to practice on the piano every day for two or three hours, because I can't let my fingers get stiff. At my age you let 'em get stiff one time and that's it. I play what I really like to play and that's mostly classical and semiclassical. I still compose every time I get a new idea, and I keep on gettin' 'em. So many of my old friends are gone, from the real old days, but that's the way the world goes, ain't it? I already wore out a couple of generations of friends, but I've still *got* so many."

Eubie doesn't seem to have done much of this assessment of the past before. In the ledger of his life he doesn't find very much on the debit side. He wonders if he's forgotten a lot of bad things because he didn't want to remember.

"It's a great pleasure," he says, "for me to see young kids comin' up and playin' not only *my* music but other composers of my early times. Mostly"—and he chuckles—"the kids play 'em better than the old-timers. There's a kid from Oslo, Norway. Mostly I don't remember names, but I remember *his* name. Morten Gunnar Larsen. He's hard to believe! He can't hardly speak English, but he knows our American music. And his *execution*, God!

"Not only him! Bolcom, Max [Morath], Terry [Waldo]. Lots of people I hear whose names I never even heard. It makes me a little sad that my own people don't take it up and carry it on. You go to a ragtime festival in St. Louis or Sedalia, and if *I* ain't there the place looks like it's Jim Crow. It ain't Jim Crow. You can't *find* Negro piano players playin' *our* music. They're still lookin' for novelties. They think they're bein' up to date. But that's not how you got to think about music.

"Ninety-six ain't too old to start doin' new things. I was ninety when I started flyin', and that did so *much* for me. I can get to so many more places. Of course I get pushed in a wheel chair around in airports. It ain't that I can't walk. It's just that I ain't fast enough any more, and that holds everybody else up. But I still step out on the stage pretty good, don't I?"

People who know I'm close to Eubie ask me how he does it. They want to know about his personal fountain of youth; they hope to find something to add to or subtract from their own regimens to facilitate a long, useful life. I'm not immune from the same curiosity, and for the same reason. Having had the opportunity to watch him for protracted periods, I can report on a number of facts. They aren't recently developed facts, either. He hasn't changed too much in all the time I've known him.

Eubie's body temperature is lower than most people's. I've never seen him perspire, even under a hot summer New Orleans sun. His hands and feet are always cold, and he always wears a head covering outdoors, usually a hand-knitted woolen cap. When he spends a long time at the piano "warming up," that's what he's doing, literally. The exercise relieves the chill in his icy, extra-long fingers.

He never drinks any alcoholic beverages. So far as I know, he hasn't touched his once-favorite "Old Overholt" rye in forty years. Even when he was drinking, he was known to be extremely moderate about it. He's not a nondrinker from moral objections. But he's full of stories about what the demon rum did to many of his old friends and associates.

Physical exercise is as abhorrent to him as it always has been.

Never stand when you can sit. Never walk when you can ride. Sports are to watch, not for participation. There's no way to imagine Eubie ever having worked on his car, fixed anything around the house, or mowed a lawn.

And he smokes. A couple of packs a day is par. Sometimes it's more. He's been doing that since he was six years old. What about the surgeon general's dictum that smoking is hazardous to your health?

"Maybe it is," Eubie replies. "For other people. It never bothered me. What does bother me is how many people are gonna see me smokin' and they say, Look at him! He's ninety-six years old. What's wrong with smokin'. That bothers me. I'll tell you what's wrong with smokin'. We ain't all built alike, and if the great scientists show you that smokin' is bad for you, you pay attention. I been lucky, but you go count the people that's dead from lung cancer and all those things.

"Inhale? Sure I inhale! Why does anybody smoke if they don't inhale? That's like takin' a shower with your clothes on."

Diet? Indulgence of his sweet tooth is not quite the whole story. At home or in restaurants Marion sees to it that a certain amount of protein finds its ways into his digestive system. They've compromised on a sliver of steak that weighs barely an ounce. Eubie diligently tries to hide it under a lettuce leaf, but she catches him at it and makes sure he eats it. He will eat fried oysters, up to six, and he loves them because, as he says, "Everybody from Baltimore loves oysters." He has never been celebrated for his appetite—until the dessert appears. Then he becomes alert and seems to be really wide awake, aware for the first time that a meal is in progress.

Water, as everyone knows, is no good for you. Oh, it's all right to do the laundry in, and you have to put up with brushing your teeth in it. For those so disposed, it's indispensable for ice skating. But drink it? Never. People have been telling him all his life he's supposed to drink plenty of water, every day. When anybody mentions it, he looks as though he's spent the last ninety-six years trying to forget what it tastes like.

I met Dr. George Liberman, Eubie's doctor, in 1977 at Eubie's home in Brooklyn. Our discussion was brief, and I was impressed with his straightforwardness and his simplicity. He is an elderly and distinguished-looking gentleman with an obvious affection for his patient.

In a letter to me, Dr. Liberman wrote: "Eubie's medical care is very personalized. When he is in Brooklyn, I see him with great regularity, always at his home except when special tests or studies require his visiting me at my office. I see him as often as necessary and if need be on very short notice. I make it a practice to forestall major problems by taking care of them while they are minor. All aspects of preventive care take total priority.

"I have worked long and hard with Marion, who has performed spectacularly as his wife, nurse, and dietician, to make her very knowledgeable about his different medical needs. He travels far and wide with a high degree of assurance that he himself, his traveling companion, or Marion will be able to handle his routine medical problems. He knows that I am as close as his telephone.

"Eubie smokes incessantly, cigarette after cigarette, and gets to bed, after working at his piano, in the early hours of the morning, and invariably sleeps till about midday. His eating habits leave much to be desired and require major effort on Marion's part to get enough and proper food into him.

"Fortunately, as a legacy from his mother and father, Eubie was blessed with a wonderful heart and blood vessel system that have stood him in good stead these many years. He is most responsive to medication in all forms, and over the years I have become totally aware of major and minor medical problems which have beset him, as well as the most effective way to handle them. Eubie's continued success is the adrenalin that keeps him young even while he grows old."

Dr. Liberman has predicted to me that "Eubie might outlive us all." He assures me that in spite of Eubie's lifelong abnormal sugar consumption, he does not have or show any tendency to diabetes. He still is in possession of his own teeth.

Eubie doesn't flaunt his vices and excesses. "I hope nobody tries to copy off of *me*." he says fervently. "I don't think I got any bad habits. They might be bad habits for other people, but they're all right for me. But if you want to stay healthy, don't look at what

I'm doin'. Do what the doctors tell you. Remember, I got a doctor too, and I do what he tells me. For myself, I don't think bad habits made me live to ninety-six, and able to stay busy and enjoy myself. I think it's because I spent my whole life doin' what I like to do best and I don't think I ever worried as much as other people. Worry can make people die before their time.

"I had an easy life, and I think that easy livin' makes you healthy."

Normally Eubie never speaks of his physical condition. He has nothing of the hypochondriac in him and is generally stoical about the minor aches and pains that everyone suffers. I'm sure what I've quoted here is the most discussion about it that I've ever heard from him.

"Health ain't the only thing I been lucky with," Eubie assures me. "It seems like all my life I had people doin' things to *help* me. Mostly they helped me with things they could do better than me. Somebody always took care of business, my clothes, my house, transportation. They made it easy for me to do what I do best, and what I *like* to do best—goin' around and playin', and entertainin' people.

"That's why I can still be booked *someplace* almost every week of the year. And I go to places I like to be in. New Orleans is one. Marion and me talk seriously about movin' to New Orleans to live there. We've got so many good friends in New Orleans.

"I enjoy playin' the White House too. It's only about fifty miles from the house where *I* was born, but it's a million miles in class. I never thought that when I was playin' in Doc Frazier's medicine show that I'd play in the White House some day.

"I'm still makin' records whenever I take a notion, and they do very well—better than they ever did. My very good friend and associate Carl Seltzer takes care of the business, and he does so many things for me that ain't got anything to do with business.

"So bein' ninety-six is easy. It's gettin' there that's supposed to be tough. But everything is so good for me now, and I'm having such a good time. You know I like to do those TV shows with good friends like Bill Cosby and Johnny Carson and Mike Douglas and Merv Griffin. Well maybe I shouldn't have mentioned *them* if I can't mention everybody. And you *saw* me in the movie about the life of Joplin. I *love* to do that stuff. I never *used* to get a chance to do all them things, and now I do. I wish I *started out* bein' ninety-six. Look at all the fun I woulda had!

"I'm still happy every time I see the curtain goin' up."

"Eubie!"

On September 23, 1978, "Eubie!" opened on Broadway at the Theater-Off-Park after a riotously successful trial run at Philadelphia's old Walnut Street Theater. In it, twenty-one first-class professionals—twelve performers and nine company musicians—offer a program of the music of Eubie Blake. The show is a beautifully mounted production showcasing twenty-three of his most successful numbers. After superlative reviews in *Time*, *Newsweek*, and on the Today show—not to mention all the enthusiastic notices in the press—it settled down to an inevitable long run. On February 7, 1979, Eubie's ninety-sixth birthday, the first road company began its tour in Baltimore, Eubie's home town. At this writing a second touring company is being organized, and the Broadway company, now at the Ambassador Theater, is still playing to packed houses.

The program is the same as on the opening night in Philadelphia:

Act 1: Good Night, Angeline (1919), Charleston Rag (1899), Shuffle Along (1921), In Honeysuckle Time (1921), I'm Just Wild about Harry (1921), Baltimore Buzz (1921), Daddy (1921), There's a Million Little Cupids in the Sky (1924), I'm a Great Big Baby (1940), My Handy Man Ain't Handy No More (1930), Low Down Blues (1921), Gee, I Wish I Had Someone to Rock Me in the Cradle of Love (1919), I'm Just Simply Full of Jazz (1919)

Act 2: High Steppin' Days (1921), Dixie Moon (1924), Weary (1940), Roll, Jordan (1930), Memories of You (1930), If You've Never Been Vamped by a Brownskin, You've Never Been Vamped at All (1921), You Got to Git the Gittin While the Gittin's Good (1956), Oriental Blues

(1921), I'm Craving for That Kind of Love (1921), Hot Feet (1958), Good Night, Angeline (1919)

Most of these numbers are on the Warner Brothers record album HS3267 performed by the original cast and orchestra.

The production closes with a finale in which the cast, first, and then the audience, sing lustily, "I'm Just Wild about Eubie." Eubie himself appeared on stage for the opening and performed. He has turned up at the theater on subsequent occasions and is unstinting in his praise for all phases of the production—the cast, the musicians, the scenery, the dances—it's all just perfect as far as he's concerned. And the public appears to share his enthusiasm.

Selected List of Compositions

The compositions named here have been selected from Eubie Blake's prolific musical output, estimated at more than 1,000 pieces. Because many of them have been lost, no list of his works can claim to be complete. This list is arranged alphabetically by title. Blake's collaborators are named in parentheses. Shows that songs were used in or composed for are named after the date of composition.

Affectionate Dan (Sissle), 1918
Ain't Cha Coming Back, Mary Ann, to Maryland (Sissle), 1919
Ain't We Got Love (Reddie and Mack), 1937; "Swing It"
Al-le-lu [Old Noah's Ark] (Sissle), 1925
Alone with Love (Sissle), 1950; unused, "Shuffle Along of 1952"
Arabian Moon (Sissle), 1933; "Shuffle Along of 1933"
As Long as You Live (Arthur Porter)
Baby Buntin' (Sissle), 1923; "Elsie"
Baltimore Blues (Sissle), 1919
Baltimore Buzz (Sissle), 1921; "Shuffle Along"
Baltimore Todolo, 1908
Bandana Days (Sissle), 1921; "Shuffle Along"
Bandana Ways (Sissle), 1933; "Shuffle Along of 1933"
Blackbirds on Parade (Razaf), 1930; "Blackbirds of 1930"

Blue Classique, 1939

Blue Rag in Twelve Keys, 1969

Blue Thoughts, 1936

Blues, Why Don't You Leave Me Alone? (Arthur Porter)

Bonga-Boola (Sissle), 1952; "Shuffle Along of 1952"

Boogie Woogie Beguine (Sissle), 1945

Breakin' 'Em Down (Sissle), 1924; "The Chocolate Dandies"

Breaking 'Em In, 1933; "Shuffle Along of 1933"

Brittwood Rag, 1911

Butterfly, 1936

Capricious Harlem, 1936

Castle of Love, 1960

Charleston Rag [originally titled Sounds of Africa], 1899

Chevy Chase, 1911

Chickens Come Home to Roost (Sissle), 1933; "Shuffle Along of 1933"

Chocolate Dandies (Sissle), 1924; "The Chocolate Dandies"

City Called Heaven (Sissle), 1952; "Shuffle Along of 1952"

Classical Rag [Eubie's Classical Rag], 1972

Cleo Zell My Creole Belle (Sissle), 1921

Corner Chestnut and Low, 1903

Daddy, Won't You Please Come Home (Sissle), 1921; "Shuffle Along"

Dear Li'l Pal (Sissle), 1923

Dictys on Seventh Avenue, 1955

Dixie Ann in Afghanistan (Razaf), 1940; "Tan Manhattan"

Dixie Moon (Sissle), 1924; "The Chocolate Dandies"

A Dollar for a Dime (Razaf), 1940; "Tan Manhattan"

Don't Love Me Blues (Sissle), 1923

Don't Make a Plaything out of My Heart (Sissle), 1958; "Happy Times" (unproduced)

Down in the Land of Dancing Pickaninnies (Sissle), 1924; "The Chocolate Dandies"

Dumb Luck (Sissle), 1924; "The Chocolate Dandies"

Dusting Around (Sissle), 1933; "Shuffle Along of 1933"

Election Day (Sissle), 1921; "Shuffle Along"

Elsie (Sissle), 1923; unused, "Elsie"

Eubie Dubie (Guarnieri), 1972

Eubie's Boogie, 1904

Everybody's Struttin' Now (Sissle), 1923; "Elsie"

Everything Reminds Me of You (Sissle), 1921; "Shuffle Along"
Falling in Love (Sissle), 1933; "Shuffle Along of 1933"
Farewell with Love (Sissle), 1952; "Shuffle Along of 1952"
Fizz Water, 1911
Florodora Girls (Sissle), 1920
Gee! I Wish I Had Someone to Rock Me in the Cradle of Love (Sissle), 1919
Gee! I'm Glad That I'm from Dixie (Sissle), 1919
Glory (Sissle), 1933; "Shuffle Along of 1933"
Good Fellow Blues (Sissle), 1921
Good Night, Angeline (Europe and Sissle), 1917; "Shuffle Along"
Good-bye, My Honey, I'm Gone (Europe and Sissle), 1918
A Great Big Baby (Razaf), 1940; "Tan Manhattan"
Green and Blue (Reddie and Mack), 1937; "Swing It"
Gypsy Blues (Sissle), 1921; "Shuffle Along"
Harlem Moon (Sissle), 1933; "Shuffle Along of 1933"
Have a Good Time Everybody (Sissle), 1924; "The Chocolate Dandies"
Here 'Tis (Sissle), 1933; "Shuffle Along of 1933"
He's Always Hanging Around (Sissle), 1917(?)
High Muck de Muck, 1972
High Steppin' Days, 1921 (Brandon, 1978)
Hot Feet (Sissle), 1958
I Can't Get You Out of My Mind (Reddie)
I Like to Walk with a Pal Like You (Sissle), 1923; "Elsie"
I Wonder Where My Sweetie Can Be (Sissle), 1925
If It's Any News to You (Sissle), 1933; "Shuffle Along of 1933"
If You've Never Been Vamped by a Brownskin, You've Never Been
    Vamped at All (Sissle), 1921; "Shuffle Along"
I'll Find My Love in D-I-X-I-E (Sissle), 1924; "The Chocolate Dandies"
I'm a Great Big Baby (Razaf), 1940; "Tan Manhattan"
I'm Craving for That Kind of Love (Sissle), 1921; "Shuffle Along"
I'm Just Simply Full of Jazz (Sissle), 1919; "Shuffle Along"
I'm Just Wild about Harry (Sissle), 1921; "Shuffle Along"
In Honeysuckle Time (Sissle), 1921; "Shuffle Along"
In the Land of Sunny Sunflowers (Sissle), 1933; "Shuffle Along of 1933"
It's Afro-American Day (Sissle), 1969
It's All Your Fault (Sissle and Nelson), 1915
It's the Gown That Makes the Girl That Makes the Guy (Sissle and Javits),
    1952; "Shuffle Along of 1952"

I've the Lovin'es' Love for You (Europe and Sissle), 1917
Jassamine Lane (Sissle), 1924; "The Chocolate Dandies"
Jazz Baby (Europe and Sissle), 1919
Jazzing Thunder Storming Dance (Sissle), 1923; unused, "Elsie"
Jazztime Dance (Sissle), 1924; "The Chocolate Dandies"
Jingle Step (Sissle), 1923; unused, "Elsie"
Jive Drill (Sissle), 1952; "Shuffle Along of 1952"
The Jockey's Life for Mine (Sissle), 1924; "The Chocolate Dandies"
Jubilee Brazilian (Reddie)
Jump Steady (Sissle), 1924; "The Chocolate Dandies"
Keep Your Chin Up (Sissle), 1933; "Shuffle Along of 1933"
Kentucky Sue (Sissle), 1921; unused, "Shuffle Along"
Kitchen Tom, 1908
Koo Wah [You Got to Have Koo Wah] (Sissle), 1933; "Shuffle Along of 1933"
Labor Day Parade (Sissle), 1933; "Shuffle Along of 1933"
Lady of the Moon (Sissle), 1925; Cochran's London Revue, "Still Dancing"
Let's Get Married Right Away (Sissle), 1926; "Cochran's Revue of 1926"
Lonesome Man (Sissle), 1933; "Shuffle Along of 1933"
Love Will Find a Way (Sissle), 1921; "Shuffle Along"
Lovin' Chile (Sissle), 1923; unused, "Elsie"
Loving You the Way I Do (Scholl), 1930; "Hot Rhythm"
Low Down Blues (Sissle), 1921; "Shuffle Along"
Magnolia Rose (Razaf), 1940; "Tan Manhattan"
Mammy's Little Choc'late Cullud Chile (Sissle), 1917(?); "The Chocolate Dandies"
Manda (Sissle), 1924; "The Chocolate Dandies"
Martin Luther King [Didn't the Angels Sing] (Sissle), 1968
Melodic Rag, 1971
Memories of You (Razaf), 1930; "Blackbirds of 1930"
Messin' Around (Sissle), 1919
Michi Mori San (Sissle), 1919
Mirandy (Europe and Sissle), 1919
Moods of Harlem, 1937
My Crinoline Girl (Sissle), 1923; "Elsie"
My Handy Man Ain't Handy No More (Razaf), 1930; "Blackbirds of 1930"
My Little Dream Toy Shop (Reddie)
My Loving Baby (Sissle), 1916

My Vision Girl (Sissle), 1920

A National Love Song (Sissle), ca. 1950

Novelty Rag, 1910

Oriental Blues, (Sissle), 1920; "Shuffle Along"

Pickaninny Shoes (Sissle), 1920

Poor Katie Redd, 1910

Rain Drops, 1924

A Regular Guy, 1923; "Elsie"

The Rhythm of America (Sissle), 1952; "Shuffle Along of 1952"

Roll, Jordan (Razaf), 1930

Run on the Bank (Sissle), 1924; "The Chocolate Dandies"

Sand Flowers (Sissle), 1923; "Elsie

Saturday Afternoon (Sissle), 1933; "Shuffle Along of 1933"

See America First (Sissle and Nelson), 1915

Serenade Blues (Sissle), 1922

Shuffle Along (Sissle), 1921; "Shuffle Along"

Sing and Dance Your Troubles Away (Sissle), 1933; "Shuffle Along of 1933"

Sing Me to Sleep, Dear Mammy (Sissle), 1921; "Shuffle Along"

The Slave of Love (Sissle), 1924; "The Chocolate Dandies"

The Sons of Old Black Joe (Sissle), 1924; "The Chocolate Dandies"

Sore Foot Blues (Sissle), 1933; "Shuffle Along of 1933"

Sounds of Africa [African Rag; retitled Charleston Rag], 1899

Swanee Moon (Sissle), 1952; "Shuffle Along of 1952"

Swingtime at the Savoy (Sissle and Langston Hughes), 1948

Sylvia (Sissle), 1950

Tahiti (Sissle), 1926; "Cochran's Revue of 1926"

Tan Manhattan (Razaf), 1940; "Tan Manhattan"

That Charleston Dance (Sissle), 1924; "The Chocolate Dandies"

That South Car'lina Jazz Dance (Sissle), 1925

There's a Million Little Cupids in the Sky (Sissle), 1924; "The Chocolate Dandies"

There's No Place as Grand as Bandana Land (Sissle), 1924; "The Chocolate Dandies"

There's One Lane That Has No Turning (Sissle), 1926

They Had to Get the Rhythm Out of Their Souls (Sissle), 1958; "Happy Times" (unproduced)

Thinking of Me (Sissle), 1924; "The Chocolate Dandies"

The Three Wise Monkeys (Sissle), 1925
To Hell with Germany (Sissle), 1918
Tricky Fingers, 1908
Trouble Seems to Follow Me Around (Reddie)
Troublesome Ivories, 1911
Two Hearts in Tune (Sissle), 1923; "Elsie"
Uncle Tom and Old Black Joe (Sissle), 1921; "Shuffle Along"
Valse Amelia, 1972
Valse Eileen, 1972
Valse Erda, 1968
Valse Ethel, 1972
Valse Marion, 1972
Valse Vera, 1972
Waiting for the Whistle to Blow (Sissle), 1933; unused, "Shuffle Along of 1933"
We Are Americans Too (Razaf), 1940; "Tan Manhattan"
Weary (Razaf), 1940; "Tan Manhattan"
What a Great Day (Sissle), 1918
Why? (Sissle), 1926
Why Did You Make Me Care? (Sissle), 1925
With You (Sissle), 1923; unused, "Elsie"
You Got to Git the Gittin While the Gittin's Good (Miller), 1956
You Ought to Know (Sissle), 1924; "The Chocolate Dandies"
You Were Born to Be Loved (Reddie)
You Were Meant for Me (Sissle), 1922(?); "London Calling," 1923; "Charlot's Revue of 1924"
You're Lucky to Me (Razaf), 1930, "Blackbirds of 1930"
You've Been a Good Little Mammy to Me (Sissle), 1919

Discography

There may never be a complete listing of all recorded appearances of Eubie Blake. This one, based on research by Robert Kimball, Mike Montgomery, and myself, is as complete as we have been able to make it. New discoveries will be welcome.

78 RPM

This list is arranged alphabetically by title. Composers' names, if known, are given in parentheses after composition titles.

Affectionate Dan (Sissle and Blake)
April 1920; Florence Emory, vocal; Eubie Blake, piano
Victor test (unissued)
1920; Sissle and Blake with orchestra   Pathé 20470

Ain't Cha Coming Back, Mary Ann, to Maryland (Sissle and Blake)
1920; Sissle and Blake with orchestra   Pathé 22284

American Jubilee (Ed Claypoole)
1917–18; piano duet with drums; Blake and Carpenter, pianos
Pathé 20326
5389

Arkansas Blues [Down Home Chant] (Williams and Lada)
August 1921; Sissle and Blake   Emerson 10443
Reissued 1923, Emerson 10605

Baltimore Buzz (Sissle and Blake)
1921; medley; Eubie Blake, piano solo   Emerson 10434
June 1921; Eubie Blake, piano, with alto and banjo   Victor test

Baltimore Buzz (*continued*)
July 1921; Eubie Blake and the "Shuffle Along" Orchestra

Victor 18791
HMV B-1297
HMV Victor 18789

July 1921; Broadway Jones, vocal; Eubie Blake, piano   Victor test
1921; Sissle and Blake   Emerson 10385
Reissued 1923, Emerson 10574

Bandana Days (Sissle and Blake)
1921; Eubie Blake and the "Shuffle Along" Orchestra   Victor 18791
HMV B-1297
HMV Victor 18789

June 1921; Eubie Blake, piano, with alto   Victor test
1922; Sissle and Blake   Paramount 12002
(take 1115-3)

Blues in My Heart
September 1931; Eubie Blake Orchestra   Crown 3197
as "Dick Robertson and His Orchestra"   Varsity 5056

Boll Weevil Blues (Hess)
1921; Sissle and Blake   Emerson 10357
Reissued 1923, Emerson 10627

Boo Hoo Hoo (Nelson, Link, Aaronson, and Lentz)
January 1922; Sissle and Blake   Emerson 10512
Regal 9180

Broadway Blues (Swanstrom and Morgan)
1920; Sissle and Blake   Emerson 10296
Medallion 8246
as "Leonard Graham and Robert Black"   Regal 911

Broken Busted Blues (Dowell and Troy)
May 1925; Sissle and Blake   Edison reject
June 1925; Sissle and Blake   Edison 51572
Edison Blue Amberol Cylinder 50141

Can't You Heah Me Callin', Caroline (Roma)
1917–18; Noble Sissle, vocal; piano assumed to be Eubie Blake
Pathé 20194

Crazy Blues (Bradford)
1920–21; Sissle and Blake   Emerson 10326
Medallion 8252
as "Willie Black and Ruby Blake"   Medallion 8305
Issued 1922, Paramount 12007
as "Leonard Graham and Robert Black"   Regal 911

Crazy Blues (*continued*)
1920–21; Sissle and Blake with orchestra — Pathé 20484
Actuelle 020484
1921; Sissle and Blake with orchestra — Edison 50754
Edison Blue Amberol Cylinder 4264
1927; Sissle and Blake with orchestra — Okeh reject

Cutie (Rudolf Friml)
1922; Eubie Blake and His Orchestra — Emerson 10519
Regal 9198

Dah's Gwinter Be er Landslide
July 1921; Broadway Jones, vocal; Eubie Blake, piano — Victor test

Dear Li'l Pal (Sissle and Blake)
August 1923; Sissle and Blake — Victor reject
January 1924; Sissle and Blake — Victor reject

'Deed I Do (Fred Rose and Walter Hirsch)
1927; Sissle and Blake — Okeh 40776
Parlophone E-5796

Dinah (Lewis, Young, and Akst)
March 1926; Sissle and Blake — Edison Bell Winner 4402

Dissatisfied Blues
December 1929; Eubie Blake, piano solo — Victor reject

Dixie Moon (Sissle and Blake)
March 1924; Sissle and Blake — Victor reject
October 1924; Sissle and Blake — Victor 19494

Don't Leave Me Blues
August 1923; Sissle and Blake — Victor reject

Downhearted Blues (Alberta Hunter and Lovie Austin)
May 1923; Sissle and Blake — Victor 19086
HMV Victor 19086
HMV B-1703

Ev'rything's Made for Love
1927; Sissle and Blake — Okeh 40776
Parlophone E-5796

Gee! I Wish I Had Someone to Rock Me in the Cradle of Love
(Sissle and Blake)
April 1920; Florence Emory, vocal; Eubie Blake, piano — Victor test
1920; Sissle and Blake with orchestra — Pathé 22394

Gee! I'm Glad That I'm from Dixie (Sissle and Blake)
1920; Sissle and Blake with orchestra — Pathé 20470

Good Night, Angeline (Sissle, Blake, and Europe)
1917–18; Sissle and Blake with Pathé orchestra   Pathé 20226
April 1920; Sissle and Blake   Victor test

Great Camp Meeting Day (Sissle and Mikell)
1920–21; Sissle and Blake with orchestra   Pathé 20484
       Actuelle 020484

He's Always Hanging Around (Sissle and Blake)
1918; Sissle and Blake with Pathé orchestra   Pathé 20280

Home, Cradle of Happiness
May 1927; Sissle and Blake   Okeh 40894
       Parlophone R-3368

House Rent Lizzie
December 1929; Eubie Blake, piano solo   Victor reject

Hungarian Rag (Lenzberg)
1917–18; Eubie Blake Trio, with Eubie Blake and Elliott
     Carpenter, pianos, and unknown drummer   Pathé 20326

I Wonder Where My Sweetie Can Be (Sissle and Blake)
ca. February 1926; Sissle and Blake   Edison Bell Winner 4371

**If You've Never Been Vamped by a Brownskin,
You've Never Been Vamped at All** (Sissle and Blake)
1922; Sissle and Blake   Paramount 12002
       (takes 1114-1, 1114-2)

I'm a Doggone Struttin' Fool (Ryan and Pinkard)
October 1921; Sissle and Blake   Emerson 10484
       Regal 9158

I'm Craving for That Kind of Love (Sissle and Blake)
January 1922; Sissle and Blake   Emerson 10512
       Regal 9203

I'm Going Away Just to Wear You Off My Mind
     (Smith, Johnson, and Smith)
July 1922; Alberta Hunter, vocal; Eubie Blake, piano   Paramount 12006
       Reissued 1923, Paramount 12043

I'm Just Simply Full of Jazz (Sissle and Blake)
April 1920; Sissle and Blake   Victor test
April 1920; Sissle and Blake with orchestra   Pathé 22284

I'm Just Wild about Harry (Sissle and Blake)
June 1921; Eubie Blake, piano, with alto   Victor test

In Honeysuckle Time (Sissle and Blake)
1921; Sissle and Blake with orchestra   Emerson 10385
     as "Leonard Graham and His Jazz Band"   Regal 9102

I've Got the Blues, but I'm Just Too Mean to Cry
(Parish, Young, and Squires)
August 1921; Sissle and Blake   Emerson 10443
                              Reissued 1923, Emerson 10605
          as "Leonard Graham and Robert Black"   Regal 9137

I've Got the Red, White and Blues (Gaskill)
October 1921; Sissle and Blake   Emerson 10484
                                                  Regal 9158

Jassamine Lane (Sissle and Blake)
March 1924; Sissle and Blake   Victor reject

Jazz Babies' Ball (Bayha and Pinkard)
1920; Sissle and Blake   Pathé 22357

The Jazz Dance (Overstreet)
1918; Blake's Jazzone Orchestra, with Eubie Blake, piano
                                                  Pathé 20430

Jazzin' Baby Blues (Richard M. Jones)
1922; Alberta Hunter, vocal; Eubie Blake, piano   Paramount 12006
                              Reissued 1923, Paramount 12043

Jimmy, I Love But You
1922; Eubie Blake and His Orchestra   Emerson 10519
                                                  Regal 9199

Life Is Just a Bowl of Cherries (Brown and Henderson)
1931; Eubie Blake   Crown 3193
                                                  Imperial 2638
                                                  Varsity 6017

Little Alabama Coon (Hattie Starr)
1917–18; Noble Sissle, vocal; Eubie Blake, presumably, piano
                                                  Pathé 20194

A Little Bit o' Honey (Carrie Jacobs Bond)
1917–18; Sissle and Blake with Pathé orchestra   Pathé 20233

Little Girl
1931; Eubie Blake, piano   Victor 22735

Long Gone (W. C. Handy)
1921; Sissle and Blake   Emerson 10365
                              Reissued 1923, Emerson 10574
                                                  Medallion 8279

Love Will a Way (Sissle and Blake)
June 1921; Sissle and Blake   Emerson 10396
                              Reissued 1923, Emerson 10604
          as "Leonard Graham and Robert Black"   Regal 9107
                                                  Symphonola 4361

Loveless Love (W. C. Handy)
1920–21; Sissle and Blake with orchestra — Pathé 20493
Actuelle 020493
1921; Sissle and Blake with orchestra — Emerson 10357
Reissued 1923, Emerson 10605
as "Leonard Graham and His Jazz Band" — Regal 946

Low Down Blues (Sissle and Blake)
1921; Sissle and Blake — Emerson 10365
Reissued 1923, Emerson 10627
as "Leonard Graham and His Jazz Band" — Regal 946

Ma! (Con Conrad)
1921; Eubie Blake, piano solo — Emerson 10450

Mammy's Little Choc'late Cullud Chile (Sissle and Blake)
1917–18; Sissle and Blake with Pathé orchestra — Pathé 20210

Mammy's Little Sugar Plum (Davis and Erdman)
1920; Sissle and Blake with orchestra — Pathé 22394

Manda (Sissle and Blake)
March 1924; Sissle and Blake — Victor reject
October 1924; Sissle and Blake — Victor 19494
Reissued on Victor LP LPV-560

Mandy Lou (Cook)
1918; Sissle and Blake with Pathé orchestra — Pathé 20295

Marching Home
December 1929; Broadway Jones, vocal; Eubie Blake, piano
Victor test

My Blue Days Blew Over (Seymour and Rich)
1931; Eubie Blake, piano solo — Victor 22735

My Fate Is in Your Hands (Razaf and Waller)
December 1929; Broadway Jones, vocal; Eubie Blake, piano
Victor test

My Mammy's Tears (Coslow, Ringle, and Schaffer)
1921; Sissle and Blake — Emerson 10367

My Vision Girl (Sissle and Blake)
1920; Noble Sissle, vocal; Eubie Blake, presumably, piano
Pathé 20463

Nobody's Sweetheart (Erdman)
1931; Eubie Blake and His Orchestra — Crown 3130
Varsity 8046

Oh, Boy! What a Girl
ca. January 1926; Sissle and Blake — Edison Bell Winner 4337

Old-fashioned Love (Mack and Johnson)
January 1924; Sissle and Blake   Victor 19253

One More Time
1931; Eubie Blake and His Orchestra   Crown 3111

Oriental Blues (Sissle and Blake)
June 1921; Sissle and Blake   Emerson 10396

Pickaninny Shoes (Sissle and Blake)
ca. January 1921; Sissle and Blake with orchestra   Pathé 20475
March 1926; Sissle and Blake   Edison Bell Winner 4402
1927; Sissle and Blake   Okeh 40917
                                          Parlophone R-186

Please Don't Talk about Me When I'm Gone (James P. Johnson)
February 1931; Eubie Blake and His Orchestra;
                Dick Robertson, vocal   Crown 3090
                as "John Martin and His Orchestra"   Broadway 1448

River, Stay 'Way from My Door (Dixon and Woods)
1931; Eubie Blake   Crown 3193
                                                  Varsity 6017

Royal Garden Blues (Williams and Williams)
1920–21; Sissle and Blake with orchestra   Emerson 10367
                          Reissued 1923, Emerson 10604
                                          Pathé 20493
                                          Actuelle 020493
        as "Willie Brown and His Sizzling Syncopators"
                                          Medallion 8286

St. Louis Blues (W. C. Handy)
1931; Eubie Blake and His Orchestra   Crown 3130
        as "Dick Robertson and His Orchestra"   Varsity 8046

Sarah from Sahara (Frey)
1917–18; Eubie Blake Trio, with Eubie Blake and Elliott
        Carpenter, pianos, and unknown drummer   Pathé 20358
                                                  5389

Slow River (Myers and Schwab)
May 1927; Sissle and Blake   Okeh 40894
                                          Parlophone R-3368

Somebody's Gona [sic] **Get You** (Morgan)
1917–18; Sissle and Blake with Pathé orchestra   Pathé 20226

Sounds of Africa [Charleston Rag] (Blake)
1921; Eubie Blake, piano solo   Emerson 10434

Sounds of Africa (*continued*)   Symphonola 4360
                                                      Paramount 14004
            Reissued on Columbia, "Sounds of Harlem"
                                        3-Col C3L-33, 41886-4, 41886-6

Stay in Your Own Back Yard (Udall)
1917–18; Sissle and Blake with Pathé orchestra   Pathé 20233

Sweet Georgia Brown (Pinkard)
1931; Eubie Blake, piano solo   Crown 3197

Sweet Henry, the Pride of Tennessee (Davis and Akst)
January 1924; Sissle and Blake   Victor 19253

Sweet Lady, medley from "Tangerine" (Johnson, Crumit, and Zoob)
1921; Irving Kaufman, vocal; Eubie Blake, piano
                                                      Symphonola 4360
                                                 Emerson 10350, 10450
            as "Billy Clark and Robert Black"   Regal 9130

That's the Kind of Baby for Me (Egan)
1918; Sissle and Blake with Pathé orchestra   Pathé 20280

There It Goes Again (Jentes)
1918; Sissle and Blake with Pathé orchestra   Pathé 20267

There's One Lane That Has No Turning (Sissle and Blake)
February 1926; Sissle and Blake   Edison Bell Winner 4371

Thumpin' and Bumpin'
June 1931; Eubie Blake, piano solo   Victor 22737

Two Little Blue Little Eyes
April 1931; Eubie Blake and His Orchestra   Crown 3111
            as "John Martin and His Orchestra"   Broadway 1460

Ukelele Baby (Meskill, Rose, Sherman, and Bloom)
ca. February 1926; Sissle and Blake   Edison Bell Winner 4356

Ukelele Lullaby (Williams)
ca. February 1926; Sissle and Blake   Edison Bell Winner 4356

Waitin' for the Evenin' Mail (Billy Baskette)
May 1923; Sissle and Blake   Victor 19086
                                                    HMV Victor 19086

When Your Lover Has Gone (E. A. Swann)
1931; Eubie Blake and His Orchestra   Crown 3086

Why? (Sissle and Blake)
January 1926; Sissle and Blake   Edison Bell Winner 4337

You Ought to Know (Sissle and Blake)

May 1925; Sissle and Blake	Edison reject
June 1925; Sissle and Blake	Edison 51572
	Edison Blue Amberol Cylinder 50141
March 1926; Sissle and Blake	Edison Bell Winner 4417

Long-Playing Records

This list is arranged chronologically by date of recording. Records issued by Eubie Blake Music, Eubie's record company, and piano-roll reissues are listed separately in the following sections.

1951 **Jammin' at Rudi's No. 1** (10-inch)   Circle LP L-467

Maryland, My Maryland   Maple Leaf Rag

1951 **Jammin' at Rudi's**   Unissued

Charleston Rag	Chevy Chase
Dictys on Seventh Avenue	The Dream
Black Keys on Parade	Mr. Johnson Turn Me Loose
Troublesome Ivories	Lovie Joe

This tape now belongs to Jazzology Records in Atlanta, Georgia.

1952 **Songs from "Shuffle Along"**   RCA Victor LPM-3514
                                                                        EPA-482

Orchestra under the direction of Eubie Blake

Love Will Find a Way (Louise Woods, Laurence Watson, vocal)
I'm Just Wild about Harry (Thelma Carpenter, Avon Long, vocal)
Bandana Days (Avon Long, vocal)
Gypsy Blues (Thelma Carpenter, Avon Long, vocal)

1958 **The Wizard of the Ragtime Piano**   Twentieth Century–Fox 3003

Eubie Blake, piano; Buster Bailey, clarinet; Bernard Addison, guitar; Milton Hinton, George Duvivier, bass; Panama Francis, Charles Persip, drums; Noble Sissle, vocal

Jubilee Tonight	Eubie's Boogie Rag
Maple Leaf Rag	Mobile Rag
Sunflower Slow Drag	I'm Just Wild about Harry
The Dream Rag	Mississippi Rag
Ragtime Rag	Carry Me Back to Old Virginny
(Troublesome Ivories)	Carolina in the Morning
Maryland	My Gal Is a High Born Lady
The Ragtime Millionaire	Bill Bailey, Won't You Please
Good Morning, Carrie	Come Home

1959   **The Marches I Played on the Old Ragtime Piano**
Twentieth Century–Fox 3039

Eubie Blake, piano; Buster Bailey, clarinet; Kenny Burrell, guitar; Milton Hinton, bass; Panama Francis, drums

Stars and Stripes Forever	Greeting to Bangor
Dunlap Commandery	On, Brave Old Army Team
Ragtime Polish Dance	High School Cadets
Our Director	Charleston Rag Dance
Semper Fidelis	Song without Words
King Cotton	Ragtime Piano "Tricks"

1962   **Golden Reunion in Ragtime**   Stereoddities c. 1900

Eubie Blake, Joe Jordan, Charles Thompson, pianos

Meet Me in St. Louis (Blake, Jordan, and Thompson)
Bunch o' Blackberries (Blake, Jordan, and Thompson)
Maori (Blake, Jordan, and Thompson)
Lovie Joe (Jordan, with Blake and Thompson)
Lily Rag (Thompson)
Memories of You (Blake)
Teasin' Rag (Jordan and Blake)
Old Black Crow (Jordan, with Blake and Thompson)
Waiting for the Robert E. Lee (Thompson, Jordan, and Blake)
That's Jelly Roll (Blake)
Until (Jordan)
Delmar Rag (Thompson)
Dora Dean (Blake, Thompson, and Jordan)
Dictys on Seventh Avenue (Blake)
Broadway in Dahomey (Blake, Jordan, and Thompson)

1962   Two-LP package issued by Stereoddities for use as an hour radio show, with cue script, but not released for retail sale

Eubie Blake, Joe Jordan, Charles Thompson, pianos

Meet Me in St. Louis (Blake, Jordan, and Thompson)
Alexander's Ragtime Band
Funeral March (demonstration)
Ragtime Funeral March Music
Won't You Come Home, Bill Bailey
Sweetie Dear (Jordan)
Tricky Fingers (Blake)
Buffet Flat Blues (Jordan)
Morocco Blues (Jordan)
Blue Thoughts (Blake)
Lovie Joe (Jordan)
Brother-in-Law Dan (Jordan)
Waiting for the Robert E. Lee (Thompson, Jordan, and Blake)
Judge Fogarty (Blake)

1968 **The Eighty-six Years of Eubie Blake**   Columbia C2S 847

Recorded December 26, 1968, February 6, 1969, and March 12, 1969; Eubie Blake, Noble Sissle, vocals; Eubie Blake, piano

Record 1, side 1
Dream Rag
Charleston Rag
Maple Leaf Rag
Semper Fidelis
Eubie's Boogie
Poor Jimmy Green
Tricky Fingers

Record 1, side 2
Stars and Stripes Forever
Baltimore Todolo
Poor Katie Redd
Kitchen Tom
Troublesome Ivories
Chevy Chase
Brittwood Rag

Record 2, side 1
Medley: Bleeding Moon;
  Under the Bamboo Tree
It's All Your Fault
"Shuffle Along" medley:
  Bandana Days; I'm
  Just Simply Full of
  Jazz; In Honeysuckle
  Time; Gypsy Blues; If
  You've Never Been
  Vamped by a Brownskin;
  Love Will Find a Way;
  I'm Just Wild about Harry
I'm Just Wild about Harry
  (waltz version)
Spanish Venus
As Long as You Live

Record 2, side 2
Medley of J. P. Johnson
  songs: Charleston;
  Old-fashioned Love;
  If I Could Be with You
You Were Meant for Me
Dixie Moon
Blues, Why Don't You
  Leave Me Alone
Blue Rag in Twelve Keys
Memories of You

1977 **Wild about Eubie**   Columbia 34504

Joan Morris, vocals; William Bolcom, piano; with guest artist Eubie Blake, piano

An album of twelve of Eubie's compositions, including "Boogie Woogie Beguine" (Blake, solo piano), "Eubie's Classical Rag" (Blake, solo piano), and "Dixie Moon" (Morris, vocal; Bolcom and Blake, pianos)

LPs Issued by Eubie Blake Music (EBM)

EBM-1 **Eubie Blake, Volume 1, Featuring Ivan Harold Browning** (1972)

Dictys on Seventh Avenue
Fizz Water
Sugar Babe
Melodic Rag
Ragtime Merry Widow
Novelty Rag
Good Night, Angeline

Jungle Nights in Gay Montmartre
Some Little Bug Is Going
  to Find You
Love Will Find a Way
Roll Them Cotton Bales
My Lindy Lou
De Gospel Train

EBM-2 **Eubie Blake: Rags to Classics** (1971)

Charleston Rag
(1971 performance)
Charleston Rag
(1921 performance)
Capricious Harlem
Rustle of Spring
You're Lucky to Me
You Do Something to Me

Rain Drops
Pork and Beans
Valse Marion
Classical Rag
Scarf Dance
Butterfly
Junk Man Rag

EBM-3 **Eubie Blake, and His Friends Edith Wilson and Ivan Harold Browning**

Side 1: Eubie Blake, piano; Edith Wilson, Ivan Harold Browning, vocals
He May Be Your Man, but He Comes to See Me Sometimes (Wilson, vocal)
There'll Be Some Changes Made (Wilson, vocal)
Black and Blue (Wilson, vocal)
Joshua Fit the Battle of Jericho (Browning, vocal)
Go Down Moses (Browning, vocal)
In That Great Gettin' Up Morning (Browning, vocal)
Exhortation (Browning, vocal)
Medley from "Shuffle Along": If You've Never Been Vamped by a Brownskin; In Honeysuckle Time; I'm Just Wild about Harry (Browning, vocal)

Side 2: Eubie Blake, piano and vocals
Eubie Dubie
I Can't Get You Out of My Mind
Memphis Blues
Corner Chestnut and Low
When Day Is Done

EBM-4 **Sissle and Blake: Early Rare Recordings, Vol. 1**

Side 1
Baltimore Buzz (July 1921)
Love Will Find a Way (June 1921)
Oriental Blues (June 1921)
I'm Craving for That Kind of Love (January 1922)
Bandana Days (July 1922)
Pickaninny Shoes (February 1927)

Side 2
Broadway Blues (September 1920)
I've Got the Blues (August 1921)
I've Got the Red, White and Blues (October 1921)
I'm a Doggone Struttin' Fool (October 1921)
Boo Hoo Hoo (January 1922)
Downhearted Blues (May 1923)
Waitin' for the Evenin' Mail (May 1923)
Sweet Henry (January 1924)

EBM-5 **Eubie Blake: Live Concert** (1973)

Eubie tells of the origins of ragtime, illustrates with brief piano demonstrations, using parts of "Tricky Fingers," "Memories of You," "J. P. Johnson Medley," "The Dream Rag," "Rhapsody in Ragtime," "I'm Just Wild about Harry," and "As Long as You Live."

EBM-6 **Eubie Blake, Introducing Jim Hession**

Eubie shares an LP with a protégé and plays solo piano on "Troublesome Ivories," "Elite Syncopations" (Joplin), "Good Morning, Carrie," "Slew Foot Nelson," and "The Man I Love."

EBM-7 **Sissle and Blake: Early Rare Recordings, Vol. 2**

Side 1
Baltimore Buzz (July 1921)
Ma! (September 1921)
Oh Me! Oh My! / Say It with Music (ca. 1933)
Sweet Lady (September 1921)
I'm Going Away Just to Wear You off My Mind (July 1922)
My Blue Days Blew Over (June 1931)
Bandana Days (July 1921)

Side 2
You Ought to Know (March 1926)
I Wonder Where My Sweetie Can Be (ca. February 1926)
Ukelele Baby (ca. February 1926)
Oh Boy! What a Girl (ca. January 1926)
Ukelele Lullaby (ca. February 1926)
Jazz Babies' Ball (ca. May 1920)
I'm Just Simply Full of Jazz (1920)
Low Down Blues (April 1921)

EBM-8 **Eubie Blake and His Protégés** (1974)

Eubie Blake, Jim Hession, Mike Lipskin, Terry Waldo, piano and vocals

A live concert, with Eubie as M.C., recorded at the Theatre De Lys, New York, including "Kitchen Tom" (Blake, piano), "That Lindy Hop" (Blake, piano), and "He's a Cousin of Mine" (Blake, piano and vocal).

EBM-9 **Eubie Blake Song Hits, with Eubie and His Girls** (1975)

Eubie Blake, Emme Kemp, piano and vocals; Mary Louise, Mable Lee, vocals

Side 1
If You've Never Been Vamped by a Brownskin (Lee, vocal)
Daddy, Won't You Please Come Home (Louise, vocal)
Loving You the Way I Do (Blake, piano and vocal)

Gee! I Wish I Had Someone to Rock Me in the Cradle of Love
  (Louise and Kemp, vocal)
Strange What Love Will Do (Louise, vocal)
I'm Craving for That Kind of Love (Lee, vocal)

Side 2
Sweet Talk (Kemp, arrangement and piano; Louise, vocal)
It Ain't Being Done No More (Kemp, piano and vocal)
My Handy Man Ain't Handy No More (Kemp, piano and vocal)
Ain't We Got Love (Louise, vocal)
You Got to Git the Gettin' While the Gettin' Is Good (Lee, vocal)
Don't Love Me Blues (Kemp, piano; Blake, Kemp, Louise, vocal)
Roll, Jordan (Kemp, arrangement, piano, and vocal)

Piano-Roll Reissues on LP

Twenty-two of Eubie Blake's thirty-nine known piano rolls (see the piano rollography) were reissued in early 1973 on long-playing records. They may be ordered directly from their producer, Arnold S. Caplin, Biograph Records, P. O. Box 109, Canaan, New York 12029, if they cannot be obtained from record stores.

1973 **Eubie Blake, Volume I: Blues and Rags**   Biograph BLP 1011Q
                                                            stereo

Eubie's earliest piano rags, 1917–21

Side 1	*Side 2*
Charleston Rag	Broadway Blues
Somebody's Done Me Wrong	Crazy Blues
Good Night, Angeline	Strut Miss Lizzie
Shubert Gaieties of 1919 (selections)	It's Right Here for You
Gee! I Wish I Had Someone to Rock Me in the Cradle of Love	Home Again Blues
	Fare Thee Honey Blues

1973 **Eubie Blake, Volume II: 1921**   Biograph BLP 1012
                                                       stereo

Rare piano rolls of early blues and spirituals

Side 1	*Side 2*
The Good Fellow Blues	Wang-Wang Blues
Don't Tell Your Monkey Man	Roumania
Boll Weevil Blues	Memphis Blues
If You Don't Want Me Blues	Dangerous Blues
Negro Spirituals (selections)	Arkansas Blues
	The Down Home Blues

Special Recording

1927 Sound track for Vitaphone short subject
                              Vitaphone "Va-464-3 Rec. 97 Vol. +5"

My Dream of the Big Parade   All God's Chillun Got Shoes

A rare 16-inch 33 1/3-RPM recording (February 1927) of Sissle and Blake with orchestra and chorus, made as the sound track for an early Vitaphone "talkie" (see the filmography). It runs about twelve minutes.

Piano Rollography

by Michael Montgomery

I compiled the first Eubie Blake piano rollography (list of player piano rolls) as an appendix to Robert Kimball and William Bolcom's book *Reminiscing with Sissle and Blake* (Viking Press, 1973). Since then, more vintage rolls played by Eubie have surfaced, and he recorded five new rolls in 1973 for QRS. In addition, the mystery surrounding two unconfirmed Blake rolls ("My Sweetie" and "Ten Little Fingers") has been solved: "Sweetie" is by Eubie, "Fingers" is not. As a result, this revised rollography includes data from my 1973 rollography plus additions and corrections. I am indebted to Myer Fishman, Sandy Libman, Mike Schwimmer, Dick Howe, and Bill Burkhardt for the new information that made this revision possible.

Dates shown, unless otherwise noted, are months in which the rolls were released for sale to the public, as indicated by lists issued by the various roll companies. Actual recording dates would normally have preceded the date of release by at least a month or two. Except for Eubie's 1973 QRS rolls, recording dates are unknown.

Eubie made a total of thirty-nine known rolls, all of which are presumed to have been issued. Of this number, five have not been found by collectors as of this writing (March 1979). These titles are preceded by an asterisk (*). Of the remaining thirty-four rolls, twenty-two appear in reissued form on two Biograph long-playing records (see the discography for details).

This list is arranged chronologically by date of release. In most cases, data shown come directly from the roll labels or from original catalogs; words known to be misspelled are followed by "[sic]." Unless noted to the contrary, the artist credit on each roll reads "Played by Eubie Blake."

Probably September 1917
Charleston Rag (Eubie Blake)   Ampico 54174-E
Played by composer   1.25

> This seems to be Eubie's first issued piano roll. The exact release date is uncertain but may have followed shortly after "Charleston Rag" was copyrighted, on August 8, 1917. In fact, it may have been copyrighted because of its appearance on a piano roll. This number has been reissued by the QRS Company in two versions, both currently available: on QRS AMP-1004, which is an exact copy of the original, including Ampico coding, and on QRS Q-1004, without the Ampico coding, for use on regular player pianos.

December 1917

My Sweetie (Irving Berlin)   Rythmodik G100703
Fox trot; key of B flat   .80

> This roll is shown in company catalogs as played by Al Sterling and Victor Arden. The original application card that the American Piano Company sent to the Library of Congress to copyright this roll also shows Sterling and Arden as the artists. However, someone has crossed through these names on the card and has written "Eubie Blake" over the entry. After this was discovered, the roll itself was found; it credits Eubie as the artist. Either there was a clerical error in the catalog or two versions of the roll were produced. Apparently, the company decided to use the Blake performance as the issued version and corrected the copyright card to ensure protection of the correct arrangement.

January 1918

*Rain Song (Will Marion Cook)   Rythmodik J19124
                                                            1.00

February 1918

*Ev'rybody's Crazy 'bout the Doggone Blues   Rythmodik X101103
(Creamer and Layton) Fox Trot; key of A flat   .85

Somebody's Done Me Wrong (Skidmore)   Rythmodik X101113
Fox trot; key of B flat   .85

August 1919

Mirandy (Europe, Sissle, and Blake)　　Rythmodik J103843
Fox trot; key of F　　　　　　　　　　　　　　1.00
Played by Eubie Blake; assisted by Edwin Williams

Good Night, Angeline (Europe, Sissle, and　　Rythmodik J103933
Blake)　Fox trot; key of G　　　　　　　　　　1.00
Played by Eubie Blake; assisted by Edgar Fairchild

The Rythmodik master was used as the basis of a later release of this roll on a reproducing Ampico roll, 200743F ($1.50), but the month of release is uncertain.

Save Your Money, John (Copeland and Rogers)　　Rythmodik J104323
Fox trot from Ziegfeld Follies, 1918; key of C　　　1.00
Played by Eubie Blake; assisted by Edwin Williams

Sometime, probably during 1919, Eubie took a train from Boston to New York. A man on the train recognized him and invited him to stop off in Meriden, Connecticut, to make rolls, which Eubie did. Apparently, Eubie recorded at this time for the Artrio-Angelus label, rolls for which were made by the Wilcox & White Company in Meriden. An Artrio-Angelus roll catalog dating from about 1922 lists six of these early Blake rolls, and all but one of them have been found.

1919(?)

Ziegfeld Follies, 1919, Selection　　　　　Artrio-Angelus 8036
(Dave Stamper)　　　　　　　　　　　　　　2.00
Introducing (1) Shimmie Town, (2) A Pretty Girl Is Like a Melody, (3) Sweet Sixteen, (4) Syncopated Cocktail, (5) Mandy, (6) Tulip Time

Dave Stamper was the "official" composer of the Follies, but most of the songs on this roll are by Irving Berlin.

Good Night, Angeline (Lieutenant Jim Europe,　　Artrio-Angelus 8037
Lieutenant Noble Sissle, and Eubie Blake)　　　　1.75

Chinese Lullaby [East Is West]　　　　　Artrio-Angelus 8038
(R. H. Bowers)

*Greenwich Village Follies, Selection　　　　Artrio-Angelus 8039
(A. Baldwin Sloane)　　　　　　　　　　　　2.50
Introducing (1) I Want a Daddy Who Will Rock Me to Sleep, (2) My Little Javanese, (3) The Message of the Cameo, (4) Red, Red as a Rose, (5) My Marionette, (6) I Want a Daddy Who Will Rock Me to Sleep

Schubert [sic] Gaieties of 1919, Selection   Artrio-Angelus 8048·
(Jean Schwartz)   2.00
Introducing (1) I've Made Up My Mind to Mind a Maid Made Up Like
You, (2) Cherry Blossom Lane, (3) Beal [sic] Street Blues, (4) I'll Be
Your Baby Vampire, (5) My Beautiful Tiger Girl, (6) I've Made Up My
Mind to Mind a Maid Made Up Like You

The authenticity of this roll has been questioned, most notably by Eubie
himself, who claims that it is not his playing.

Gee! I Wish I Had Someone to Rock Me in   Artrio-Angelus 8049
the Cradle of Love (Blake)   1.50

Eubie's remaining rolls were made for the Mel-O-Dee label, which
was first introduced by the Aeolian Corporation in January 1920.
Mel-O-Dee rolls were word rolls or song rolls, with the words
printed along the right-hand edge of the roll. Many of Eubie's Mel-
O-Dee rolls were heavily edited, with extra notes that either Eubie
or some anonymous arranger added after the initial recording to
give the rolls a jazzy, fuller sound.

Of the twenty rolls Eubie recorded for Aeolian (on the Mel-O-
Dee and Duo Art labels), only one is his own composition: "The
Good Fellow Blues." Musicologists have often wondered why
Eubie did not make any rolls of the tunes from his show "Shuffle
Along," which opened in 1921 in New York. My own theory is
that Eubie recorded what Aeolian asked him to record—numbers
that were expected to be commercially successful. Either his tunes
were unknown to Aeolian at that time or they were considered important only to a small market. It is also likely that after "Shuffle
Along" opened, Eubie stopped making rolls because of the
demands on his time. The Mel-O-Dee rolls that Aeolian continued
to issue for the rest of that year could well have been recorded by
Eubie early in 1921.

January 1921

Broadway Blues (Morgan)   Mel-O-Dee 4153
Fox trot; key of F   1.25
Played by Ubie [sic] Blake

The January 1921 Mel-O-Dee bulletin used the correct spelling of Eubie's
name. QRS reissued this roll a few years ago as QRS Q-194 but no longer lists
it in the company catalog. It is available only on special order, meaning that
one would have to order a complete production run of sixteen copies.

February 1921

Crazy Blues (Bradford)   Mel-O-Dee 4199
Fox trot; key of B flat   1.25

Strut Miss Lizzie (Creamer and Layton)   Mel-O-Dee 4241
Fox trot; key of B flat   1.25

During this period the Wilcox & White Company was issuing certain rolls of popular tunes for a new word-roll series on their Artrio-Angelus label. "Strut Miss Lizzie," the only Blake recording to so appear, was released on Artrio-Angelus 2035 in May 1921, but it is the identical recording issued by Mel-O-Dee. The Artrio version, however, includes extra expression perforations along the edge and was designed to reproduce on Artrio-Angelus players.

It's Right Here for You (Bradford)   Mel-O-Dee S2948
Fox trot; key of F   1.25

This roll, like most of the rest of Eubie's rolls, was assigned an "S" serial number. Apparently, this signified rolls of special-interest music and meant that the rolls were not automatically shipped on standing orders from Mel-O-Dee dealers. Dealers had to order these rolls specially to get them.

Home Again Blues (Berlin and Akst)   Mel-O-Dee S2949
Fox trot; key of G   1.25

Fare Thee Honey Blues (Bradford)   Mel-O-Dee S2950
Fox trot; key of B flat   1.25

March 1921

The Good Fellow Blues (Blake)   Mel-O-Dee S2959
Fox trot; key of F   1.25

***Useless Blues** (Martin and Le Blanc)   Mel-O-Dee S2960
Fox trot; key of C   1.25

War Bride Blues (Le Blanc)   Mel-O-Dee S2961
Fox trot; key of F   1.25

***Sweet Mama, Papa's Getting Mad** (Rose)   Mel-O-Dee S2963
Fox trot–blues; key of F   1.25

Don't Tell Your Monkey Man [Monkey Man Blues] Mel-O-Dee S2966
(L. Johnson)   Fox trot; key of E flat   1.25

No listing in catalogs can be found for Mel-O-Dee S2962, so the possibility exists that it is another undiscovered Blake performance. Rolls S2964 and S2965 are by other artists.

Boll Weevil Blues (Hess)   Mel-O-Dee 4259
Fox trot; key of G   1.25

April 1921

If You Don't Want Me Blues (Brabford [*sic*])   Mel-O-Dee S2980
Fox trot; key of C   1.25

Wang-Wang Blues (Mueller, Johnson, and Busse)   Mel-O-Dee S2985
Fox trot; key of F   1.25

Roumania (Williams)   Mel-O-Dee S2988
Fox trot; key of E flat   1.25

> No listing in catalogs can be found for Mel-O-Dee S2982 or S2986, so the possibility exists that these may be undiscovered Blake performances. Rolls S2981, S2983, S2984, S2987, and S2989 are by other artists.

Negro Spirituals   Duo Art Song Roll 10091
   Go Down Moses   1.75
   I'm a-Rolling   Metro-Art Song Roll 250716
   Nobody Knows de Trouble I See, Lord   1.50
   I Got Shoes
Played by Ubie [*sic*] Blake

> This roll is sometimes listed as Duo Art 100917, the last digit indicating the size and price of the roll. The misspelling of Eubie's name on this, his only Duo Art roll, and on the first Mel-O-Dee roll, issued in January, indicates the possibility that both rolls were among the first he recorded, with the erroneous spelling following the Duo Art master roll all the way through production until final issuance several months later, in April 1921.

May 1921

Memphis Blues (Handy)   Mel-O-Dee 4371
Fox trot; key of F   1.25

September 1921

Dangerous Blues (Brown,   Mel-O-Dee 4427
Fox trot–blues; key of F   1.25

November 1921

Arkansas Blues (Lada)   Mel-O-Dee 4549
Fox trot; key of F   1.25

December 1921

The Down Home Blues (Delaney)   Mel-O-Dee S3001
Fox trot–blues; key of C   1.25

In May 1973 Eubie went to Buffalo, New York, to record some new piano rolls for the QRS Company. Eubie performed five of his own compositions of May 19, 1973, as listed below. The rolls were released over a period of months. In this instance the release dates are less important, since we know the actual recording date. All five rolls are still in the QRS catalog as of this writing.

Eubie's QRS rolls were recorded on the old Melville Clark recording apparatus, Clark being the master inventor who founded the Melville Clark Piano Company in 1900 in Chicago and who developed a hand-played roll-recording system to make his own QRS rolls for the Clark piano line. As Eubie played at the keyboard of the recording piano, a master roll of blank paper revolved around a special marking drum located just a few feet away. As each note was played, a corresponding carbon mark, like a pencil line, was drawn on the master roll. To make such rolls into production masters, an editor uses a special two-bladed knife to cut slots where the carbon marks appear on the master roll. After judicious editing to correct errors and to smooth out any rough spots, the master roll is ready for production. The process is manual and time-consuming, however.

May 1973

Rhapsody in Ragtime (Blake)	QRS CEL-123 3.40
Troublesome Ivories (Blake)	QRS CEL-124 3.40
Merry Widow Rag (Blake)	QRS CEL-125 3.40
Memories of You (Blake)	QRS CEL-126 3.40
I'm Just Wild about Harry (Blake)	QRS CEL-127 3.40

Filmography

Sissle and Blake's Snappy Songs (1923)

This was the first musical film. Produced by Lee De Forest. First shown at the Rivoli Theater on Broadway. Sissle and Blake perform "All God's Chillun Got Shoes" and "Affectionate Dan." The film survives. It was shown on NBC's "Today" show on February 7, 1978, Eubie's ninety-fifth birthday.

Vitaphone (Warner Brothers) short subject (1927)

The film itself, an extravaganza with a large cast and expensive production numbers, has not surfaced in recent years, but the sound track survives (it is listed at the end of the discography). I myself saw the film before 1930. Sissle and Blake perform, with orchestra, singing chorus, and dancers, "All God's Chillun Got Shoes" and "My Dream of the Big Parade."

Harlem Is Heaven (1932)

Eubie Blake and His Orchestra in support of comedian-dancer Bill Robinson. This is a full-length feature film produced by Lincoln Pictures, Inc. Robinson does the "step dance" that made him famous as the orchestra plays "Swanee River."

Pie, Pie, Blackbird (1932)

Warner Brothers one-reel musical. Eubie Blake and His Orchestra provide the music for the dance routines of the headline attraction, the Nicholas Brothers.

Eubie Blake (1974)

Four hours of documentary film on Eubie's life and music produced by Jean-Cristophe Averty for French television (Channel 3). A superb film.

Scott Joplin, King of Ragtime (1976)

A spectacularly beautiful film, made for television but also shown in some theaters. Eubie Blake plays the role of Will Williams, proprietor of the Maple Leaf Club in Sedalia, Missouri. Art Carney plays John Stark, the music publisher.

Index

A

A&P Gypsies, 108
Abba Labba (Richard McLean), 151
Abyssinian Baptist Church (New York), 136
Academy of Music (New York), 30
Actors Equity, 128
Aeolian Corporation, 192
"Affectionate Dan," 88
"African Dip," 78
"Afro-American Symphony," 2
"After the Ball," 23
"Alabama Blossom," 47
Albright, William, 139
"Alexander's Ragtime Band," 51
Alhambra Theater (Harlem), 113
Alice Tully Hall (New York), xii, 132, 140
"All Coons Look Alike to Me," 29, 63
"All God's Chillun Got Shoes," 89
"All I Wants Is My Chickens," 36
"All of No Man's Land Is Ours," 60
Allen, Richard B. (Dick), 140
Allen's, Ben (Atlantic City), 40, 52
"Alone with Love," 123
Ambassador Theater (New York), 166
"American Ambassadors of Syncopation," 95
American Guild of Authors and Composers, 139

American Symphony Orchestra, 37
"Amos 'n' Andy," 107, 108, 123
Anderson, Eddie (Rochester), 114, 121
Anderson, T.V., 132
"Annie Get Your Gun," 121
Antoine's (New Orleans), 142
"Any Rags," 22
Apollo Theater (Harlem), 113, 114
"Apple Blossom Time," 71
Armstrong, Louis, 108, 114, 121, 156
Armstrong Park (New Orleans), 136
Arpin, John, xv, 151
ASCAP, 51, 63, 99, 120, 122, 123, 128, 133
Atlantic City, N.J., 39, 40, 46, 47, 48, 49, 50, 51, 52, 147, 148, 150
Audiophile Records, 126
Averty, Jean Cristophe, 90, 139
"Awake and Sing," 110

B

"Back, Back, Back to Baltimore," 47
Baden, Germany, 136
Bailey, Buster, 103, 126
Bailey, Pearl, 125
Bailey and Fletcher, 26
Baker, Josephine, 75, 96, 141
Ball, Ernest R., 62
Baker, Phil, 88

Parker, Dr. John W.(Knocky), xv, 126, 129, 131, 132, 139, 151
Patapsco River, 5
Patchogue, L.I., 99
Peabody Institute, 133
Pemberton, Jimmy, 114
Penrose, Jack, 79
Pensacola Kid (Paul Wyer), 116, 150
"Perfect Fool, The," 73
Perlis, Vivian, xiv
Philadelphia, Pa., 111, 138, 149, 155, 166
"Pickaninny Shoes," 70
Pickett, Jesse, 12, 17, 19, 23, 29, 150, 155
Pictorial History of the American Theater, A, 71
Pimlico (race track), 39, 140
Piquir, Conchita, 88
Pistorius, Steve, 139
"Plantation Club Review, Lew Leslie's," 82
Playbill, 73
"Poor Katie Redd," 46, 141
Porter, Arthur, 55, 77
Porter, Cole, 96, 97, 111
Porter, Joe, 57
Potts, Roberta, 143
"Pousse Cafe," 123
Pratt Institute, 51, 140
Preservation Hall (New Orleans), 140
President (steamer), 142
Primary School No. 2 (Baltimore), 5, 24
Presley, Elvis, xii
Primus, Pearl, 113
Prince of Wales (later Edward VIII), 95
Princeton Club (New York), 140
Princeton Harpsichord Festival, 136, 138
Pritchett, Teeny, 23, 24
Puck, Eva, 88
"Put on Your Old Gray Bonnet," 12, 47

Q

Q.R.S. (piano rolls), 153, 189, 194, 195
Quina, Pat, 140

R

RCA Victor Records, 126, 140
Rag Times, 132, 154
"Raggin' the Scale," 40, 41
Rags and Ragtime, xiv
Ragtimer, 132
"Rain Drops," 157, 158
"Rain Song," 43
Rainey, Ma, 94
Rasch, Charlie, 129
Razaf, Andy, vii, 82, 85, 100, 101, 102, 103, 105, 111, 156
Reddie, Joshua Milton, 110, 111, 156
Redman, Don, 108, 114
Reed, Madison, 47, 51
Rembrandt Peale Museum (Baltimore), 4
"Reminiscin' with Sissle and Blake" (TV film), 137
Reminiscing with Sissle and Blake, xiv, 37, 133, 189
Reser, Harry, 108
"Rhapsody in Blue," 155
Riverview Park (Baltimore), 55
Rivkin, Joshua, 132
Rivoli Theater (New York), 89
Roberts, Luckey, 40, 45, 116, 117, 127, 149, 155
Robeson, Paul, 75
Robinson, Bill, 89, 94, 113, 149
Rochester (Eddie Anderson), 114, 121
"Roll Those Roly Boly Eyes," 73
Romberg, Sigmund, 62
Roosevelt, Eleanor, 110
Roosevelt, Franklin Delano, 110
"Roots" (film), 140
Rose, Al, ix, 142